THE ZERO DAY FILES:

CYBERSECURITY UNVEILED

A B2B BOOK SERIES ON
MODERN CYBERSECURITY
THREATS AND SOLUTIONS

Damian Davis

First Edition
Printed in the United States of America

For information about special discounts for bulk purchases or permissions requests, please contact:

marketing@disrisksolutions.com

Table of Contents

Acknowledgments

This work would not have been possible without the unwavering love and support of my parents, **Wilbert Davis** and **Carol Davis**. Your guidance and encouragement through the years have been my foundation, and for that, I am forever grateful.

To **Armie Shah**, thank you for your invaluable insights and contributions, both to this work and to the field of cybersecurity as a whole. Your expertise and dedication are truly inspiring.

To **Michael Allen**, from **Data by Drones**, thank you for your exceptional work on the cover art and audio/visual elements. Your creativity and technical expertise have brought this project to life in ways I could not have imagined.

To **Bob Curran**, a trusted friend, mentor, and accomplished business leader, thank you for your thoughtful review of this book. Your valuable feedback and insightful perspective have been instrumental in shaping this work into a resource that resonates with a diverse audience.

To the entire **DIS Risk Solutions team**, I extend my deepest gratitude. Your hard work, commitment, and passion for what we do are at the heart of our success.

Finally, to all the readers who have chosen to explore this work, thank you. Your curiosity and engagement drive the mission to create a safer, more secure digital world.

This book is as much yours as it is mine.

FOREWARD (Inspirational)

In every age, there are silent guardians—those who stand between order and chaos, safety and vulnerability. Today, those guardians are not only soldiers or first responders; they are cybersecurity professionals. *The Zero Day Files: Cybersecurity Unveiled* is a tribute to that frontline, illuminating the hidden war raging behind every login screen, data packet, and line of code.

This book invites you to go beyond the headlines and into the architecture of digital defense—to understand the unseen, anticipate the unknown, and respond to the unpredictable. At the heart of this journey lies the concept of the *zero day*: the silent breach, the undisclosed fla , the invisible enemy. But more than a technical term, *zero days* represent the urgent need for vigilance, innovation, and resilience in a world where trust is the currency and time is the most valuable defense.

The author guides us through this landscape with both precision and purpose. Every page reminds us that cybersecurity is not just about systems—it's about people. It's about protecting critical infrastructure, preserving privacy, enabling innovation, and ensuring that digital progress does not come at the cost of security.

For those just stepping into the field, this book will ignite a sense of purpose. For seasoned experts, it will reinforce why this mission matters. Behind every disclosed exploit, contained breach, and secured network lies a greater truth: we are the architects of digital trust.

The Zero Day Files doesn't just unveil cybersecurity—it redefines it as a calling. Dive into its pages with curiosity, reflect on its lessons with responsibility, and act on its insights with courage. In an age where every second counts and every system is a potential target, the stakes have never been higher. The future depends on it.

Armie Shah
Vice President (VP) of Cybersecurity Operations

PREFACE

The Gap Between Technical Security and Business Understanding

In my years as a cyber insurance broker, one truth has become increasingly clear: the gap between technical security requirements and business understanding continues to challenge organizations of all sizes. While technical teams grapple with evolving threats, business leaders struggle to translate security concepts into actionable business decisions. This disconnect not only affects security implementations but also impacts an organization's ability to properly transfer and manage cyber risk.

The Origin and Purpose of The Zero Day Files

The Zero Day Files emerged from countless conversations with clients across different industries – from healthcare providers protecting patient data to manufacturers securing their supply chains, and from financial services safeguarding transactions to technology companies protecting their innovations. Each conversation revealed a common need: a practical guide that bridges the gap between technical security requirements and business operations.

Unique Approach to Security and Risk Transfer

This book takes a unique approach. Rather than presenting abstract security concepts or purely technical solutions, we explore real-world security incidents through the lens of both business impact and technical response. Each chapter examines a specific industry scenario, drawing from actual incidents to illustrate not just what went wrong, but how proper security controls, insurance coverage, and response protocols can work together to protect an organization.

Book Structure and Target Audience

The structure of this book is designed to cater to both business leaders and technical teams, progressing through three key sections:

- **Section I: Critical Infrastructure and Healthcare** explores the unique challenges faced by industries like healthcare, manufacturing, and financial services, where securing critical operations is paramount
- **Section II: Public Sector and Emerging Industries** delves into the cybersecurity needs of government services, IoT security, and cryptocurrency, highlighting the evolving threat landscape in these sectors.
- **Section III: Enterprise and Consumer Operations** focuses on retail, cloud security, and professional services, offering insights into protecting dynamic, customer-facing environments.

Each section builds upon the lessons of the previous one while remaining self-contained for easy reference. This progression allows readers to explore industry-specific challenges and solutions while gaining a comprehensive understanding of cybersecurity and risk management.

Practical Tools and Implementation

What makes this book different is its integrated approach to security and risk transfer. As cyber threats evolve and regulatory requirements increase, organizations need more than just technical solutions or insurance policies – they need a comprehensive understanding of how these elements work together. The included appendices provide practical tools, templates, and guidelines that you can adapt and implement in your organization.

Author's Vision for Industry Impact

While writing this book, I've kept in mind the CISO explaining security needs to the board, the CFO evaluating security investments, the risk manager assessing coverage options, and the technical team implementing security controls. Each perspective matters, and each plays a crucial role in building a resilient organization.

The cyber threat landscape will continue to evolve, but the fundamental principles of protecting your organization – through both security controls and risk transfer – remain constant. This book aims to help you understand and apply these principles effectively, regardless of your role or industry.

My hope is that *The Zero Day Files* serves not just as a guide, but as a practical tool in your organization's security journey. Whether you're evaluating your security investments, considering cyber insurance coverage, implementing new controls, or responding to an incident, you'll find relevant insights and actionable guidance in these pages

The scenarios and guidance presented here reflect real-world experiences and lessons learned. While the technical details matter, ultimately this book is about protecting your organization's ability to operate, innovate, and succeed in an increasingly complex threat landscape.

Damian Davis
Managing Partner
DIS Risk Solutions

INTRODUCTION: THE NEW BATTLEFIELD

State of Cybersecurity in 2024

The cybersecurity landscape of 2024 bears little resemblance to what organizations faced even a few years ago. The traditional boundaries between physical and digital operations have dissolved, creating an environment where every business decision has security implications, and every security choice has business consequences.

We've entered an era where artificial intelligence accelerates both attack and defense capabilities, where cloud technologies expand attack surfaces beyond traditional network boundaries, and where the Internet of Things connects critical infrastructure to the digital realm in unprecedented ways. The result is a battlefield that extends far beyond IT departments into boardrooms, factory floors, and customer interactions.

The statistics tell a compelling story. Ransomware attacks now target manufacturing control systems as frequently as they do corporate networks. Healthcare providers face sophisticated attacks that threaten both patient data and clinical operations. Financial services companies confront API vulnerabilities that can compromise millions in transactions within minutes. Even local governments and critical infrastructure providers find themselves on the front lines of nation-state cyber operations.

Yet perhaps most significantl , the nature of cyber risk has fundamentally changed. What was once primarily a technical concern has evolved into a core business risk that demands attention at every organizational level. The question is no longer if an organization will face a cyber incident, but when – and more importantly, how prepared they are to respond and recover.

Business Risk Landscape

Today's business risk landscape reflects this new reality. Organizations face a complex matrix of interconnected risks that defy simple solutions:

Operational Risks:
- Business interruption from cyber incidents now averages 21 days
- Supply chain attacks can cascade through multiple organizations
- Cloud service disruptions can paralyze operations globally
- Connected systems mean localized incidents can have enterprise-wide impacts

Financial Risks:
- Average breach costs exceed $4.5 million
- Ransomware demands regularly reach eight figure
- Business interruption costs often exceed direct damage
- Regulatory fines can approach 4% of global revenu

Strategic Risks:
- Cyber incidents can derail mergers and acquisitions
- Innovation requires balancing security with agility
- Digital transformation introduces new vulnerabilities
- Competitive advantage depends on trust and resilience

Reputational Risks:
- Customer trust, once lost, proves difficult to rebuil
- Media scrutiny of cyber incidents intensifie

- Stakeholder expectations for security continue to rise
- Brand damage can persist long after technical recovery

This risk landscape demands a new approach to security and risk management. Organizations need to integrate security considerations into their business strategy while ensuring their security programs align with business objectives. This requires understanding not just the technical aspects of security but also the business implications of security decisions.

How to Use This Book

The Zero Day Files is designed to serve as both a strategic guide and a practical resource. The book is organized to support different reading approaches based on your role and immediate needs:

Section Organization:
- Section I (Chapters 1-4) focuses on Critical Infrastructure and Healthcare, examining fundamental security challenges in highly regulated industries
- Section II (Chapters 5-8) explores Public Sector and Emerging Industries, addressing unique challenges in rapidly evolving sectors
- Section III (Chapters 9-12) covers Enterprise and Consumer Operations, providing insights into common business security challenges

Each chapter follows a consistent structure:

1. Incident Scenario: A detailed examination of a real-world security incident
2. Technical Analysis: In-depth exploration of attack vectors and security controls
3. Business Impact: Assessment of operational, financial, and strategic consequences

4. Response Protocol: Practical guidance for incident handling
5. Risk Transfer: Insurance considerations and coverage implications

For Business Leaders:
- Focus on the business impact sections
- Review risk transfer considerations
- Understand strategic implications
- Evaluate security investments

For Technical Teams:
- Examine technical analysis sections
- Study response protocols
- Implement security controls
- Support business objectives

Practical Application:
The appendices provide actionable tools and templates:
- Security Implementation Guide (Appendix A)
- Incident Response Templates (Appendix B)
- Risk Assessment Tools (Appendix C)
- Regulatory Compliance Checklist (Appendix D)
- Insurance Considerations (Appendix E)

These resources are designed to help you:
- Evaluate your current security posture
- Implement improved controls
- Respond to incidents effectively
- Transfer risk appropriately

As you progress through the book, you'll encounter recurring themes that emphasize the integration of security with business operations. Each chapter builds upon previous lessons while remaining self-contained enough for reference based on your specific needs or industr .

The scenarios presented are drawn from real incidents, modified to protect confidentiality while preserving the critical lessons learned. The guidance provided reflects both industry best practices and practical experience in helping organizations navigate the complexities of modern cyber risk.

Whether you're a business leader seeking to understand security investments, a technical professional implementing controls, or a risk manager evaluating coverage options, The Zero Day Files offers insights and guidance relevant to your role in protecting your organization's ability to operate and thrive in today's threat landscape.

SECTION I

CRITICAL INFRATRUCTURE AND HEALTHCARE

Chapter 1

The Silent Breach

PART 1: NARRATIVE CASE STUDY

Company Profile: GlobalTrade Financial
Annual Revenue: $2.1B
Industry: Financial Services
Employees: 5,800
Client Base: 15,000+ institutional and retail clients
Market Position: Top 15 global trading platform provider specializing in institutional trading services and retail investment solutions
Geographic Presence: Global operations across major financial centers in North America, Europe, and Asia

0600 Hours - GlobalTrade Financial, New York Office

Sarah Chen's phone buzzed just as she was reviewing the Asian markets' overnight trading data. As Chief Risk Office , early morning alerts weren't unusual, but this one made her pause. The SOC team had flagged an anomaly: a series of micro-transactions, each just below standard monitoring thresholds, executed during the Tokyo trading window.

"Jenkins," she called to her senior risk analyst, "pull up the pattern recognition logs for the last twelve hours."

Tom Jenkins, a veteran of financial cybersecurity, was already ahead of her. “Looking at it now, Sarah. Something’s off with the API calls to the trading platform. They’re legitimate credentials, but the pattern...” He trailed off, fingers flying across his keyboard.

0615 Hours - Security Operations Center

Marcus Rodriguez, SOC Team Lead, was already assembling his team when Sarah arrived. The glass-walled command center hummed with activity, dozens of screens displaying real-time security feeds, including dedicated monitors for their CyberGuard Solutions’ advanced threat detection system.

“Talk to me, Marcus,” Sarah demanded, scanning the main display.

“We’ve got unusual API behavior across multiple endpoints,” Marcus explained, pulling up a network map. “Started around 0300 EST. Initially looked like normal trading activity, but the integrated AI pattern recognition from CyberGuard caught something the standard monitors missed.”

Dr. Emily Wong, their Advanced Threat Hunter, interrupted. “The transactions are a smokescreen. Look at this.” She projected her screen, showing a deep packet analysis, sharing it simultaneously with DataDefend’s forensics team through their secure channel. “They’re using the API calls to mask data exfiltration. Whoever this is, they’re good.”

0630 Hours - Incident Response Team Activation

Within minutes, the full incident response team assembled in their designated war room:

Internal Team:
- David Patel - Lead Forensics Analyst
- Jennifer Martinez - Malware Specialist
- Keith Robinson - Network Security Engineer

- Lisa Chang - Compliance Officer
- Michael O'Brien - Legal Counsel

DIS Risk Solutions Team (Virtual):
- Damian Davis - Strategic Response Coordinator
- Rachel Torres - Claims Protocol Manager
- Mark Stevens - Technical Integration Lead

Partner Teams:
- CyberGuard Solutions (Virtual):
  • Alex Zhang - Advanced Threat Response
  • Victoria Rodriguez - Network Defense Lead
- DataDefend (Virtual):
  • Dr. James Wilson - Enterprise Forensics Lead
  • Samantha Park - Financial Services Specialist

Sarah took command, the large displays showing both in-person and virtual participants in their practiced formation. "Let's execute Protocol Alpha-7. David, coordinate with DataDefend on those API calls. Jennifer, work with CyberGuard's team on code analysis. Keith, prepare for network segmentation with CyberGuard's NDR team. Lisa, start documentation - Damian's team will handle carrier notifications. Michael, work with DIS's legal network on client notification drafts."

0645 Hours - Technical Investigation

The integrated teams moved with practiced precision. David Patel and Dr. Wilson from DataDefend simultaneously announced their findings. "It's a zero-day," David explained, as Dr. Wilson's analysis appeared on the shared screen. "They're exploiting a previously unknown vulnerability in our API authentication protocol."

"The code is elegant," Jennifer Martinez added, her cursor moving in sync with Alex Zhang's from CyberGuard Solutions. "It's modifying memory allocation in a way that bypasses our logging."

Damian Davis spoke up from the DIS virtual panel. "This matches a pattern we've seen in recent attacks against other financial institutions. Rachel, activate our financial services incident response protocol. Mark, coordinate with CyberGuard on expanded threat hunting across our other clients' networks."

Rachel Torres immediately began drafting the carrier notification. "I'll have the initial notice out within the hour. Given the sophistication of the attack and our early detection, we should have good carrier support for our response actions."

0700 Hours - Crisis Escalation

Sarah knew the protocol. She nodded to Damian, who had already begun carrier notifications through DIS's dedicated channels. She then dialed James Davidson, CISO, on his secure line.

"Jim, Sarah Chen. We have a situation that meets escalation criteria. DIS and partners are already engaged. Zero-day targeting our trading platform. No confirmed data loss yet, but evidence of sophisticated attack attempt."

Davidson's response was immediate and measured. "Good. Damian briefed me on the carrier notifications. I'll get Margaret [CTO] for technical resources. How are CyberGuard and DataDefend integrating with our team?"

"Seamlessly. Dr. Wilson's team at DataDefend is running parallel forensics, and CyberGuard's NDR team is prepped for network segmentation if needed."

0715 Hours - C-Suite Integration

James Davidson arrived with Margaret Wu, the CTO. The command center had transformed into a fully integrated war room, with virtual panels showing DIS, CyberGuard, and DataDefend teams in constant coordination.

Margaret immediately engaged with the technical leads. "Show me the API anomalies. All of them." She and Dr. Wong huddled over the threat analysis while Alex Zhang from CyberGuard shared additional pattern recognition data from their threat intelligence network.

Davidson pulled Sarah aside. "What's our exposure window?"

"Four hours from first detected anomaly," Sarah replied. "But the pattern suggests they might have been probing longer. Damian's team is already coordinating with the carriers, and DataDefend's forensics will help establish the full timeline."

0730 Hours - Executive Briefing

The executive briefing was conducted via secure video conference. Robert Williams, CEO, and Elizabeth Morgan, CFO, joined virtually, along with Damian Davis representing DIS Risk Solutions.

Sarah led the briefing: "We have a confirmed zero-day exploit attempting to compromise our trading platform. Our integrated response team, including DIS Risk Solutions and their partners, has contained the immediate threat. DataDefend's forensics confirms no data breach, but shows evidence of attempted exfiltration. Margaret's team is developing a patch, but we need to make decisions about trading operations."

Elizabeth Morgan, CFO, leaned forward in her video feed. "What's our potential exposure?"

"Current analysis shows $2.3 million across 1,547 client accounts," Sarah reported. "But that's just the identified transactions. We need a trading halt to prevent further exposure."

Damian Davis interjected, "I've already briefed our primary carrier. Given the sophisticated nature of the attack and our rapid response, they're fully supporting our mitigation strategy. CyberGuard's threat intelligence suggests this may be part of a broader campaign targeting financial institutions."

Robert Williams nodded grimly. “Margaret, how long for the patch?”

“Two hours to develop, one hour to test, another for deployment,” the CTO responded, glancing at the CyberGuard team’s virtual panel. “Alex, your team can validate in parallel?”

Alex Zhang nodded. “Yes, we’ll run simultaneous testing through our financial services simulation environment. It’ll cut validation time by 40%.”

“Reputational impact?” Williams asked.

James Davidson stepped in. “Better to take the hit on a preventative trading halt than risk client data compromise. We can position this as proactive security maintenance. Damian, your thoughts?”

“Agreed,” Davis responded. “We’ve managed similar situations with other financial institutions. A brief, controlled halt for ‘system enhancement’ typically sees positive market response, especially when compared to potential alternatives. Rachel’s team has already drafted messaging templates that worked well in similar scenarios.”

Williams made the call. “Execute the halt. Elizabeth, work with Damian on insurance protocols. James, coordinate PR with DIS’s team. Sarah, I want updates every 30 minutes. Margaret, you have your timeline – make it happen.”

0745 Hours - Response Implementation

As the team mobilized to implement the CEO’s decisions, the integrated response showed years of preparation and planning. Each group moved with precision:

Internal Leadership:
- Margaret Wu (CTO) - Leading technical response
- James Davidson (CISO) - Managing security operations
- Elizabeth Morgan (CFO) - Handling financial implications
- Robert Williams (CEO) - Strategic oversight

- Sarah Chen (CRO) - Risk management and coordination

DIS Risk Solutions Team:
- Damian Davis - Coordinating overall response and carrier communications
- Rachel Torres - Managing claims protocols and documentation
- Mark Stevens - Synchronizing technical teams

Partner Operations:
CyberGuard Solutions:
- Alex Zhang - Running parallel security testing
- Victoria Rodriguez - Implementing enhanced network defense

DataDefend:
- Dr. Wilson - Leading forensics investigation
- Samantha Park - Managing financial systems analysis

PART 2: TECHNICAL DEEP DIVE

Investigation Timeline:

0300-0600: Initial Compromise - Anomalous API calls detected by integrated CyberGuard monitoring - Pattern recognition alert triggered through dual-layer detection - Initial data analysis begun by SOC and CyberGuard teams - DataDefend forensics team activated remotely

0600-0700: Initial Response - SOC team activation and DIS Risk Solutions notification - Preliminary investigation with partner coordination - Integrated team assembly and secure channel establishment - Initial findings shared across response platform

0700-0900: Full Investigation - Coordinated forensic analysis (Internal/DataDefend) - Parallel malware reverse engineering (Internal/CyberGuard) - Multi-team network traffic analysis - Comprehensive impact assessment

Technical Analysis:

1. Attack Vector Identification Primary Findings (Internal Team/DataDefend): - Zero-day vulnerability in API authentication - Memory buffer overflow exploitation - Custom malware deployment - Data exfi - tration attempt

CyberGuard Analysis: - Similar attack patterns observed across fina - cial sector - Advanced persistent threat (APT) indicators - Sophisticated evasion techniques - Custom exploit development

2. Malware Analysis Component Analysis (Internal/CyberGuard): - Primary payload: Custom API interceptor - Secondary payload: Data exfiltration module - Tertiary component: Anti-detection mechanism

Behavior Analysis (DataDefend): - Dynamic API call modification - Threshold-aware transaction splitting - Memory manipulation techniques - Advanced evasion capabilities

3. Network Analysis Traffic Patterns (CyberGuard Assessment): - Disguised data exfiltration attempts - Modified API calls matching known APT behaviors - Hidden command and control channels - Encrypted data transmission patterns

System Impact (Internal/DataDefend Review): - Trading platform compromise attempts - API endpoint manipulation - Memory allocation anomalies - Log manipulation signatures

CyberGuard Threat Intelligence Correlation: - Similar attacks against financial institutions - Pattern matching with known threat actors - Industry-wide attack campaign indicators - Real-time threat feed integration

4. Forensic Investigation Evidence Collection (Coordinated Approach): Internal Team: - Network traffic captures - System memory dumps - API call logs - Transaction records

DataDefend Analysis: - Advanced memory forensics - Malware behavior analysis - Timeline reconstruction - Attack chain mapping

CyberGuard Intelligence: - Threat actor attribution - Attack pattern correlation - Industry-wide indicators - Strategic threat context

Analysis Findings (Combined Teams): - Attack origin indicators suggest state-sponsored activity - Compromise timeline shows sophisticated reconnaissance - Data access patterns reveal targeted approach - System vulnerabilities identified and documente

5. Solution Development Technical Response (Multi-team Approach): Internal Team: - Emergency patch development - API security enhancement - Monitoring improvement - System hardening

CyberGuard Solutions: - Enhanced detection rules - Network defense upgrades - Threat hunting protocols - Security control validation

DataDefend Recommendations: - Forensic-based improvements - Architecture hardening - Evidence preservation - Future prevention measures

Implementation Strategy: Phase 1 - Immediate (CyberGuard Lead): - Phased deployment approach - Real-time testing methodology - Rollback procedures - Validation process

Phase 2 - Strategic (DIS Risk Solutions Coordination): - Long-term security improvements - Control enhancement implementation - Monitoring upgrade deployment - Process refinemen

PART 3: IMPLEMENTATION GUIDE

1. IMPACT ASSESSMENT

Financial Impact: Direct Costs: $2.3M potential exposure Indirect Costs: $450,000 response costs Potential Future Losses: $5M+ if unaddressed Recovery Costs: $750,000 estimated Insurance Implications: Cyber policy activation required

Insurance Implications:

Primary Coverage: $250M cyber insurance tower structured as: • Primary Layer: $25M Carrier A: 100% ($25M)

• First Excess: $50M xs $25M Carrier B: 30% ($15M) Carrier C: 25% ($12.5M) Carrier D: 25% ($12.5M) Carrier E: 20% ($10M)

• Second Excess: $50M xs $75M Carrier F: 30% ($15M) Carrier G: 25% ($12.5M) Carrier H: 25% ($12.5M) Carrier I: 20% ($10M)

• Third Excess: $50M xs $125M Carrier J: 35% ($17.5M) Carrier K: 35% ($17.5M) Carrier L: 30% ($15M)

• Fourth Excess: $50M xs $175M Carrier M: 40% ($20M) Carrier N: 35% ($17.5M) Carrier O: 25% ($12.5M)

• Fifth Excess: $25M xs $225M Carrier P: 50% ($12.5M) Carrier Q: 50% ($12.5M)

Program Manager: DIS Risk Solutions - Strategic Response Coordination - Claims Protocol Management - Technical Integration Leadership - Carrier Communications

Retention/Deductible: $10M per cyber incident • Applies to each and every claim • Annual aggregate retention: $20M • Retention applies across all trading platforms • Time deductible: 12 hours for BI • Maintenance deductible: $10M for PCI

Coverage Triggers: • Data breach • System compromise • Trading platform failure • Business interruption • Financial fraud

Notification Timeline: 24 hours for cyber incidents

Claims Process: • Coordinated through DIS Risk Solutions • Dedicated financial services cyber claims unit • Integrated partner response protocols • Real-time carrier updates

Expected Coverage: • Incident response costs • Business interruption • System restoration • Client notification • Legal defens

Additional Coverage Features: • Financial fraud coverage • Social engineering coverage • Trading platform failure • Reputational harm • Regulatory defense

Systems Affected: Primary Systems: - Trading Platform, API Infrastructure - Monitored by CyberGuard Solutions' advanced detection - Forensics by DataDefend

Secondary Systems: - Transaction Processing, Logging - Real-time monitoring integration - Enhanced security protocols

Dependencies: - Market Data Feeds, Client Portals - Partner system interfaces - Third-party connections

Third-Party Systems: - Trading Partners, Clearing Houses - Integrated security monitoring - Cross-platform validation

Recovery Status: - Full restoration required - Partner-verified security - Enhanced monitoring implementation

Business Disruption: Duration: 4 hours critical, 24 hours total Departments Affected: Trading, Risk, Operations Service Interruptions: Trading Platform Access Customer Impact: 1,547 client accounts Recovery Time: 24 hours to full restoration

Regulatory Impact: Compliance Violations: Potential SEC reporting required Reporting Requirements: 72-hour notification window Regulatory Bodies: SEC, FINRA Filing Deadlines: Immediate notific - tion required Potential Penalties: Under assessment

Reputation Risk: Public Exposure: Controlled through proactive halt Media Coverage: Preventative maintenance story Customer Trust Impact: Minimal if contained Brand Damage: Potentially positive if handled well Recovery Strategy: Proactive communication plan

2. TECHNICAL RESPONSE

Immediate Actions:
Initial Response:
- Trading platform isolation
- CyberGuard Solutions activation
- DataDefend forensics initiation
- DIS Risk Solutions coordination

Containment Measures:
- Network segmentation (CyberGuard-led)
- Enhanced monitoring deployment
- Partner system integration
- Cross-platform security

Evidence Preservation:
- Full system imaging (DataDefend)
- Chain of custody documentation
- Partner activity logging
- Integrated response timeline

Team Activation:
- Complete IR team assembly
- Partner resource deployment
- Carrier notification protocol
- Stakeholder communications

Investigation Steps:
Forensics Process:
- Memory dump analysis (DataDefend lead)
- Integrated tool deployment
- Multi-team correlation
- Partner findings synthesi

Evidence Collection:
- Network traffic capture (CyberGuard/Internal
- System state documentation
- Partner system logs
- Integrated timeline creation

Analysis Procedures:
- Malware reverse engineering
- Cross-platform investigation
- Threat intelligence correlation
- Partner expertise leveraging

Documentation:
- Chain of custody maintenance
- DIS Risk Solutions protocols
- Partner activity logging
- Integrated response records

Solution Development:
Technical Solutions:
- Emergency patch creation (Internal/CyberGuard)
- Enhanced monitoring implementation

- Partner system integration
- Security control upgrades

Process Changes:
- Enhanced monitoring protocols
- Partner communication channels
- Integrated response procedures
- Cross-team coordination

Policy Updates:
- API security protocols
- Partner access controls
- Integrated monitoring rules
- Response team procedures

Control Enhancement:
- Authentication improvements
- Partner system integration
- Multi-layer validation
- Cross-platform security

Implementation Process:
Deployment Plan:
- Phased patch rollout (CyberGuard validated)
- Partner system coordination
- Integrated testing approach
- Staged implementation

Testing Procedures:
- Staging environment validation
- Partner system verificatio
- Integration testing
- Security control validation

Rollback Plan:
- System restore points
- Partner system coordination
- Recovery procedures
- Business continuity measures

Monitoring Plan:
- Enhanced detection rules
- Partner system integration
- Cross-platform visibility
- Continuous assessment

3. IMPLEMENTATION TIMELINE

Immediate (0-24 hours): Hour 1: - Initial assessment - DIS Risk Solutions activation - Partner team engagement - Preliminary containment

Hours 2-4: - Forensic analysis (DataDefend) - Containment measures (CyberGuard) - Initial carrier notifications - Stakeholder communications

Hours 4-8: - Patch development - Partner system testing - Integration validation - Security enhancement

Hours 8-16: - Deployment and validation - Partner coordination - System restoration - Enhanced monitoring

Hours 16-24: - System restoration - Partner verificati n - Security validation - Operational confirmatio

Short-term (1-7 days): Day 1: - Enhanced monitoring implementation (CyberGuard) - Full forensics report (DataDefend) - DIS Risk Solutions carrier updates - Stakeholder briefing

Days 2-3: - Additional security measures deployment - Partner system integration refinement - Cross-platform security validation - Team coordination protocols

Days 4-5: - Process documentation updates - Partner integration procedures - Security control validation - Response capability enhancement

Days 6-7: - Team training on new procedures - Partner coordination refinement - System optimization - Security posture validatio

Review Points: - Daily security assessments - Partner performance evaluation - Integration effectiveness - Response capability validation

Long-term (8-30 days): Week 2: - Comprehensive security review - Partner system optimization - Integration enhancement - Control refinemen

Week 3: - Process improvement implementation - Partner coordination enhancement - Security control optimization - Response capability strengthening

Week 4: - Long-term monitoring enhancement - Partner integration finalization - System optimization completion - Security posture confirmatio

Milestones: - Weekly progress assessments - Partner performance reviews - Integration validation - Security enhancement confirmatio

Success Criteria: - No further anomalies - Partner system stability - Integration effectiveness - Enhanced security posture

4. KEY TAKEAWAYS

Business Lessons: Strategic Insights: - Early detection crucial - Partner integration valuable - DIS Risk Solutions coordination essential - Integrated response effectiveness

Operational Changes: - Enhanced monitoring needed - Partner communication improvements - Cross-platform integration - Response coordination refinemen

Process Improvements: - Faster escalation protocols - Partner engagement optimization - Integration enhancement - Communication streamlining

Resource Allocation: - IR team expansion required - Partner resource optimization - Tool integration investment - Training enhancement needs

Future Prevention: - Regular penetration testing - Partner capability enhancement - Integration testing - Response capability strengthening

Technical Insights: Security Gaps: - API authentication weakness - Integration point vulnerabilities - Partner access controls - Monitoring thresholds

Technical Debt: - Legacy system vulnerabilities - Integration limitations - Partner system compatibility - Security tool optimization

Architecture Changes: - Enhanced segmentation needed - Partner system integration - Cross-platform security - Monitoring enhancement

Tool Effectiveness: - AI detection successful - Partner tool integration - Cross-platform visibility - Response capability validation

Capability Needs: - Advanced threat hunting - Partner expertise leverage - Integration optimization - Response tool enhancement

Process Improvements: Policy Updates: - API security enhancement - Partner integration procedures - Response coordination - Security control standards

Procedure Modifications: - Escalation protocols - Partner engagement process - Integration workflows - Communication channel

Training Needs: - Technical team upskilling - Partner coordination training - Integration management - Response capability development

Documentation Updates: - IR playbook revision - Partner integration guides - Security procedures - Response protocols

Control Enhancements: - Authentication protocols - Partner access management - Integration security - Monitoring capabilities

5. ROI ANALYSIS

Prevention Costs: Technology Investment: - Security infrastructure: $42M - Partner integration: $8M - Tool enhancement: $12M - Platform optimization: $5.8M

Staff Training: - Internal teams: $3.2M - Partner coordination: $1.4M - Integration management: $1.2M - Response capability: $2M

Process Implementation: - Security enhancement: $5M - Partner integration: $3M - Tool deployment: $2M - Response optimization: $2M

Ongoing Maintenance: - Annual security: $4M - Partner coordination: $2M - Integration management: $1M - Response capability: $1M

Total Prevention Cost: $67.8M

Incident Costs: Direct Response: - Emergency response: $5M - Partner activation: $3M - Forensics investigation: $4M - System restoration: $3M Total Direct Response: $15M

Business Impact: - Trading disruption: $45M - Client impact: $22M - Reputation management: $12M - Recovery operations: $5M Total Business Impact: $84M potential

Recovery Efforts: - System hardening: $12M - Partner integration enhancement: $6M - Security upgrades: $7M - Process improvement: $3M Total Recovery: $28M

Long-term Effects: - Security posture enhancement - Partner relationship strengthening - Integration optimization - Response capability improvement Total Impact: Under assessment

Total Incident Cost: $162M+

Future Savings: Risk Reduction: - Incident prevention: $45M annually - Partner efficiency: $25M annually - Integration benefits: $20M annually - Response optimization: $15M annually Total Risk Reduction: $105M annually

Efficiency Gains: - Operational improvement: $18M annually - Partner coordination: $12M annually - Integration effectiveness: $8M annually - Response capability: $4M annually Total Effici ncy Gains: $42M annually

Prevention Benefits: - Security enhancement: $25M annually - Partner value: $18M annually - Integration advantage: $12M annually - Response readiness: $8M annually Total Prevention Benefits: $63M annually

Resource Optimization: - Staff efficiency: $8M annually - Partner leverage: $6M annually - Integration benefits: $4M annually - Response capability: $3M annually Total Resource Optimization: $21M annually

Total Projected Savings: $231M annually

6. ACTION CHECKLIST

Immediate Response: - Incident Declaration • Activate IR protocol • Notify DIS Risk Solutions • Engage partner teams • Document initial finding

- Team Activation • Internal IR team assembly • CyberGuard Solutions engagement • DataDefend forensics activation • DIS coordination establishment

- Initial Containment • Trading platform isolation • Partner system integration • Evidence preservation • Communication channels establishment

- Evidence Collection • System logs capture • Partner activity documentation • Chain of custody maintenance • Timeline creation

Assessment Tasks: - Impact Analysis • Financial exposure assessment • Partner system review • Client impact evaluation • Regulatory implications

- System Review • Technical vulnerability assessment • Partner integration check • Security control evaluation • Response capability assessment

- Data Assessment • Breach scope determination • Partner data review • Privacy impact analysis • Regulatory requirements

- Risk Evaluation • Current threat assessment • Partner risk review • Integration vulnerability check • Future exposure analysis

- Compliance Check • Regulatory requirement review • Partner compliance verificat on • Documentation completeness • Reporting obligations

7. C-SUITE COMMUNICATION PROTOCOL

Executive Notification Sequence

CISO (James Davidson) - Initial incident assessment - Security response coordination - Partner integration oversight - Ongoing security updates

CTO (Margaret Wu) - Technical impact assessment - Resource allocation - Partner system coordination - Recovery timeline development

CFO (Elizabeth Morgan) - Financial exposure assessment - DIS Risk Solutions coordination - Insurance activation - Cost impact analysis

CEO (Robert Williams) - Strategic decisions - Public communications approval - Stakeholder management - Final authority on major actions

DIS Risk Solutions (Damian Davis) - Insurance coordination - Partner response management - Carrier communications - Strategic response guidance

Communication Templates: - Initial Notification • Incident overview • Partner engagement status • Immediate actions taken • Required decisions

- Status Updates • Response progress • Partner activities • Risk assessment • Next steps

- Decision Requests • Options analysis • Partner recommendations • Risk implications • Required actions

- Executive Summaries • Situation overview • Partner contribution • Current status • Strategic implications

- Public Statements • Approved messaging • Partner coordination • Stakeholder communications • Media response

Decision Matrix: - Trading Halt Criteria • Impact thresholds • Partner input • Risk assessment • Business implications

- System Shutdown Authority • Decision hierarchy • Partner consultation • Recovery implications • Business continuity

- Client Notification Triggers • Regulatory requirements • Partner guidance • Legal obligations • Communication timing

- Media Response Guidelines • Message approval process • Partner coordination • Spokesperson designation • Response timing

- Recovery Milestones • Technical restoration • Partner verification • Business resumption • Long-term enhancement

Chapter 2

Supply Chain Compromise

PART 1: NARRATIVE CASE STUDY

Company Profile: TechManufacture Global
Annual Revenue: $175M
Industry: Advanced Manufacturing (Electric Vehicle Components)
Employees: 550
Client Base: Regional automotive manufacturers (Tier 2 Supplier)
Market Position: Mid-sized supplier of precision EV components specializing in automated manufacturing solutions
Geographic Presence: Primary manufacturing facility in Detroit, with satellite operations in Singapore

0430 Hours - TechManufacture Global, Detroit Operations Center
Alex Rivera's production monitoring dashboard lit up like a Christmas tree. As Operations Technology (OT) Security Manager, he immediately noted that TechDefend's advanced monitoring system, implemented as part of their DIS Risk Solutions security package, had caught microscopic deviations that shouldn't exist.

"Park," he called to his senior systems analyst, "pull up the ICS logs for Lines 3 through 7."

Michelle Park, recently transferred from their Singapore facility, was already analyzing the data. "These deviations... they're systematic. The robots are operating within normal parameters, but their movements are off by 0.03 millimeters. TechDefend's baseline monitoring caught it before quality control."

0445 Hours - Manufacturing Floor

The massive production floor hummed with the synchronized dance of hundreds of robotic arms, assembling electric vehicle components with precision that should have been perfect. Alex and Michelle stood before Line 4, tablets in hand, watching the real-time security feeds from both internal systems and TechDefend's monitoring platform.

"There," Michelle pointed. "The compensation algorithm is adjusting for the deviation, but it shouldn't need to. Something's manipulating the baseline coordinates."

0500 Hours - Initial Investigation

Dr. William Foster, Head of Industrial Control Systems, joined them on the floo . His expertise in OT/IT convergence had helped design their segmented network architecture, working closely with TechDefend to implement DIS Risk Solutions' recommended security controls.

"The deviations started appearing in the third shift," William explained, pulling up historical data. "But here's the concerning part – the changes came through a validated vendor update package. All signatures check out."

0515 Hours - Security Operations Center

The facility's integrated SOC team, led by Sarah Rodriguez, began their investigation, combining internal expertise with TechDefend's managed security services:

Internal Team: • Marcus Lee - OT Security Specialist • Dr. Patricia Wong - Supply Chain Security Lead

TechDefend Team: • Richard Johnson - OT Security Response • David Nguyen - Threat Hunter • Victoria Liu - System Restoration Specialist

Sarah's team had already initiated their OT incident response protocol, a framework developed jointly with DIS Risk Solutions. "The vendor update came from AutomatePro," she reported. "They're our primary robotics software provider. All digital signatures are valid, but the update pattern is unusual. TechDefend's threat intelligence is showing similar patterns across the automotive sector."

0530 Hours - Technical Discovery

David Nguyen's analysis revealed the first critical insight. "The update package is genuine, but it's been tampered with post-signature. Someone compromised AutomatePro's distribution network. The modification is subtle – it's adjusting the robotic arm's base calibration by introducing a dynamic variable in the positioning algorithm."

Dr. Patricia Wong added, "This could affect every component manufactured since the update. We're looking at potentially thousands of defective parts. I've already notified CyberForensics to begin their supply chain analysis."

0545 Hours - Crisis Assessment

Alex knew they needed to escalate. The potential impact was massive – defective components could affect multiple global auto manufacturers. He reached for his phone to initiate the executive notification protocol, which included Damian Davis from DIS Risk Solutions.

"We need to wake up Michael Anderson," Alex stated. "Damian's team is already coordinating with the carriers, and CyberForensics is starting their investigation."

Rachel Torres had already begun preparing the carrier notification. "The combined cyber and product liability implications require careful documentation," she noted. "I'll have the initial notice to carriers within the hour, including the potential safety implications."

Sarah nodded. "I'll start the incident response documentation. TechDefend's team is already pulling forensics data for CyberForensics to analyze. Dr. Amanda Foster's team has experience with similar supply chain compromises."

0600 Hours - C-Suite Notification

Alex made two simultaneous calls - one to Michael Anderson, CISO, and another to Damian Davis at DIS Risk Solutions. Both answered immediately.

"Michael, it's Alex Rivera. We have a critical supply chain incident. Compromised vendor update affecting production quality. Multiple lines impacted. Damian's already coordinating with carriers and CyberForensics is starting their analysis."

Anderson's response was sharp and focused. "Scope of impact?"

"Potentially thousands of components since 2300 hours," Alex reported. "The deviation is subtle enough to bypass standard quality control, but TechDefend's enhanced monitoring caught it. We need to notify Jennifer [CTO] and consider a production halt."

"Good catch by TechDefend," Anderson replied. "I'm calling Jennifer now. Damian, what's our insurance position on this?"

Damian Davis, already reviewing the initial data, responded, "Our blended cyber and product liability coverage will respond. I've activated our claims protocols, and Rachel Torres is preparing the carrier notifications. Mark Stevens is coordinating the technical response between TechDefend and CyberForensics."

0615 Hours - Technical Response Team Assembly

Jennifer Park, CTO, arrived at the facility within fifteen minutes of Anderson's call. The war room was already configured with TechDefend's integrated security feeds and CyberForensics' analysis platforms:

Command Center Displays: - Real-time production monitoring (TechDefend) - Vendor update analysis (CyberForensics) - Component quality data - Supply chain mapping - Client delivery schedules - Insurance and regulatory compliance tracking (DIS Risk Solutions)

Dr. Amanda Foster from CyberForensics joined virtually, her team already deep into the supply chain analysis. "We're seeing similarities to other recent automotive supplier compromises. Dr. William Foster's forensics team is mapping the attack path through AutomatePro's distribution network."

0630 Hours - Executive Briefing

The emergency executive briefing convened via secure conference. Robert Mitchell, CEO, and Sandra Wong, CFO, joined virtually, along with Thomas Schmidt, COO, who was already on-site. Damian Davis and key partner leads were patched in through their dedicated incident response channel.

Alex led the briefing: "At 0430 hours, TechDefend's advanced monitoring system detected systematic deviations in robotic assembly precision. CyberForensics' preliminary analysis reveals a compromised vendor update from AutomatePro, affecting component quality across multiple production lines. The deviation is 0.03 millimeters – subtle enough to bypass standard quality control but potentially critical in final assembly."

Sandra Wong interrupted, "Quantify the exposure."

"Approximately 3,200 components produced since 2300 hours," Alex reported. "These components are destined for three major auto manufacturers. The deviation could affect critical safety systems."

Damian Davis interjected, "I've already initiated both cyber and product liability claims. Rachel Torres has engaged our crisis management coverage, and Mark Stevens is coordinating the technical response teams. Given the potential safety implications and our early detection, we're in a strong position with carriers."

Thomas Schmidt leaned forward. "Jennifer, what's the technical assessment?"

"The attack is sophisticated," Jennifer Park responded. "TechDefend's analysis, led by Richard Johnson, shows they compromised AutomatePro's software distribution system, modified a legitimate update, but maintained valid signatures. Dr. Amanda Foster's team at CyberForensics found evidence this may be part of a larger campaign targeting automotive suppliers. We need to halt production, roll back the update, and implement manual quality checks on all affected components."

"Timeline for resolution?" Mitchell asked.

"Victoria Liu from TechDefend estimates four hours to roll back the update, another two for system validation," Jennifer replied. "But quality inspection of existing components will take at least 48 hours. Kevin Zhang from CyberForensics is already coordinating with AutomatePro's security team to expedite the process."

"Regulatory implications?" Mitchell turned to Anderson.

"We have a 24-hour notification requirement to the NTSB," the CISO explained. "Rachel Torres is already preparing the necessary documentation through DIS's regulatory response protocols. Given the safety implications, we should notify them immediately."

Damian Davis added, "Our crisis management team has experience with similar situations in the automotive sector. Early transparency typically yields the best results. We can coordinate all stakeholder communications through our established channels."

Mitchell made the decision. "Execute the halt. Sandra, work with Rachel Torres on financial impact assessment. Thomas, activate our supply chain contingency plan. Michael, have CyberForensics continue their investigation with AutomatePro. Jennifer, you have six hours for the rollback and validation. Alex, I want hourly updates from all teams."

0645 Hours - Response Implementation

The integrated response team moved with practiced precision, each group executing their designated responsibilities:

Internal Leadership: Jennifer Park (CTO) - Leading technical response Michael Anderson (CISO) - Managing security operations Sandra Wong (CFO) - Handling financial implications Thomas Schmidt (COO) - Managing operational impact Robert Mitchell (CEO) - Strategic oversight Alex Rivera (OT Security) - Technical coordination

DIS Risk Solutions Team: Damian Davis - Strategic Response Coordinator Rachel Torres - Claims Protocol Manager Mark Stevens - Technical Integration Lead

Partner Operations: TechDefend: Richard Johnson - Leading OT security response David Nguyen - Managing threat hunting operations Victoria Liu - Coordinating system restoration

CyberForensics: Dr. Amanda Foster - Leading supply chain investigation Dr. William Foster - Managing forensics analysis Kevin Zhang - Coordinating vendor investigation

PART 2: TECHNICAL DEEP DIVE

Investigation Timeline:

2300-0430: Initial Compromise Window

- Vendor update deployment
- Initial deviations begin
- Quality control bypass
- Production continuation
- TechDefend's monitoring system logs anomalies
- Component manufacturing affected

0430-0600: Detection and Analysis

- TechDefend's system flags deviation
- DIS Risk Solutions notificatio
- CyberForensics activation
- System log analysis
- Vendor package verificatio
- Initial impact assessment
- Integrated team activation

0600-0900: Full Investigation

- CyberForensics supply chain analysis
- TechDefend OT system assessment
- Vendor coordination through DIS channels
- Impact quantificatio
- Mitigation strategy development

Technical Analysis:
1. Attack Vector Identificatio
Compromise Method (CyberForensics Findings):
- Software supply chain infiltratio
- Post-signature package modificatio

- Valid certificate manipulatio
- Distribution network compromise
- Update mechanism exploitation

TechDefend Analysis:
- Precision deviation patterns
- Authentication bypass methods
- Update validation failures
- Distribution chain mapping
- Control system impacts

2. Industrial Control System (ICS) Analysis
Component Analysis (TechDefend/Internal):
- Primary Impact: Robotic arm calibration
- Secondary Impact: Quality control systems
- Tertiary Impact: Production logging
- Affected PLCs: Series 7000 controllers
- Compromised Updates: Version 3.2.1.45

Behavior Analysis (Joint TechDefend/CyberForensics Assessment):
- Dynamic variable injection patterns
- Calibration drift implementation
- Error compensation manipulation
- Quality check evasion techniques
- Log consistency maintenance methods

3. Supply Chain Impact Analysis
Vendor Systems (CyberForensics Investigation):
- AutomatePro update server compromise patterns
- Distribution network vulnerabilities
- Certificate management weaknesse
- Package validation bypass methods
- Deployment system infiltration point

Production Impact (TechDefend Assessment):
- Assembly precision deviation mapping
- Component quality variation analysis
- Production line vulnerability assessment
- Quality control bypass mechanisms
- Downstream implications modeling

4. Forensic Investigation
Evidence Collection (Coordinated Approach):
TechDefend OT Forensics:
- Update package analysis
- System logs extraction
- Network traffic captur
- PLC memory dumps
- Configuration backup

CyberForensics Supply Chain Analysis:
- Modification timestamp
- Package alteration signatures
- Distribution path mapping
- Attack methodology documentation
- Persistence mechanism identificatio

5. OT/IT Convergence Analysis
Network Segmentation (TechDefend Review):
- IT/OT boundary assessment
- DMZ configuration analysi
- Access control validation
- Update mechanism security
- Security zone effectiveness

Security Controls (Joint Assessment):
- Authentication system review
- Package validation protocols

- Signature verification method
- Change management procedures
- Update distribution security

6. Quality Impact Assessment

Manufacturing Precision (TechDefend Analysis):
- Standard tolerance: ±0.01mm
- Induced deviation: 0.03mm
- Cumulative effect modeling
- Component stress analysis
- Safety implications assessment

Testing Methodology (Integrated Approach):
- Automated inspection protocols
- Manual verification procedure
- Stress testing parameters
- Component analysis methods
- Safety validation requirements

7. Solution Development

Technical Response (TechDefend Lead):
- Update rollback procedure development
- System recalibration protocols
- Quality control enhancement
- Monitoring improvement strategy
- Validation protocol design

Implementation Strategy (Coordinated Approach):

DIS Risk Solutions Oversight:
- Production halt coordination
- Insurance notification managemen
- Regulatory compliance tracking
- Stakeholder communication

TechDefend Implementation:
- System restoration procedures
- Component quarantine protocols
- Testing methodology
- Verification process managemen

CyberForensics Support:
- Supply chain vulnerability remediation
- Vendor system hardening recommendations
- Future attack prevention measures
- Long-term security improvements

PART 3: IMPLEMENTATION GUIDE

1. IMPACT ASSESSMENT

Financial Impact: Direct Costs: $2.1M production halt Indirect Costs: $750,000 quality inspection Potential Future Losses: $15M+ liability exposure Recovery Costs: $500,000 estimated Insurance Implications: Cyber and liability policies activated

Insurance Implications:

Primary Coverage: $50M cyber and product liability tower structured as: • Primary Layer: $10M Carrier A: 100% ($10M) Cyber/Product Liability Blend

• First Excess: $20M xs $10M Carrier B: 35% ($7M) Carrier C: 35% ($7M) Carrier D: 30% ($6M)

• Second Excess: $20M xs $30M Carrier E: 40% ($8M) Carrier F: 30% ($6M) Carrier G: 30% ($6M)

Program Manager: DIS Risk Solutions - Strategic Response Coordination: Damian Davis - Claims Protocol Management: Rachel Torres - Technical Integration: Mark Stevens

Retention/Deductible: $1M per cyber incident, $1M per product recall • Applies to each and every claim • Annual aggregate retention: $2M cyber, $2M product recall • Retention applies across all manufacturing operations • Time deductible: 12 hours for BI • Maintenance deductible: $1M for PCI

Coverage Triggers: • Cyber attack • Product defect • Manufacturing halt • Supply chain incident • Quality control failure

Notification Timeline: 12 hours for cyber events, immediate for safety issues

Claims Process: • Coordinated through DIS Risk Solutions • Dual-track activation (cyber and product liability) • Integrated partner response protocols • Real-time carrier updates

Expected Coverage: • Business interruption • Product recall expenses • System restoration • Third-party liability • Crisis management

Additional Coverage Features: • Supply chain contingent coverage • Vendor liability • Quality control failure • Regulatory defense • Crisis management expenses

1. IMPACT ASSESSMENT

Systems Affected: Primary Systems: - Robotic Assembly Lines 3-7 (TechDefend monitored) - Quality Control Systems (Joint monitoring) - Production Logging Systems

Secondary Systems: - Vendor Update Management - Quality Assurance Platforms - Production Tracking - Supply Chain Management

Dependencies: - AutomatePro Infrastructure - TechDefend Security Monitoring - CyberForensics Analysis Platforms - DIS Risk Solutions Integration Systems

Third-Party Systems: - AutomatePro Update Servers - Supplier Network Connections - Client Integration Points - Regulatory Reporting Systems

Recovery Status: - Full system rollback required - Partner-verified security - Enhanced monitoring implementation - Quality control validation

Business Disruption: Duration: 6 hours critical, 48 hours total Departments Affected: Production, Quality, Supply Chain Service Interruptions: Full production halt Customer Impact: Three major auto manufacturers Recovery Time: 48-72 hours estimated

Regulatory Impact: Compliance Violations: NTSB reporting required Reporting Requirements: 24-hour notification window Regulatory Bodies: NTSB, ISO, Quality Certifications Filing Deadlines: Immediate NTSB notification Potential Penalties: Under assessmen

Reputation Risk: Public Exposure: High - safety implications Media Coverage: Potential industry news Customer Trust Impact: Major manufacturers affected Brand Damage: Significant if not handled properly Recovery Strategy: - DIS Risk Solutions crisis management - Proactive transparency approach - Coordinated stakeholder communications - Integrated partner response

2. TECHNICAL RESPONSE

Immediate Actions: Initial Response: - Production halt initiation - TechDefend system isolation - CyberForensics activation - DIS Risk Solutions coordination

Containment Measures: - Network segmentation (TechDefend) - Update rollback procedures - Evidence preservation protocols - Partner system integration

Investigation Steps: Forensics Process: - TechDefend OT System Analysis • Memory dump collection • System log extraction • Configuration backup • Network traffic capture - CyberForensics Supply Chain Investigation • Vendor package analysis • Distribution path tracking • Compromise timeline creation • Attack pattern documentation - DIS Risk Solutions Coordination • Evidence preservation protocols • Chain of custody maintenance • Documentation standards • Regulatory compliance tracking

Solution Development: Technical Solutions: - TechDefend Implementation • System restoration planning • Security control enhancement • Monitoring improvement • Quality check automation

- CyberForensics Recommendations • Supply chain hardening • Vendor security requirements • Distribution security • Update validation protocols - DIS Risk Solutions Oversight • Solution validation • Compliance verification • Insurance alignment • Documentation revie

Implementation Process: Deployment Plan: - Phase 1: Immediate Response • Production system isolation • Initial containment measures • Evidence preservation • Stakeholder notification - Phase 2: Investigation • Forensic analysis • Impact assessment • Root cause determination • Exposure quantification - Phase 3: Remediation • System restoration • Security enhancement • Process improvement • Control validation

3. IMPLEMENTATION TIMELINE

Immediate (0-24 hours): Hour 1: - Production halt initiation - DIS Risk Solutions activation - Partner team engagement - Initial containment

Hours 2-4: - TechDefend system rollback - CyberForensics analysis - Evidence preservation - Stakeholder communications

Hours 4-8: - System restoration - Security validation - Quality control testing - Partner coordination

Hours 8-16: - Component inspection - Process verification - Documentation review - Status updates

Hours 16-24: - Production resumption planning - Enhanced monitoring implementation - Partner system integration - Compliance verificatio

Short-term (1-7 days): Day 1: - Complete quality inspection (TechDefend oversight) - Full forensics report (CyberForensics) - DIS Risk Solutions carrier updates - Initial regulatory filing

Days 2-3: - Additional security measures deployment - TechDefend enhanced monitoring - CyberForensics vendor coordination - Stakeholder progress reports - DIS Risk Solutions documentation review

Days 4-5: - Process documentation updates - Security control validation - Partner integration refinement - Response capability enhancement - Insurance claim documentation

Days 6-7: - Team training on new procedures - System optimization verification - Quality control validation - Partner coordination protocols - Compliance documentation review

Review Points: - Daily security assessments (TechDefend) - Supply chain analysis updates (CyberForensics) - Insurance position reviews (DIS Risk Solutions) - Partner performance evaluation - Integration effectiveness checks

Long-term (8-30 days): Week 2: - Comprehensive security review • TechDefend system assessment • CyberForensics recommendations • DIS Risk Solutions compliance audit • Partner integration validation

Week 3: - Process improvement implementation • Enhanced monitoring protocols • Supply chain security measures • Updated response procedures • Partner coordination refinemen

Week 4: - Long-term monitoring enhancement • TechDefend platform optimization • CyberForensics threat intelligence integration • DIS Risk Solutions program updates • Partner capability enhancement

Milestones: - Weekly progress assessments - Partner performance reviews - Insurance program updates - Security enhancement confirm - tion - Compliance validation checks

Success Criteria: - No further anomalies - Partner system stability - Insurance program optimization - Enhanced security posture - Documented compliance

4. KEY TAKEAWAYS

Business Lessons: Strategic Insights: - Early detection crucial - Partner integration valuable - DIS Risk Solutions coordination essential - Supply chain security critical

Operational Changes: - Enhanced monitoring needed (TechDefend-led) - Supply chain validation protocols (CyberForensics-guided) - Insurance program optimization (DIS Risk Solutions) - Cross-platform integration requirements - Response coordination refinemen

Process Improvements: - Faster escalation protocols - Partner engagement optimization - Integration enhancement - Communication streamlining - Documentation standards

Resource Allocation: - IR team expansion required - Partner resource optimization - Tool integration investment - Training enhancement needs - Compliance capability building

Future Prevention: - Regular penetration testing (TechDefend) - Supply chain audits (CyberForensics) - Insurance program reviews (DIS Risk Solutions) - Partner capability enhancement - Response capability strengthening

Technical Insights: Security Gaps: - Supply chain validation weaknesses - Integration point vulnerabilities - Update distribution security - Quality control monitoring - Partner access controls

Technical Debt: - Legacy system vulnerabilities - Integration limitations - Monitoring capabilities - Security tool optimization - Documentation systems

Architecture Changes: - Enhanced segmentation needed - Partner system integration - Cross-platform security - Monitoring enhancement - Access control refinemen

Tool Effectiveness: - TechDefend monitoring success - CyberForensics analysis capability - DIS Risk Solutions coordination tools - Partner platform integration - Response system efficienc

Capability Needs: - Advanced threat hunting - Supply chain monitoring - Insurance program integration - Partner expertise leverage - Response tool enhancement

Process Improvements: Policy Updates: - Supply chain security requirements - Partner integration procedures - Insurance program alignment - Response coordination - Documentation standards

Procedure Modifications: - Escalation protocols - Partner engagement process - Integration workflows - Communication channels - Quality control procedures

Training Needs: - Technical team upskilling - Partner coordination training - Insurance program awareness - Integration management - Response capability development

Documentation Updates: - IR playbook revision - Partner integration guides - Insurance program procedures - Security protocols - Compliance requirements

Control Enhancements: - Supply chain validation - Partner access management - Insurance program controls - Integration security - Monitoring capabilities

5. ROI ANALYSIS

Prevention Costs: Technology Investment: - TechDefend Security Infrastructure: $350,000 - CyberForensics Supply Chain Tools: $200,000 - DIS Risk Solutions Integration: $100,000 - Platform Optimization: $100,000 Subtotal: $750,000

Staff Training: - Internal Teams: $75,000 - Partner Coordination: $35,000 - Insurance Program: $15,000 - Integration Management: $25,000 Subtotal: $150,000

Process Implementation: - Security Enhancement: $100,000 - Partner Integration: $75,000 - Insurance Program Updates: $25,000 - Response Optimization: $50,000 Subtotal: $250,000

Ongoing Maintenance: - Annual Security: $150,000 - Partner Coordination: $75,000 - Insurance Program: $25,000 - Integration Management: $50,000 Subtotal: $300,000/year

Total Prevention Cost: $1.45M

Incident Costs: Direct Response: - Emergency Response: $200,000 - Partner Activation: $150,000 - Forensics Investigation: $100,000 - System Restoration: $50,000 Total Direct Response: $500,000

Business Impact: - Production Halt: $1.2M - Quality Inspection: $400,000 - Client Impact: $300,000 - Recovery Operations: $200,000 Total Business Impact: $2.1M

Recovery Efforts: - System Hardening: $300,000 - Partner Integration: $200,000 - Security Upgrades: $150,000 - Process Improvement: $100,000 Total Recovery: $750,000

Long-term Effects: - Security Posture Enhancement - Partner Relationship Strengthening - Insurance Program Optimization - Response Capability Improvement Total Impact: Under assessment

Total Incident Cost: $3.35M+

Future Savings: Risk Reduction: - Incident Prevention: $4M annually - Partner Efficiency: $3M annually - Insurance Optimization: $2M annually - Response Improvement: $1M annually Total Risk Reduction: $10M+ annually

Efficiency Gains: - Operational Improvement: $750,000 annually - Partner Coordination: $400,000 annually - Insurance Program: $150,000 annually - Response Capability: $200,000 annually Total Efficiency Gains: $1.5M annually

Prevention Benefits: - Security Enhancement: $1M annually - Partner Value: $500,000 annually - Insurance Program: $250,000 annually - Response Readiness: $250,000 annually Total Prevention Benefits: $2M annually

Resource Optimization: - Staff Efficiency: $300,000 annually - Partner Leverage: $200,000 annually - Insurance Program: $100,000 annually - Response Capability: $150,000 annually Total Resource Optimization: $750,000 annually

Total Projected Savings: $14.25M annually

6. ACTION CHECKLIST

Immediate Response:

- Incident Declaration • Activate IR protocol • Notify DIS Risk Solutions • Engage TechDefend and CyberForensics • Document initial finding

- Team Activation • Internal IR team assembly • DIS Risk Solutions coordination • TechDefend security response • CyberForensics investigation • Partner resource deployment

- Initial Containment • Production system isolation (TechDefend) • Evidence preservation (CyberForensics) • Insurance notification (DIS Risk Solutions) • Communication channel establishment • Partner system integration

- Evidence Collection • System logs capture (TechDefend) • Supply chain analysis (CyberForensics) • Insurance documentation (DIS Risk Solutions) • Chain of custody maintenance • Timeline creation

Assessment Tasks:

- Impact Analysis • Financial exposure assessment (DIS Risk Solutions) • Technical system review (TechDefend) • Supply chain impact (CyberForensics) • Client impact evaluation • Regulatory implications

- System Review • Technical vulnerability assessment • Partner integration check • Security control evaluation • Response capability assessment • Insurance program review

- Quality Assessment • Component inspection protocols • Production line validation • Quality control review • Safety impact analysis • Compliance verificatio

- Risk Evaluation • Current threat assessment • Partner risk review • Insurance coverage analysis • Integration vulnerability check • Future exposure analysis

- Compliance Check • Regulatory requirement review • Partner compliance verification • Insurance program validation • Documentation completeness • Reporting obligations

7. C-SUITE COMMUNICATION PROTOCOL

Executive Notification Sequence

CISO (Michael Anderson)
- Initial incident assessment • Security response coordination • Partner integration oversight • Ongoing security updates • DIS Risk Solutions liaison

CTO (Jennifer Park)
- Technical impact assessment • Resource allocation • Partner system coordination • Recovery timeline development • Solution validation

COO (Thomas Schmidt)
- Operational impact assessment • Production decisions • Supply chain management • Customer communications • Business continuity oversight

CFO (Sandra Wong)
- Financial exposure assessment • DIS Risk Solutions coordination • Insurance activation • Cost impact analysis • Resource allocation

CEO (Robert Mitchell)
- Strategic decisions • Public communications approval • Stakeholder management • Final authority on major actions • Partner relationship oversight

DIS Risk Solutions (Damian Davis)
- Insurance coordination • Partner response management • Carrier communications • Strategic response guidance • Crisis management oversight

Communication Templates:
- Initial Notification • Incident overview • Partner engagement status • Insurance activation status • Immediate actions taken • Required decisions

- Status Updates • Response progress • Partner activities • Insurance claims status • Risk assessment • Next steps

- Decision Requests • Options analysis • Partner recommendations • Insurance implications • Risk assessment • Required actions

- Executive Summaries • Situation overview • Partner contribution • Insurance position • Current status • Strategic implications

- Public Statements • Approved messaging • Partner coordination • Insurance alignment • Stakeholder communications • Media response

Decision Matrix:

- Production Halt Criteria • Impact thresholds • Partner input • Insurance implications • Risk assessment • Business implications

- System Shutdown Authority • Decision hierarchy • Partner consultation • Insurance consideration • Recovery implications • Business continuity

- Client Notification Triggers • Regulatory requirements • Partner guidance • Insurance obligations • Legal requirements • Communication timing

- Media Response Guidelines • Message approval process • Partner coordination • Insurance alignment • Spokesperson designation • Response timing

- Recovery Milestones • Technical restoration • Partner verification • Insurance validation • Business resumption • Long-term enhancement

Chapter 3

The Human Factor

PART 1: NARRATIVE CASE STUDY

Company Profile: Metropolitan Medical Center
Annual Revenue: $225M
Industry: Healthcare (Regional Medical Center)
Employees: 1,200
Client Base: 250,000+ annual patients
Market Position: Leading regional healthcare provider specializing in oncology and clinical research
Geographic Presence: Main hospital campus with multiple satellite clinics in metropolitan area

0845 Hours - Metropolitan Medical Center, Information Security Operations

Rachel Martinez's morning coffee nearly hit the floor when the alert popped up on her screen. As Information Security Manager for one of the largest healthcare networks in the region, she was grateful for HealthGuard IT's enhanced monitoring system, implemented as part of their DIS Risk Solutions security package. The alert pattern was unlike typical phishing attempts.

"Zhang," she called to her senior security analyst, "pull up the email logs for the oncology department. HealthGuard's behavioral analysis is showing unusual access patterns."

Kevin Zhang, a veteran healthcare security specialist, was already analyzing the data. "These login credentials... they're valid, but the access locations are scattered across different IP ranges. Multiple simultaneous logins from different locations. HealthGuard's AI flagged it as potential credential compromise."

0900 Hours - Security Operations Center

The hospital's integrated SOC team, combining internal staff with HealthGuard IT's managed security services, assembled quickly:

Internal Team:
Dr. Sarah Anderson - Chief Medical Information Officer
James Liu - Security Analyst
Maria Ramirez - Compliance Officer
David Wright - Network Security Engineer
Lisa Nguyen - Incident Response Specialist

HealthGuard IT Team:
Michael Chen - Healthcare Security Lead
Victoria Adams - Network Defense Specialist
Robert Taylor - System Integration Lead

"Show me what we've got," Rachel demanded, scanning the main display.

James Liu pulled up the analysis. "It started with a targeted spear-phishing campaign. Very sophisticated - personalized emails to oncology staff, appearing to come from Dr. Anderson herself, requesting urgent patient record reviews. HealthGuard's threat intelligence has seen similar patterns targeting other healthcare facilities."

Dr. Anderson leaned forward, frowning. "I never sent those emails. When did this start?"

"First wave hit about 48 hours ago," James replied. "The attackers did their homework. They referenced actual patient appointment schedules, used proper medical terminology. Several staff members have already entered their credentials."

Michael Chen from HealthGuard IT added, "Our behavioral analysis shows they've been studying your email patterns and medical workflows. This isn't opportunistic - it's a targeted campaign."

0915 Hours - Initial Assessment

Lisa Nguyen's preliminary analysis, coordinated with CyberForensics' healthcare team, revealed the scope. "We're looking at potential unauthorized access to over 5,000 patient records. The attackers are using compromised credentials to extract data systematically. They're focusing on high-profile patients and those involved in clinical trials."

Maria Ramirez, already documenting for HIPAA compliance, interjected. "This is a reportable breach. We have 60 days to notify affected patients, but given the sensitivity of oncology data, we should act faster. I'll coordinate with DIS Risk Solutions on the notification requirements."

Rachel Torres from DIS Risk Solutions was already drafting the initial carrier notification. "Given the HIPAA implications and the nature of the compromised data, we need to be thorough," she noted. "I'll have the preliminary notice to carriers within the hour, including the potential clinical trial data exposure."

0930 Hours - Pattern Recognition

David Wright and Victoria Adams from HealthGuard IT identified the attack pattern. "They're smart," David explained. "They're spacing out the access requests to avoid triggering standard threshold alerts. Each compromised account is being used to access just enough records to stay under the radar. But when you look at the aggregate pattern..."

Victoria gestured to her screen, showing a spider web of data access points spreading across the hospital's network. "Our enhanced monitoring caught it because we're correlating behavior across all access points. Dr. Amanda Foster's team at CyberForensics is already mapping the data extraction patterns."

0945 Hours - Crisis Escalation

Rachel knew it was time to notify the executive team and DIS Risk Solutions. She reached for her phone to make two calls - one to Katherine Song, the hospital's CISO, and another to Damian Davis.

"We need to lock this down now," Rachel announced to her team. "David and Victoria, start isolating the affected accounts. Maria, begin breach documentation with DIS. Lisa, coordinate with CyberForensics for full incident response. James, get me a complete list of compromised records. Dr. Anderson, we'll need your help with the medical staff."

1000 Hours - Executive Notification

Katherine Song answered on the first ring. Rachel's calls were always priority, especially with DIS Risk Solutions' alert protocols in place.

"Katherine, it's Rachel. We have a confirmed social engineering breach in oncology. HealthGuard IT detected a sophisticated spear-phishing campaign that compromised multiple staff credentials. Over 5,000 patient records potentially exposed, including clinical trial data. Damian Davis is already coordinating with carriers."

"Severity assessment?" Katherine's tone was sharp.

"Critical. They're specifically targeting high-profile patients and research data. Well-planned, well-executed. HealthGuard's analysis suggests this is part of a larger campaign targeting healthcare facilities. CyberForensics is already mapping the data extraction patterns."

"Understood. I'm activating the incident response team. Have you started containment?"

"Yes, HealthGuard's team is isolating affected accounts now. But Katherine... this is going to require department-wide access resets. Possibly network-wide."

"Agreed. I'm calling Emma [CTO] and William [CEO]. Get your team ready for a full briefing in 30 minutes. We'll need options for maintaining critical care access during the reset."

1015 Hours - Technical Response Team Assembly

The hospital's integrated incident response team gathered in the main conference room. Emma Richardson, CTO, arrived with William Hayes, CEO, and Dr. Jennifer Williams, Chief Medical Office . Damian Davis and the partner team leads joined virtually through their secure incident response channel.

The situation room displays showed:
- Compromised account status (HealthGuard IT)
- Patient record access logs
- Phishing email analysis (CyberForensics)
- Network access patterns
- Department impact assessment
- Insurance and compliance tracking (DIS Risk Solutions)

1030 Hours - Executive Briefing

Rachel led the briefing: "At 0845 hours, HealthGuard IT's enhanced monitoring detected anomalous access patterns in our Electronic Health Records system. Investigation reveals a sophisticated spear-phishing campaign targeting oncology staff. Attackers impersonated Dr. Anderson, using accurate patient scheduling details and medical terminology to establish credibility."

Emma Richardson interrupted, "Current exposure?"

"Approximately 5,200 patient records accessed through compromised credentials," Rachel reported. "CyberForensics has confirmed they're primarily targeting high-profile patients and those in clinical trials. The attack shows clear knowledge of our internal procedures and medical workflows."

Damian Davis added, "I've already initiated our cyber insurance response protocols. Rachel Torres is preparing the carrier notifications, and Mark Stevens is coordinating the technical response teams. Given the sensitivity of oncology data, we're treating this as a critical incident under our policy."

Dr. Williams leaned forward. "Impact on patient care?"

"We need to reset all oncology department access credentials immediately," Rachel explained. "This will disrupt EHR access for approximately 200 medical staff. HealthGuard IT has prepared emergency protocols for paper-based contingency, but it will slow down care delivery."

"Regulatory implications?" Hayes turned to Katherine.

"This is a reportable HIPAA breach," the CISO confirmed. "DIS Risk Solutions' compliance team is already preparing the necessary documentation. We have 60 days to notify patients, but given the sensitivity and profile of the affected records, we should accelerate that timeline. Rachel Torres is coordinating with our carriers, and CyberForensics is preserving evidence for law enforcement notification."

Hayes considered the options. "Do we have any indication of the attackers' identity or motivation?"

"The sophistication suggests a well-funded group," Katherine responded. "HealthGuard IT's threat intelligence team has identified similar patterns at other healthcare facilities. Michael Chen's analysis suggests this could be part of a coordinated campaign targeting clinical research data."

Dr. Amanda Foster from CyberForensics joined in virtually. "We're seeing sophisticated data extraction patterns focused specifically on oncology research and high-profile patient records. This aligns with recent attacks we've investigated at other medical facilities."

Hayes made the decision. "Execute the credential reset. Katherine, coordinate with FBI healthcare cybercrime division through CyberForensics. Emma, implement emergency access protocols for critical care. Dr. Williams, activate medical staff contingency procedures. Rachel, coordinate hourly updates through DIS Risk Solutions' incident management platform."

1045 Hours - Response Implementation

As the team mobilized to execute the CEO's directives, the integrated response showed years of preparation and planning. Each group moved with practiced precision:

Internal Leadership:
- Katherine Song (CISO) - Leading security response
- Emma Richardson (CTO) - Managing technical systems
- Dr. Williams (CMO) - Coordinating medical staff
- William Hayes (CEO) - Directing overall response
- Rachel Martinez - Technical coordination
- Maria Ramirez - Compliance documentation

DIS Risk Solutions Team:
- Damian Davis - Strategic Response Coordinator
- Rachel Torres - Claims Protocol Manager
- Mark Stevens - Technical Integration Lead

HealthGuard IT Team:
- Michael Chen - Leading security operations
- Victoria Adams - Managing network defense
- Robert Taylor - Coordinating system restoration

CyberForensics Team:
- Dr. Amanda Foster - Leading investigation
- Sarah Wilson - Healthcare forensics analysis
- Thomas Lee - Compliance investigation

Action Teams:
Technical Response:
- HealthGuard IT implementing access resets
- CyberForensics conducting forensic analysis
- Internal IT managing clinical systems
- DIS Risk Solutions coordinating documentation

Clinical Operations:
- Medical staff moving to contingency procedures
- Paper-based backup systems activated
- Critical care access maintained
- Patient care continuity preserved

Compliance and Communications:
- HIPAA documentation initiated
- Patient notification planning
- Law enforcement coordination
- Stakeholder communications prepared

PART 2: TECHNICAL DEEP DIVE

Investigation Timeline:

0845-1000: Initial Detection and Analysis

- HealthGuard IT monitoring alert
- DIS Risk Solutions notificatio
- Email log analysis
- Credential compromise verificatio
- Initial impact assessment
- Partner team activation
- CyberForensics engagement

1000-1200: Full Investigation

- HealthGuard IT behavioral analysis
- CyberForensics phishing investigation
- Access pattern mapping
- Data exfiltration trackin
- DIS Risk Solutions documentation
- Breach scope determination
- Impact quantificatio

1200-1500: Comprehensive Response

- Account containment (HealthGuard IT)
- Forensic preservation (CyberForensics)
- System hardening
- Access restructuring
- Insurance coordination (DIS Risk Solutions)
- Recovery implementation
- Documentation completion

Technical Analysis:

1. Attack Vector Identificatio
Phishing Campaign Analysis (HealthGuard IT):
- Email crafting sophistication
- Social engineering elements
- Medical terminology usage
- Schedule integration
- Authority impersonation
- AI-driven behavioral patterns

CyberForensics Findings:
- Attack methodology mapping
- Targeting analysis
- Credential harvesting techniques
- Data extraction patterns
- Campaign infrastructure

2. Electronic Health Records (EHR) Analysis
Access Pattern Study (HealthGuard IT):
- Login location diversity
- Access timing patterns
- Record selection criteria
- Data extraction methods
- System interaction patterns
- Behavioral anomalies

Compromised Systems Assessment:
HealthGuard IT Analysis:
- EHR access portals
- Authentication systems
- Medical records database
- Clinical trial data

- Patient scheduling systems
- Access control infrastructure

3. Data Exfiltration Analysis
CyberForensics Findings:
- Credential utilization patterns
- Access timing coordination
- Data selection criteria
- Export methodologies
- Evasion techniques
- Exfiltration path

Target Data Categories:
- Patient demographics
- Treatment records
- Clinical trial data
- Research information
- High-profile case
- Care protocols

4. Forensic Investigation
Evidence Collection (CyberForensics Lead):
- Email server logs
- Access credentials
- System logs
- Network traffi
- Authentication records
- HIPAA audit trails

HealthGuard IT Support:
- Real-time monitoring data
- Behavioral analysis logs
- System configuration state

- Access control logs
- Security tool outputs

Analysis Findings:
- Attack timeline reconstruction
- Compromise methodology
- Data access patterns
- Exfiltration route
- Attack sophistication level
- Campaign infrastructure

5. Healthcare-Specific Impac
Clinical Operations Analysis:
- Patient care disruption assessment
- Access limitation impact
- Workflow modification requiremen
- Documentation contingencies
- Treatment delay risk analysis

Research Impact Evaluation:
- Clinical trial data compromise
- Research integrity assessment
- Data confidentiality breac
- Study implications analysis
- Protocol adherence verificatio

6. Security Control Analysis
Authentication Systems (HealthGuard IT):
- Credential management review
- Access control assessment
- Multi-factor authentication evaluation
- Session monitoring analysis
- Login validation protocols

System Monitoring Enhancement:
- Access pattern detection refinemen
- Behavioral analysis improvement
- Anomaly identification threshold
- Alert trigger optimization
- Response protocol updates

7. Solution Development
Technical Response Strategy:
HealthGuard IT Implementation:
- Access reset protocols
- System hardening measures
- Monitoring enhancement
- Authentication strengthening
- Control implementation

CyberForensics Recommendations:
- Forensic analysis finding
- Security control improvements
- Evidence preservation protocols
- Investigation methodology
- Future prevention measures

DIS Risk Solutions Coordination:
- Insurance compliance alignment
- Documentation requirements
- Regulatory reporting needs
- Evidence preservation standards
- Claims process integration

Implementation Strategy:
Phase 1 - Immediate Response:
- Critical system isolation
- Access control reset

- Evidence preservation
- Patient care continuity
- Initial notification

Phase 2 - Investigation:
- Forensic analysis
- Impact assessment
- Documentation collection
- Regulatory compliance
- Insurance coordination

Phase 3 - Recovery:
- System restoration
- Access reestablishment
- Control enhancement
- Training implementation
- Long-term monitoring

PART 3: IMPLEMENTATION GUIDE

1. IMPACT ASSESSMENT

Financial Impact: Direct Costs: $2.45M potential exposure Indirect Costs: $750,000 response costs Potential Future Losses: $5M+ if unaddressed Recovery Costs: $850,000 estimated HIPAA Penalties: Up to $1.5M per violation category Insurance Implications: Cyber and medical malpractice policies activated

Insurance Implications:

Primary Coverage: $75M cyber liability and medical malpractice tower structured as: • Primary Layer: $15M Carrier A: 100% ($15M) Cyber/ Medical Malpractice Blend

• First Excess: $25M xs $15M Carrier B: 30% ($7.5M) Carrier C: 25% ($6.25M) Carrier D: 25% ($6.25M) Carrier E: 20% ($5M)

• Second Excess: $35M xs $40M Carrier F: 35% ($12.25M) Carrier G: 35% ($12.25M) Carrier H: 30% ($10.5M)

Program Manager: DIS Risk Solutions - Strategic Response Coordination: Damian Davis - Claims Protocol Management: Rachel Torres - Technical Integration: Mark Stevens

Retention/Deductible: $2.5M per cyber incident • Applies to each and every claim • Annual aggregate retention: $5M • Retention applies across all facilities • Time deductible: 12 hours for BI • Maintenance deductible: $2.5M for PCI

Coverage Triggers: • Data breach • HIPAA violations • Patient notification costs • Regulatory defense • Business interruption • Medical malpractice implications • Clinical trial liability

Notification Timeline: • 24 hours for cyber events • Immediate for patient safety issues • 60 days maximum for HIPAA breach notification • State-specific requirements as applicabl

Claims Process: • Coordinated through DIS Risk Solutions • HIPAA breach documentation • Patient notification protocols • Regulatory reporting requirements • Medical malpractice considerations

Expected Coverage: • Breach response costs • Patient notification expenses • Regulatory defense • Crisis management • Legal defense • Clinical trial liability • Business interruption • Reputational harm

Additional Coverage Features: • HIPAA compliance coverage • Regulatory investigation defense • Patient notification costs • Crisis management expenses • Clinical trial protection • Research data liability • Medical malpractice integration

Patient Data Impact:

Records Affected: - 5,200+ patient records compromised • Oncology department focus • Clinical trial data exposed • High-profile patient information • Research protocol data • Treatment planning documentation

Data Categories: - Protected Health Information (PHI) • Electronic Health Records (EHR) • Clinical trial protocols • Research participant data • Treatment histories • Patient demographics

Systems Affected:

Primary Systems: - Electronic Health Records (EHR) platform • HealthGuard IT monitoring infrastructure • Clinical trial management system • Patient scheduling platform • Oncology department systems • Authentication infrastructure

Secondary Systems: - Medical imaging systems • Laboratory information system • Pharmacy management platform • Research databases • Patient portal • Documentation systems

Dependencies: - HealthGuard IT security monitoring • CyberForensics analysis platforms • DIS Risk Solutions integration • Clinical workflow systems • Research data repositories • Regulatory compliance tracking

Business Disruption:
Clinical Impact: - 200+ medical staff affected • Oncology department access limited • Clinical trial documentation delayed • Patient care workflow modified • Treatment planning adjusted • Research activities impacted

Operational Effect: - EHR access restrictions • Paper-based contingency activation • Modified clinical workflows • Extended appointment times • Research protocol delays • Documentation backlog

Duration: - Critical Phase: 6 hours • Full Recovery: 72 hours • System Restoration: 48 hours • Documentation Catch-up: 96 hours • Training/ Updates: 2 weeks

Regulatory Impact:
HIPAA Compliance: - Reportable breach confirmed • 60-day notific - tion requirement • OCR reporting mandatory • State AG notifications required • Documentation requirements • Patient notification plannin

Additional Regulations: - State data breach laws • Clinical trial regulations • Research protocol compliance • Medical board requirements • FDA reporting (clinical trials) • Joint Commission standards

Documentation Requirements: - Breach investigation records • Patient impact assessment • Notification documentation • Response timeline logs • Corrective action plans • Training updates

Reputation Risk:
Stakeholder Impact: - Patient trust concerns • Clinical trial participant confidence • Research partner relationships • Medical staff morale • Community reputation • Industry standing

Media Exposure: - Healthcare sector coverage • Clinical research implications • Patient privacy concerns • Industry reputation impact • Public trust considerations • Research integrity questions

Recovery Strategy: - DIS Risk Solutions crisis management • Proactive patient communication • Research partner engagement • Staff transparency • Community outreach • Media response planning

2. TECHNICAL RESPONSE

Immediate Actions:
Initial Response: - EHR access containment • HealthGuard IT monitoring escalation • CyberForensics activation • DIS Risk Solutions notification • Clinical workflow modification • Patient care continuity maintenance

Containment Measures: - Credential deactivation (HealthGuard IT) • System isolation protocols • Access control enhancement • Evidence preservation (CyberForensics) • Patient data protection • Clinical service continuity

Investigation Steps:
Technical Analysis: - HealthGuard IT security assessment • CyberForensics investigation • Access pattern analysis • Data exposure mapping • System vulnerability review • Attack vector identificatio

Clinical Impact Analysis: - Patient care assessment • Treatment delay evaluation • Research impact review • Documentation gaps • Workflow disruption • Recovery planning

Solution Development:
Technical Remediation: - Access control enhancement • Authentication strengthening • Monitoring improvement • System hardening • Training development • Documentation updates

Clinical Continuity: - Patient care protocols • Research protection measures • Documentation procedures • Staff access management • Treatment planning • Quality assurance

Implementation Process:
Phase 1 - Critical Response: - Patient care continuity • System security • Evidence preservation • Staff communication • Regulatory compliance • Partner coordination

Phase 2 - Recovery: - System restoration • Access reestablishment • Documentation catch-up • Training execution • Process improvement • Compliance verificatio

Phase 3 - Enhancement: - Security improvement • Process refinement • Training enhancement • Documentation update • Partner integration • Long-term monitoring

3. IMPLEMENTATION TIMELINE

Immediate (0-24 hours): Hour 1: - HealthGuard IT containment initiation - DIS Risk Solutions activation - Clinical workflow modification - Initial patient care adjustments - Partner team engagement - Preliminary documentation

Hours 2-4: - CyberForensics investigation launch - Access control implementation - Critical patient data protection - Staff communication initiation - HIPAA documentation start - Clinical contingency activation

Hours 4-8: - System access restructuring - Patient care protocol adjustment - Research data protection - Documentation system setup - Partner coordination refinement - Regulatory compliance initiatio

Hours 8-16: - Access reset implementation - Clinical workflow stabilization - Investigation progression - Staff training initiation - Documentation continuation - Patient care monitoring

Hours 16-24: - System restoration planning - Enhanced monitoring deployment - Clinical process verification - Partner system integration - Compliance verification - Documentation revie

Short-term (1-7 days): Day 1: - Complete access reset - Full forensics assessment (CyberForensics) - Clinical workflow normalization - DIS Risk Solutions carrier updates - Initial regulatory filings - Patient notification plannin

Days 2-3: - Enhanced security deployment (HealthGuard IT) - Clinical staff retraining - Research protocol review - Documentation catch-up - Partner coordination enhancement - Compliance documentation

Days 4-5: - Process documentation updates - Security control validation - Clinical workflow refinement - Response capability enhancement - Insurance claim documentation - Patient communication preparation

Days 6-7: - Staff training completion - System optimization - Clinical process validation - Partner coordination protocols - Compliance verification - Documentation finalizatio

Long-term (8-30 days): Week 2: - Comprehensive security review - Clinical process enhancement - Research protocol updates - Partner integration validation - Training program refinement - Documentation system upgrade

Week 3: - Process improvement implementation - Enhanced monitoring protocols - Clinical workflow optimization - Updated response procedures - Partner coordination refinement - Compliance enhancemen

Week 4: - Long-term monitoring enhancement - Clinical process stabilization - Research protection verification - Partner capability enhancement - Documentation system optimization - Compliance program updates

4. KEY TAKEAWAYS

Business Lessons: Strategic Insights: - Healthcare-specific detection crucial - Partner integration valuable - DIS Risk Solutions coordination essential - Clinical continuity critical - Patient care priority maintenance - Research protection importance

Operational Changes: - Enhanced monitoring needed (HealthGuard IT) - Clinical workflow protection (Internal) - Insurance program optimization (DIS Risk Solutions) - Research data security (CyberForensics) - Patient care continuity - Documentation enhancement

Process Improvements: - HIPAA compliance enhancement - Clinical access management - Partner engagement optimization - Research protection protocols - Patient care documentation - Staff training programs

Healthcare-Specific Insights: Clinical Impact: - Patient care continuity essential - Research integrity protection - Treatment documentation importance - Clinical workflow resilience - Staff access management - Quality care maintenance

Technical Considerations: - EHR system protection - Clinical data security - Research data safeguards - Patient privacy protection - Access control enhancement - Documentation system security

Compliance Requirements: - HIPAA regulation adherence - Research protocol compliance - Clinical trial protection - Patient notification protocols - Documentation standards - Regulatory reporting needs

5. ROI ANALYSIS

Prevention Costs: Technology Investment: - HealthGuard IT Security Infrastructure: $400,000 - CyberForensics Healthcare Tools: $250,000 - DIS Risk Solutions Integration: $100,000 - EHR Security Enhancement: $200,000 - Clinical System Protection: $150,000 - Research Data Security: $150,000 Subtotal: $1.25M

Staff Training: - Clinical Staff Security: $100,000 - IT Team Enhancement: $75,000 - Partner Coordination: $50,000 - HIPAA Compliance: $50,000 - Research Protocol Security: $50,000 - Documentation Procedures: $25,000 Subtotal: $350,000

Process Implementation: - Security Enhancement: $150,000 - Clinical Workflow Integration: $100,000 - Partner System Integration: $75,000 - Documentation Systems: $50,000 - Compliance Procedures: $75,000 - Research Protection: $50,000 Subtotal: $500,000

Ongoing Maintenance: - Annual Security: $200,000 - Clinical System Updates: $150,000 - Partner Coordination: $100,000 - Compliance Management: $100,000 - Documentation Systems: $50,000 - Research Security: $50,000 Subtotal: $650,000/year

Total Prevention Cost: $2.75M

Incident Costs: Direct Response: - Emergency Response: $300,000 - Partner Activation: $200,000 - Forensics Investigation: $150,000 - System Restoration: $100,000 - Clinical Workflow Adjustment: $100,000 - Documentation Recovery: $50,000 Total Direct Response: $900,000

Clinical Impact: - Patient Care Disruption: $500,000 - Research Delay Costs: $400,000 - Documentation Backlog: $200,000 - Staff Overtime:

$150,000 - Quality Assurance: $100,000 - Protocol Adjustments: $150,000 Total Clinical Impact: $1.5M

Recovery Efforts: - System Hardening: $400,000 - Clinical Process Enhancement: $300,000 - Partner Integration: $200,000 - Security Upgrades: $250,000 - Documentation Systems: $150,000 - Training Programs: $200,000 Total Recovery: $1.5M

Long-term Effects: - Patient Trust Impact - Research Credibility - Clinical Trial Delays - Regulatory Scrutiny - Partner Relationships - Industry Reputation Total Impact: Under assessment

Total Incident Cost: $3.9M+

Future Savings: Risk Reduction: - Incident Prevention: $5M annually - Clinical Protection: $3M annually - Research Security: $2M annually - Compliance Management: $1M annually - Partner Efficiency: $1M annually Total Risk Reduction: $12M annually

Efficiency Gains: - Clinical Operations: $2M annually - Research Productivity: $1.5M annually - Documentation Efficiency: $1M annually - Partner Coordination: $500,000 annually - Compliance Management: $500,000 annually Total Efficiency Gains: $5.5M annuall

Prevention Benefits: - Patient Trust Value: $3M annually - Research Integrity: $2M annually - Clinical Quality: $1.5M annually - Partner Relations: $1M annually - Industry Standing: $1.5M annually Total Prevention Benefits: $9M annuall

Resource Optimization: - Staff Efficiency: $1M annually - Clinical Systems: $750,000 annually - Partner Integration: $500,000 annually - Documentation Systems: $500,000 annually - Compliance Programs: $250,000 annually Total Resource Optimization: $3M annually

Total Projected Savings: $29.5M annually

6. ACTION CHECKLIST

Immediate Response: - Incident Declaration • Activate IR protocol • Notify DIS Risk Solutions • Engage HealthGuard IT and CyberForensics • Alert clinical leadership • Document initial findings • Initiate HIPAA protocols

- Team Activation • Internal IR team assembly • Clinical staff notification • DIS Risk Solutions coordination • HealthGuard IT security response • CyberForensics investigation • Research team alert • Partner resource deployment

- Clinical Containment • EHR access restriction • Patient care contingency • Research data protection • Clinical workflow modification • Documentation protocol activation • Quality assurance measures

- Evidence Collection • System logs capture (HealthGuard IT) • Clinical access records • EHR activity documentation • Research data audit trails • HIPAA compliance evidence • Chain of custody maintenance

Assessment Tasks: - Impact Analysis • Patient care assessment • Research protocol review • Clinical workflow evaluation • Data breach scope • HIPAA violation check • Regulatory implications

- System Review • EHR security assessment • Clinical system check • Research data protection • Access control evaluation • Documentation systems • Partner integration verificatio

7. C-SUITE COMMUNICATION PROTOCOL

Executive Notification Sequence

CISO (Katherine Song) - Initial incident assessment - Security response coordination - Partner integration oversight - HIPAA compliance monitoring - Ongoing security updates

CTO (Emma Richardson) - Technical impact assessment - System modification approval - Clinical system coordination - Resource allocation - Recovery timeline development

CMO (Dr. Jennifer Williams) - Clinical impact assessment - Patient care implications - Research protocol oversight - Medical staff coordination - Quality assurance management

CEO (William Hayes) - Strategic decisions - Public communications approval - Stakeholder management - Regulatory oversight - Final authority on major actions

DIS Risk Solutions (Damian Davis) - Insurance coordination - Partner response management - Carrier communications - Strategic response guidance - Crisis management oversight

Communication Templates: - Initial Notification • Incident overview • Clinical impact assessment • Partner engagement status • HIPAA implications • Required decisions

- Status Updates • Response progress • Patient care status • Research impact • Partner activities • Compliance status

- Clinical Advisories • Patient care modifications • Workflow changes • Documentation requirements • Quality measures • Staff instructions

- Executive Summaries • Situation overview • Clinical impact • Partner contribution • Compliance status • Strategic implications

Decision Matrix: - Clinical Impact Criteria • Patient care priorities • Research continuity • Quality thresholds • Documentation requirements • Staff access needs

- System Modification Authority • EHR access changes • Clinical workflow adjustments • Research protocol modifications • Documentation requirements • Partner system integration

- Patient Notification Triggers • HIPAA requirements • Clinical implications • Research impact • Legal obligations • Communication timing

- Media Response Guidelines • Message approval process • Clinical information release • Partner coordination • Spokesperson designation • Response timing

- Recovery Milestones • Clinical restoration • System verification • Research validation • Partner confirmation • Compliance documentation

Chapter 4

Cloud Under Siege

PART 1: NARRATIVE CASE STUDY

Company Profile: CloudScale Technologies
Annual Revenue: $300M+
Industry: Cloud Services Provider
Employees: 850
Client Base: Enterprise and mid-market companies
Market Position: Leading provider of cloud infrastructure and platform services
Geographic Presence: Primary operations in US, with global data centers

0715 Hours - CloudScale Technologies, Cloud Security Operations Center

Michael Zhao's monitoring dashboard erupted with alerts. As Cloud Security Operations Manager, he immediately recognized that CloudGuard's advanced threat detection system, implemented as part of their DIS Risk Solutions security package, had caught something unusual in their container orchestration platform.

"Kumar," he called to his lead cloud security engineer, "check the Kubernetes cluster metrics. CloudGuard's behavioral analysis is showing anomalous pod creation patterns."

Aisha Kumar, having recently led their cloud-native security implementation, was already analyzing the data. "These containers... they're spawning with valid credentials, but the resource consumption patterns are completely abnormal. CloudGuard's AI flagged it as potential credential compromise in our cloud management plane."

0730 Hours - Cloud Operations Floor

The massive operations center displayed wall-to-wall monitoring dashboards, tracking thousands of customer workloads across multiple cloud regions. Michael and Aisha stood before the security operations display, watching real-time feeds from both internal systems and CloudGuard's cloud-native security platform.

"There," Aisha pointed. "The containers are being created with legitimate service accounts, but they're immediately establishing outbound connections to unknown endpoints. Something's compromised our IAM infrastructure."

0745 Hours - Initial Investigation

Dr. Rebecca Morrison, Cloud Architecture Lead, joined them at the security operations center. Her expertise in cloud-native security architecture had helped design their zero-trust implementation, working closely with CloudGuard to implement DIS Risk Solutions' recommended security controls.

The integrated SOC team, combining internal staff with CloudGuard's managed security services, assembled quickly:

Internal Team: Jason Cho - Security Analysis Manager Tom Peterson - Network Security Lead Maya Singh - Compliance Director Claire O'Connor - Customer Security Liaison

CloudGuard Team: Daniel Wilson - Cloud Security Lead Victoria Chen - Cloud Defense Specialist Robert Adams - Platform Integration Lead

"Show me what we've got," Rebecca demanded, studying the attack patterns.

Jason Cho pulled up the analysis. "It started in our staging environment. Sophisticated attack - they compromised a CI/CD pipeline, injected malicious container images that passed our signature verific - tion. CloudGuard's behavioral detection caught the anomalous runtime patterns."

Daniel Wilson from CloudGuard added, "Our cloud threat intelligence shows similar patterns in recent attacks against other cloud providers. This isn't a random attack - it's a coordinated attempt to compromise customer workloads."

0800 Hours - Technical Discovery

Tom Peterson's analysis, coordinated with CyberForensics' cloud team, revealed the scope. "We're looking at potential compromise of our container orchestration platform. The attackers are using valid credentials to deploy malicious workloads across multiple customer clusters. They're specifically ta geting financial services and healthcare customers.

Maya Singh, already documenting for compliance, interjected. "This affects our SOC 2 compliance and potentially our FedRAMP authorization. We need to notify affected customers within our SLA windows. I'll coordinate with DIS Risk Solutions on the notification requirements.

Rachel Torres was already mobilizing DIS Risk Solutions' claims protocols. "With compromised container orchestration affecting regulated industries, we need to activate both our cyber and technology E&O coverage," she explained. "I'll submit the initial carrier notification package, focusing on the platform-wide exposure and potential customer business interruption."

0815 Hours - Pattern Recognition

Victoria Chen from CloudGuard identified the attack progression. "They're smart," she explained. "The malicious containers are designed to look like normal microservices. Each compromised cluster is running just enough malicious pods to stay under standard resource quotas. But when you look at the aggregate behavior..."

She gestured to her screen, showing a complex web of container communications spreading across multiple customer namespaces. "Our enhanced monitoring caught it because we're correlating behavior across all orchestration layers. Dr. Amanda Foster's team at CyberForensics is already mapping the attack infrastructure."

0830 Hours - Crisis Escalation Michael knew this required immediate escalation. The potential impact on customer workloads was massive. He reached for his phone to make two simultaneous calls - one to Amanda Sullivan, CISO, and another to Damian Davis at DIS Risk Solutions.

"We need to contain this now," Michael announced to his team. "Tom and Victoria, start isolating affected clusters. Maya, begin customer impact analysis with DIS. Claire, prepare for customer communications. Jason, get me a complete list of compromised workloads. Dr. Morrison, we'll need your team for platform validation."

Robert Adams from CloudGuard added, "We're already deploying containment measures across the orchestration layer. Our platform security team is ready to assist with customer workload validation."

0845 Hours - Executive Notification

Amanda Sullivan answered immediately, with Damian Davis already patched into the secure conference line.

"Amanda, it's Michael. We have a confirmed supply chain compromise in our container platform. CloudGuard detected sophisticated malicious workloads bypassing our CI/CD controls. Multiple customer clusters affected, primarily in financial services and healthcare sectors. Damian's team is already coordinating with carriers."

"Blast radius?" Amanda's tone was focused.

"Potentially thousands of customer containers across multiple regions," Michael reported. "The attack passed our standard security controls, but CloudGuard's behavioral analysis caught the runtime anomalies. CyberForensics is already mapping the attack infrastructure. This looks like part of a larger campaign targeting cloud providers."

Damian Davis interjected, "I've initiated our cyber insurance and technology E&O response protocols. Rachel Torres is preparing carrier notifications, and Mark Stevens is coordinating the technical response teams. Given the customer impact, we're treating this as a critical incident under our policy."

"Understood. Have you started containment?" Amanda asked.

"Yes, CloudGuard is implementing cluster isolation now. But Amanda... this will require a full platform-wide security scan and potential customer workload rebuilds."

"Agreed. I'm calling David [CTO] and Jennifer [CEO]. Get your team ready for a full briefing in 30 minutes. We'll need options for maintaining customer workload continuity during remediation."

0900 Hours - Technical Response Team Assembly

The integrated incident response team gathered in the main conference room. David Marshall, CTO, arrived with Jennifer Blake, CEO, and Mark Edwards, COO. Damian Davis and the partner team leads joined virtually through their secure incident response channel.

The situation room displays showed: - Compromised cluster status (CloudGuard) - Customer workload impact analysis - Container security scanning results (CyberForensics) - Platform access patterns - Customer environment mapping - Insurance and compliance tracking (DIS Risk Solutions)

0915 Hours - Executive Briefing

Michael led the briefing: "At 0715 hours, CloudGuard's advanced behavioral detection identified anomalous container creation patterns in our orchestration platform. Investigation reveals a sophisticated supply chain attack compromising our CI/CD pipeline. Attackers injected malicious container images that passed our standard security controls but exhibit suspicious runtime behavior."

David Marshall interrupted, "Current exposure?"

"Approximately 3,000 customer containers affected across 200+ clusters," Michael reported. "CyberForensics has confirmed they're primarily targeting financial services and healthcare workloads. The attack shows deep understanding of container orchestration and our platform architecture."

Amanda Sullivan added, "The sophistication suggests a well-funded threat actor. CloudGuard's threat intelligence team has identified similar patterns at other cloud providers. This appears to be part of a coordinated campaign targeting critical infrastructure customers."

"Customer impact?" Jennifer Blake asked sharply.

"We need to implement immediate cluster isolation and customer workload validation," Michael explained. "CloudGuard has prepared automated containment procedures, but customers will need to rebuild affected workloads from verified images. CyberForensics is already validating our golden container registry."

Damian Davis spoke up, "From an insurance perspective, we're looking at both cyber and technology E&O exposure. Our policy is structured for this type of platform-wide incident. Rachel Torres is coordinating with carriers, and Mark Stevens is working with CloudGuard on the technical evidence preservation."

"Regulatory implications?" Blake turned to Amanda.

"This affects our SOC 2 compliance and FedRAMP authorization," the CISO confirmed. "DIS Risk Solutions' compliance team is already preparing the necessary documentation. Given our customer base, we have various regulatory notification requirements. We should accelerate our customer communication timeline."

Dr. Amanda Foster from CyberForensics joined virtually. "Our analysis shows sophisticated supply chain manipulation focused specifically on the CI/CD pipeline. The attackers understood how to bypass traditional container security controls while maintaining seemingly legitimate behavior patterns."

Blake made the decision. "Execute the containment plan. Amanda, coordinate with affected customers through Claire's team. David, implement emergency customer workload protocols. Mark, activate our platform contingency plan. Michael, I want hourly updates through DIS Risk Solutions' incident management platform."

0930 Hours - Response Implementation

As the team mobilized to execute the CEO's directives, the integrated response showed the value of their prepared incident response strategy. Each group moved with practiced precision:

Internal Leadership: - Amanda Sullivan (CISO) - Leading security response - David Marshall (CTO) - Managing platform operations - Mark Edwards (COO) - Coordinating customer impact - Jennifer Blake (CEO) - Directing overall response - Michael Zhao - Technical coordination - Maya Singh - Compliance documentation

DIS Risk Solutions Team: - Damian Davis - Strategic Response Coordinator - Rachel Torres - Claims Protocol Manager - Mark Stevens - Technical Integration Lead

CloudGuard Team: - Daniel Wilson - Leading cloud security operations - Victoria Chen - Managing defense implementation - Robert Adams - Coordinating platform restoration

CyberForensics Team: - Dr. Amanda Foster - Leading investigation - Brian Taylor - Cloud forensics analysis - Stephen Wang - Compliance investigation

Action Teams: Platform Response: - CloudGuard implementing cluster isolation - CyberForensics conducting forensic analysis - Internal teams managing customer environments - DIS Risk Solutions coordinating documentation

Customer Operations: - Workload continuity procedures activated - Emergency communication channels opened - Technical support teams mobilized - Account management teams engaged

Compliance and Communications: - SOC 2 documentation initiated - Customer notification planning - Regulatory coordination - Stakeholder communications prepared

PART 2: TECHNICAL DEEP DIVE

Investigation Timeline:

0715-0845: Initial Detection and Analysis

- CloudGuard behavioral alert
- Container anomaly detection
- CI/CD pipeline analysis
- Kubernetes cluster scanning
- Initial impact assessment
- Partner team activation
- Customer workload analysis

0845-1045: Full Investigation

- CloudGuard platform analysis
- CyberForensics container forensics
- Supply chain compromise mapping
- Customer impact quantificatio
- Cluster isolation planning
- Evidence preservation
- Attack infrastructure analysis

1045-1400: Comprehensive Response

- Container platform isolation
- Customer workload validation
- CI/CD pipeline hardening
- Registry verificatio
- Golden image validation
- Platform restoration planning
- Customer environment protection

Technical Analysis:

1. Attack Vector Identificatio
Container Supply Chain Analysis (CloudGuard):
- CI/CD pipeline compromise
- Image tampering techniques
- Registry manipulation
- Build system infiltratio
- Deployment automation abuse
- Runtime behavior anomalies

CyberForensics Findings:
- Attack infrastructure mapping
- Malicious image analysis
- Container escape attempts
- Lateral movement patterns
- Data exfiltration method
- Persistence mechanisms

2. Container Platform Analysis
Kubernetes Environment Assessment:
- Cluster compromise patterns
- Pod security violations
- Service account abuse
- RBAC manipulation
- Network policy bypass
- Resource quota evasion

Platform Security Analysis (CloudGuard):
- Control plane integrity
- API server access patterns
- etcd data validation
- Kubelet compromise check

- Admission controller status
- CNI security assessment

3. Supply Chain Impact Analysis
CI/CD Pipeline Investigation:
- Build system compromise
- Image signing bypass
- Registry manipulation
- Deployment automation
- GitOps workflow analysi
- Artifact validation

Customer Environment Impact:
- Workload compromise assessment
- Namespace isolation status
- Service mesh security
- Ingress/egress patterns
- Data plane analysis
- Multi-tenant boundaries

4. Forensic Investigation
Container Analysis (CyberForensics):
- Image layer examination
- Runtime behavior analysis
- System call patterns
- Network communication
- Resource utilization
- Persistence mechanisms

Infrastructure Evidence:
- Kubernetes audit logs
- Container runtime logs
- CI/CD pipeline trails
- Registry access logs

- Platform metrics
- Service mesh telemetry

5. Cloud-Native Security Analysis
Platform Controls:
- Image scanning effectiveness
- Admission control validation
- Pod security standards
- Network policy enforcement
- RBAC configuratio
- Service account management

Runtime Security:
- Container behavior monitoring
- Workload isolation
- Privilege escalation detection
- Network segmentation
- Resource management
- Threat detection capabilities

6. Customer Impact Assessment
Workload Analysis:
- Container compromise scope
- Service disruption mapping
- Data access patterns
- Application dependencies
- Performance impact
- Security boundary validation

Compliance Implications:
- SOC 2 requirements
- FedRAMP controls
- PCI DSS considerations
- HIPAA requirements

- Customer SLA impact
- Regulatory reporting

7. Solution Development
Technical Response:
CloudGuard Implementation:
- Container platform isolation
- Cluster security hardening
- Runtime protection enhancement
- Network policy enforcement
- Monitoring improvement
- Access control strengthening

CyberForensics Recommendations:
- Supply chain security
- Image validation processes
- Build system hardening
- Registry security controls
- Deployment validation
- Runtime monitoring

DIS Risk Solutions Coordination:
- Evidence preservation standards
- Documentation requirements
- Customer notification protocol
- Regulatory compliance
- Insurance alignment
- Recovery validation

Implementation Strategy:
Phase 1 - Platform Protection:
- Control plane isolation
- Customer workload containment
- Evidence preservation

- Initial communication
- Partner coordination

Phase 2 - Investigation:
- Forensic analysis
- Impact assessment
- Customer environment review
- Documentation collection
- Compliance validation

Phase 3 - Recovery:
- Platform restoration
- Customer workload rebuild
- Security enhancement
- Process improvement
- Long-term monitoring

PART 3: IMPLEMENTATION GUIDE

1. IMPACT ASSESSMENT

Financial Impact: Direct Costs: $3.5M platform remediation Indirect Costs: $1.2M customer support Potential Future Losses: $25M+ liability exposure Recovery Costs: $2.5M estimated Customer SLA Credits: $5M+ potential exposure Insurance Implications: Cyber and Technology E&O policies activated

Insurance Implications:

Primary Coverage: $100M blended Technology E&O (errors & omissions) and Cyber Liability insurance tower structured as: • Primary Layer: $10M Carrier A: 100% ($10M) Tech E&O/Cyber Blend

• First Excess: $50M xs $10M Carrier B: 30% ($15M) Tech E&O/Cyber Blend Carrier C: 25% ($12.5M) Tech E&O/Cyber Blend Carrier D: 25% ($12.5M) Tech E&O/Cyber Blend Carrier E: 20% ($10M) Tech E&O/Cyber Blend

• Second Excess: $40M xs $60M Carrier F: 35% ($14M) Tech E&O/Cyber Blend Carrier G: 35% ($14M) Tech E&O/Cyber Blend Carrier H: 30% ($12M) Tech E&O/Cyber Blend

Program Manager: DIS Risk Solutions - Strategic Response Coordination: Damian Davis - Claims Protocol Management: Rachel Torres - Technical Integration: Mark Stevens

Retention/Deductible: $2.5M per incident • Applies to each and every claim • Annual aggregate retention: $5M • Retention applies to both E&O and Cyber claims • Time deductible: 12 hours for BI • Maintenance deductible: $2.5M for PCI

Coverage Triggers: • Platform security breach • Customer data compromise • Service interruption • Technology E&O claims • Regulatory investigations • Customer notification costs • SL violation claims

Notification Timeline: • 24 hours for security events • Immediate for customer impact • SLA-specific requirements • Regulatory timeframes by jurisdiction • FedRAMP reporting requirements

Claims Process: • Coordinated through DIS Risk Solutions • Platform incident documentation • Customer impact assessment • Technical evidence preservation • Regulatory reporting requirements • SLA violation tracking

Expected Coverage: • Platform restoration costs • Customer notification expenses • Business interruption • Technology E&O defense • Regulatory defense • Crisis management • Customer remediation

Additional Coverage Features: • Supply chain security • Multi-tenant liability • Customer workload protection • Regulatory investigation • FedRAMP compliance • SOC 2 requirements • Technology E&O extension

Platform Impact:

Primary Systems:

- Container orchestration platform
- CI/CD pipeline infrastructure
- Image registry systems
- Kubernetes control planes
- Service mesh infrastructure
- Platform monitoring systems

Secondary Systems:

- Customer cluster management
- Identity and access management
- Secrets management platform

- API gateway infrastructure
- Log aggregation systems
- Backup infrastructure

Dependencies:
- CloudGuard security monitoring
- CyberForensics analysis platforms
- DIS Risk Solutions integration
- Customer authentication systems
- Multi-cloud connectors
- Platform automation tools

Customer Environment Impact:
Workload Status:
- 3,000+ affected containers
- 200+ customer clusters
- Multiple cloud regions
- Production workloads
- Development environments
- Staging systems

Service Disruption:
Duration: 6 hours critical, 72 hours total
Scope: Container platform services
Customer Impact: Production workloads
Recovery Time: 48-96 hours estimated
Documentation: Platform-wide audit required

Compliance Impact:
Regulatory Requirements:
- SOC 2 Type II controls
- FedRAMP authorization
- ISO 27001 certificatio
- PCI DSS compliance

- HIPAA requirements (healthcare customers)
- GDPR considerations (EU customers)

Documentation Requirements:
- Platform incident timeline
- Customer impact assessment
- Control effectiveness review
- Remediation documentation
- Evidence preservation
- Regulatory notification

TECHNICAL RESPONSE

Immediate Actions:
Platform Containment:
- Container orchestration isolation
- CI/CD pipeline suspension
- Registry access restriction
- Control plane lockdown
- Service mesh quarantine
- API gateway controls

Partner Integration:
CloudGuard Implementation:
- Runtime security enforcement
- Container behavior monitoring
- Network policy enforcement
- Workload isolation
- Platform telemetry
- Access control validation

CyberForensics Support:
- Container image analysis
- Supply chain investigation

- Pipeline compromise assessment
- Evidence preservation
- Attack pattern analysis
- Infrastructure forensics

DIS Risk Solutions Coordination:
- Evidence documentation
- Customer notification protocol
- Regulatory compliance tracking
- Insurance claim preparation
- Partner communication
- Recovery validation

3. IMPLEMENTATION TIMELINE

Immediate (0-24 hours): Hour 1-4: - Platform containment execution - CloudGuard security activation - CyberForensics engagement - Customer communication initiation - Evidence preservation - Initial assessment completion

Hours 4-8: - Container platform isolation - Customer workload assessment - Registry validation - Pipeline analysis - Partner coordination - Documentation initiation

Hours 8-16: - Security control implementation - Customer environment validation - Evidence collection - Impact assessment - Communication updates - Recovery planning

Hours 16-24: - Platform restoration preparation - Security enhancement deployment - Customer workload validation - Documentation review - Partner integration verification - Compliance assessmen

Short-term (1-7 days): Day 1: - Complete platform assessment - Full forensics report - Customer impact analysis - Initial regulatory filings - Insurance documentation - Recovery implementation

Days 2-3: - Enhanced security deployment - Customer workload restoration - Pipeline security hardening - Documentation updates - Partner coordination - Compliance verificatio

Days 4-5: - Process documentation - Security control validation - Platform optimization - Customer support - Training preparation - Recovery validation

Days 6-7: - Final security verification - Customer environment validation - Documentation completion - Training execution - Partner integration review - Compliance confirmatio

Long-term (8-30 days): Week 2: - Comprehensive security review - Platform architecture assessment - Customer feedback integration - Partner capability enhancement - Documentation refinement - Training program expansion

Week 3: - Process improvement implementation - Security control optimization - Customer support enhancement - Partner integration refin - ment - Documentation updates - Compliance program review

Week 4: - Long-term monitoring enhancement - Platform security optimization - Customer relationship management - Partner program updates - Documentation finalization - Compliance validatio

4. KEY TAKEAWAYS

Business Lessons: Strategic Insights: - Container platform security critical - Supply chain validation essential - Partner integration valuable - Customer communication crucial - Multi-tenant protection vital - Compliance documentation critical

Operational Changes: - Enhanced CI/CD security needed - Container registry hardening required - Platform monitoring improvement

- Customer isolation enhancement - Partner coordination refinement - Documentation standards upgrade

Process Improvements: - Security validation protocols - Customer notification procedures - Partner engagement optimization - Compliance documentation - Training enhancement - Recovery procedures

Technical Insights: Platform Security: - Container orchestration vulnerabilities - CI/CD pipeline weaknesses - Registry security gaps - Control plane exposure - Service mesh protection - API gateway controls

Architecture Changes: - Enhanced segmentation needed - Multi-tenant isolation - Pipeline security controls - Registry validation - Platform monitoring - Access management

5. ROI ANALYSIS

Prevention Costs: Technology Investment: - CloudGuard Security Infrastructure: $2.5M - CyberForensics Platform Tools: $1.5M - DIS Risk Solutions Integration: $500K - Container Security Enhancement: $1.5M - Platform Monitoring Upgrade: $1M - CI/CD Security Tools: $1M Subtotal: $8M

Staff Training: - Platform Security: $750K - Customer Support: $500K - Partner Coordination: $250K - Compliance Management: $250K - Documentation Procedures: $250K Subtotal: $2M

Process Implementation: - Security Enhancement: $1M - Platform Integration: $750K - Partner Coordination: $500K - Documentation Systems: $500K - Compliance Procedures: $250K Subtotal: $3M

Ongoing Maintenance: - Annual Security: $2M - Platform Updates: $1.5M - Partner Coordination: $750K - Compliance Management: $750K - Documentation Systems: $500K Subtotal: $5.5M/year

Total Prevention Cost: $18.5M

Incident Costs: Direct Response: - Emergency Response: $2M - Partner Activation: $1.5M - Platform Recovery: $2.5M - Customer Support: $1.5M - Documentation: $500K Total Direct Response: $8M

Business Impact: - Service Interruption: $15M - Customer Credits: $10M - Reputation Impact: $20M - Recovery Operations: $5M Total Business Impact: $50M

Future Savings: Risk Reduction: - Incident Prevention: $25M annually - Customer Protection: $15M annually - Compliance Management: $5M annually - Partner Efficiency: $5M annually Total Risk Reduction: $50M annually

Efficiency Gains: - Platform Operations: $10M annually - Customer Management: $5M annually - Partner Integration: $3M annually - Documentation Systems: $2M annually Total Efficiency Gains: $20M annually

Total Projected Savings: $70M annually

6. ACTION CHECKLIST

Immediate Response: - Incident Declaration • Activate platform IR protocol • Notify DIS Risk Solutions • Engage CloudGuard and CyberForensics • Alert customer success team • Document initial fin - ings • Initiate compliance protocols

- Team Activation • Internal platform team assembly • Customer support mobilization • DIS Risk Solutions coordination • CloudGuard security response • CyberForensics investigation • Partner resource deployment

- Platform Containment • Container orchestration isolation • CI/CD pipeline suspension • Registry access restriction • Customer workload protection • Evidence preservation • Partner system integration

- Evidence Collection • Platform logs capture • Container runtime data • CI/CD pipeline logs • Registry access records • Customer impact data • Compliance documentation

Assessment Tasks: - Impact Analysis • Platform service assessment • Customer workload review • Data exposure evaluation • Compliance implications • Partner integration check • Documentation requirements

- System Review • Container platform security • CI/CD pipeline integrity • Registry system status • Customer environment check • Partner system integration • Documentation completeness

7. C-SUITE COMMUNICATION PROTOCOL

Executive Notification Sequence

CISO (Amanda Sullivan) - Initial incident assessment - Security response coordination - Partner integration oversight - Platform security status - Ongoing security updates - Compliance monitoring

CTO (David Marshall) - Technical impact assessment - Platform modification approval - Resource allocation - Recovery timeline development - Customer service continuity - Architecture decisions

COO (Mark Edwards) - Operational impact assessment - Customer relationship management - Service delivery coordination - Business continuity oversight - Partner coordination - Resource management

CEO (Jennifer Blake) - Strategic decisions - Public communications approval - Stakeholder management - Final authority on major actions - Customer relationship oversight - Partner relationship management

DIS Risk Solutions (Damian Davis) - Insurance coordination - Partner response management - Carrier communications - Strategic response guidance - Crisis management oversight - Documentation coordination

Communication Templates: - Initial Notification • Incident overview • Platform impact assessment • Customer exposure status • Partner engagement status • Required decisions • Immediate actions

- Status Updates • Response progress • Platform status • Customer impact • Partner activities • Compliance status • Next steps

- Decision Requests • Options analysis • Risk assessment • Partner recommendations • Customer implications • Required actions • Timeline implications

- Executive Summaries • Situation overview • Technical impact • Customer status • Partner contribution • Compliance position • Strategic implications

Decision Matrix: - Platform Impact Criteria • Service interruption thresholds • Customer impact levels • Security risk assessment • Partner consultation • Compliance requirements • Communication timing

- System Modification Authority • Platform changes • Customer environment impact • Partner integration • Security controls • Compliance implications • Recovery procedures

- Customer Notification Triggers • Impact thresholds • Regulatory requirements • SLA obligations • Security implications • Partner consultation • Communication timing

- Media Response Guidelines • Message approval process • Customer consideration • Partner coordination • Compliance alignment • Spokesperson designation • Response timing

- Recovery Milestones • Platform restoration • Customer service resumption • Partner verification • Compliance validation • Documentation completion • Long-term enhancement

SECTION II

PUBLIC SECTOR AND EMERGING INDUSTRIES

Chapter 5

The City of Millbrook Ransomware Attack

PART 1: NARRATIVE CASE STUDY

Company Profile: City of Millbrook
Annual Budget: $125M (Municipal)
Industry: Local Government/Municipality
Employees: 850 (City Workers)
Constituent Base: 175,000 residents
Market Position: Mid-sized city providing essential public services including emergency services, utilities, and administrative functions
Geographic Presence: Main city center with multiple service locations (police, fire, utilities, parks & recreation)

2330 Hours - City of Millbrook IT Department

Mike Peterson stared at his screen in disbelief. The ransomware message glowed mockingly: "Your systems are encrypted. Payment required: 2.5 million in Bitcoin."

His hands shook as he dialed Andrea Sullivan, the City Manager. "We're compromised. Everything's locked - police dispatch, traffic control, utility management, payment systems. Even our backups."

2345 Hours - Emergency Operations Center

"What do you mean 'everything's locked'?" Andrea demanded, staring at the increasingly panicked IT admin.

Jennifer Koslowski, Finance Director, burst into the room with a paper copy of their insurance policy. "I keep hard copies of all our critical documents. We have serious coverage issues - only $500,000 in coverage with a $50,000 retention, and the sub-limits are far too low for a city our size."

"Those limits won't begin to cover this," Andrea responded, running her hands through her hair. "What are our options?"

"I remember that cyber insurance broker from last year - DIS Risk Solutions," Jennifer said, pulling a folder from her cabinet. "Their president, Damian Davis, spent hours explaining our exposures and even provided a detailed security assessment. They offered a $5 million program specifically designed for municipalities, plus pre-breach services through their cybersecurity partnerships. But we went with the lower premium option instead."

0000 Hours (12:00 AM) - Crisis Response Initiation

Jennifer found Damian Davis's business card, still paper-clipped to the DIS Risk Solutions proposal. Despite the late hour, he answered on the second ring.

"Mr. Davis, this is Jennifer Koslowski from the City of Millbrook. I wish we'd gone with your proposal last year. We're in the middle of a ransomware attack, and our coverage is completely inadequate. We need help."

"I remember the City of Millbrook well," Damian replied. "Before we proceed, I need to explain something important. To work directly with your carriers and properly advocate on your behalf, we'll need what's called a Broker of Record letter, or BOR. This officially transfers authority to DIS as your insurance broker."

"I'll sign whatever you need," Jennifer said. "How quickly can you send it?"

"I'll send our standard BOR letter to your personal email right now," Damian replied. "While you're signing that, I need you to read me your current policy information - especially the binder letter with your underwriter's contact information. I'm also going to make some calls to TechDefend - they're our preferred Municipal MSP partner - and CyberForensics. You need expert help regardless of the insurance situation."

0015 Hours - Emergency Response Mobilization

While Jennifer read off the policy details, Damian was already coordinating response teams. "I've got TechDefend's emergency response unit heading your way. They'll establish secure temporary systems for critical services. CyberForensics will join remotely to begin their investigation."

"What about the ransom demand?" Andrea asked.

"First, we need to stabilize essential services," Damian explained. "TechDefend will prioritize emergency response systems. Once we have the BOR processed in the morning, we can engage with your carrier about the ransom and coverage implications."

0030 Hours - City Hall Emergency Meeting

Andrea gathered the available department heads:
- Chief Michael Romano - Police Department
- Chief Linda Nakamura - Fire Department
- David Reeves - Public Works Director
- Mike Peterson - IT Administrator
- Tom Reilly - Emergency Management Coordinator

0045 Hours - Response Strategy

"The ransom is $2.5 million in Bitcoin," Andrea announced to the group. "Our coverage is only $500,000 with a $50,000 retention."

"What's our immediate plan?" Chief Romano asked, concerned about his dispatch systems.

"DIS Risk Solutions has already mobilized help," Jennifer explained. "TechDefend's municipal response team is on the way to restore emergency services, and CyberForensics will investigate the attack."

0100 Hours - Technical Response Arrival

Marcus Thompson from TechDefend arrived with his team, immediately unloading equipment. "Our first priority is emergency services - police, fire, and critical infrastructure. We're bringing in temporary CAD systems and secure communications gear."

Dr. Amanda Foster from CyberForensics joined virtually. "We're starting our investigation. I'll need access to any offline system logs or backup documentation you might have."

0115 Hours - Initial Assessment

"Here's our immediate strategy," Damian outlined via speakerphone:

"First Priority - Critical Services:
- Emergency response systems
- Water treatment controls
- Essential communications
- Public safety functions

Second Priority - Investigation:
- Attack vector identificatio
- System compromise assessment
- Evidence preservation
- Recovery planning

TechDefend and CyberForensics will handle the technical response while we work on the insurance and vendor coordination through SecureResponse once we have the BOR processed in the morning."

0130 Hours - Emergency Services Focus
Chief Romano watched as TechDefend's team began setting up temporary dispatch systems. "How long until we're operational?"

"We should have basic emergency dispatch running within two hours," Marcus replied. "It won't be full functionality, but it will handle critical calls and coordinate response units."

Chief Nakamura added, "We need to notify our mutual aid partners about our communication limitations."

"We'll set up secure alternative channels for inter-agency communication," Marcus assured her.

0200 Hours - Initial Cost Assessment

Marcus Thompson provided his preliminary estimate:
"Based on what we're seeing:
- Emergency response systems: $750,000
- Critical infrastructure recovery: $1.2M
- Investigation and remediation: $500,000

Plus additional costs for notification and legal requirements.

"That's well over $2 million," Jennifer calculated, "and we only have $500,000 in coverage after our retention."

"This is where SecureResponse comes in," Damian explained. "Their vendor network typically reduces overall costs by 25-30% through preferred pricing and coordinated services. Once we have the BOR processed in the morning, they'll help manage costs both within and beyond our coverage limits."

0215 Hours - Cost Management Strategy

"Let me outline how SecureResponse will help," Damian explained. "Their vendor network includes:
- Legal teams for compliance requirements
- PR firms for crisis communicatio
- Forensics specialists
- System recovery experts
All at preferred rates, which will be crucial given our coverage situation."

0230 Hours - Response Coordination

Marcus Thompson from TechDefend reported progress:
"We've established temporary emergency dispatch. Moving on to:
- Water treatment system controls
- Critical infrastructure access
- Essential payment systems"

Dr. Foster from CyberForensics added, "We're seeing evidence of sophisticated attack vectors. Full investigation and recovery will be extensive."

0245 Hours - Strategic Planning

"Here's how we'll structure this," Damian outlined:

"Immediate Response:
- TechDefend focusing on critical systems
- CyberForensics handling investigation
- SecureResponse coordinating vendor network
This coordinated approach through SecureResponse's preferred vendors should help reduce that $2 million estimate by about half a million, but we'll still need to discuss emergency funding options with the council in the morning."

0300 Hours - Department Updates

Chief Romano: "Emergency dispatch is functioning on temporary systems. Response times will be slower but manageable."

Chief Nakamura: "We need to maintain clear communication with mutual aid partners about our limitations."

David Reeves: "Water treatment systems are secure on manual controls. We need to discuss timeline for full automation restoration."

0315 Hours - Morning Preparation

"Before the council meeting," Andrea noted, "we need clear numbers on:
- Current response costs
- Expected recovery expenses
- Available coverage
- SecureResponse savings
- Emergency funding needs"

0330 Hours - Documentation Preparation

Jennifer organized materials for the emergency council meeting:
- Current policy details
- DIS Risk Solutions' previous proposal
- Initial damage assessments
- TechDefend's preliminary estimates
- Emergency funding requirements

0400 Hours - Early Progress

Marcus Thompson reported, "Emergency dispatch is now operating at 60% capacity. We're prioritizing life-safety calls and coordinating with neighboring jurisdictions for backup."

"The temporary systems are holding," Dr. Foster added. "We're seeing evidence this attack was specifically designed for municipal ta gets."

0500 Hours - Department Head Briefing

Andrea gathered the team for a status update:
- Police: Operating on temporary dispatch
- Fire: Managing emergency responses
- Public Works: Manual infrastructure control
- IT: Supporting TechDefend's deployment
- Finance: Preparing council presentation

0600 Hours - BOR Processing

With business hours beginning on the East Coast, Damian initiated the formal BOR process. "Once this processes, we can fully engage SecureResponse's vendor network and begin coverage discussions with the carriers."

0700 Hours - Council Preparation

Andrea and Jennifer prepared for the emergency council session:

"We need to present three things," Andrea outlined. "Current situation, immediate costs, and recommended actions."

"I've prepared the numbers," Jennifer replied. "Including TechDefend's estimates and potential savings through SecureResponse's vendor network."

0800 Hours - Emergency Council Session

Councilwoman Aaron and Councilman Lewis joined the emergency meeting. Andrea presented the situation:
- Complete system compromise
- Limited insurance coverage
- Emergency response costs
- Immediate funding needs

"The coverage gap is significant," Jennifer explained. "But DIS Risk Solutions has already mobilized their partner network to help manage costs."

0900 Hours - BOR Confirmation

"The Broker of Record change is official," Damian announced. "We can now fully deploy SecureResponse's vendor network and begin carrier negotiations."

"What's our first priority?" Andrea asked.

"Getting you proper coverage going forward," Damian replied. "But for now, let's focus on managing this incident with our partner resources."

1000 Hours - Expanded Response

With the BOR in place, SecureResponse's full vendor network activated:
- Legal teams for compliance
- PR firms for communicatio
- Additional forensics support
- Crisis management specialists

1100 Hours - Strategic Planning

"With SecureResponse's vendors now engaged," Damian explained, "we can implement a more structured recovery plan."

Marcus from TechDefend outlined the priorities:
- Strengthen temporary systems
- Begin permanent recovery planning
- Enhance security protocols
- Document all response actions

1200 Hours - Midday Assessment

Dr. Foster presented initial findings: "The attack shows sophisticated targeting of municipal systems. They specifically went after emergency services and revenue-generating functions."

Chief Romano added, "We're maintaining essential services, but we need to plan for extended operations under these temporary systems."

1300 Hours - Resource Coordination

Jennifer reviewed the financial implications: "With SecureResponse's vendor network now active, we're seeing significant cost reductions
- Coordinated response efforts
- Preferred vendor pricing
- Streamlined processes
- Optimized resource allocation"

1400 Hours - Recovery Planning

TechDefend and CyberForensics presented their joint recovery strategy:
- Phase 1: Strengthen temporary systems
- Phase 2: Begin permanent restoration
- Phase 3: Implement enhanced security
- Phase 4: Return to normal operations

1415 Hours - Response Coordination

"We need to maintain this momentum," Andrea noted, reviewing progress with the response team.

Marcus Thompson reported: "TechDefend has:
Stabilized critical systems
Secured temporary networks
Protected essential data
Begun recovery planning"

1430 Hours - FBI Engagement

Special Agent Matthews joined via secure line: "We're tracking similar attacks on municipalities. Your decision to maintain rather than immediately pay shows good judgment. We'll provide ongoing guidance as the investigation develops."

1445 Hours - Cost Management

Jennifer updated the financial tracking: "SecureResponse's vendor network is already showing value:
Coordinated response reducing duplication
Preferred pricing lowering costs
Streamlined processes saving time
Resource optimization improving efficiency

1500 Hours - Public Update

Andrea delivered the afternoon briefing: "Our response continues to progress. Emergency services remain operational. We've established temporary payment centers for utility bills and permits. While some services are slower than normal, essential city operations continue."

1515 Hours - Security Implementation

"This is our opportunity," Damian noted to Andrea, "to build back better than before. The security improvements we're implementing now will strengthen the city's position for proper coverage going forward."

1530 Hours - Strategic Assessment

"Our first day response is on track," Andrea told her team. "Marcus, what's next for our temporary systems?"

Marcus Thompson outlined the progression: "We're moving from emergency stabilization to enhanced temporary operations. This gives Dr.

Foster's team time for thorough investigation while maintaining city services."

1545 Hours - Investigation Update

Dr. Foster reported remotely: "We're making progress mapping the attack vector. This will be crucial both for recovery and preventing future incidents."

Special Agent Matthews added, "This intelligence helps protect other municipalities too. Your structured response provides valuable data."

1600 Hours - End-of-Day Planning

Andrea gathered department heads:

Chief Romano: "Dispatch systems stable. Officers adapting to temporary protocols."

Chief Nakamura: "Emergency response times holding steady. Manual systems functioning."

David Reeves: "Infrastructure controls secure. Teams adjusted to 24-hour manual monitoring."

1615 Hours - Tomorrow's Priorities

Damian outlined next steps:

"Day Two focuses on:
Response Enhancement:
Expand temporary capabilities
Begin permanent recovery planning
Implement security improvements
Continue investigation

Cost Management:
Deploy additional SecureResponse vendors

Optimize resource allocation
Document all expenses
Track recovery metrics"

1630 Hours - Evening Transition Planning
"We need 24-hour coverage until critical systems are restored," Andrea announced. "Let's review shift assignments."

Marcus Thompson outlined staffing
"Three shifts established:
Day: 0600-1400
Swing: 1400-2200
Night: 2200-0600

Each shift maintains:
Technical response team
Infrastructure monitoring
Security oversight"

1645 Hours - Public Communication

Andrea prepared the evening update:
"Residents should know:
Emergency services fully functional
Critical infrastructure secure
Temporary payment centers operating
Essential services maintained
Regular updates continuing"

1700 Hours - Day Two Preparation

Damian reviewed priorities with Jennifer:

"Tomorrow we focus on:
System Recovery:

Expand temporary operations
Begin permanent restoration
Enhance security measures

Cost Control:
Maximize SecureResponse benefit
Track expenses by category
Document all decisions
Manage resource allocation"

1715 Hours - Security Implementation

"The silver lining," Damian noted to Andrea, "is that these security improvements position the city for better coverage options once we're through this. Every measure we implement now strengthens your risk profile.

1730 Hours - First Day Assessment

As the evening shift took over, Andrea gathered with Damian for a final review of their first 24 hours

"We've come a long way since midnight," Andrea reflected. "Emergency services stable, critical infrastructure secure, and a clear path forward."

"The city's response has been exemplary," Damian noted. "Quick decisions, structured approach, and proper resource deployment. While we have challenging days ahead, we've laid the groundwork for both recovery and future protection."

Looking at the darkening sky outside her office window, Andrea managed a tired smile. "I suppose there's a lesson here about preparation and proper coverage."

"There is," Damian agreed. "But right now, let's focus on the fact that the City of Millbrook is still serving its residents, despite everything that's happened in the last twenty-four hours. That's what matters most."

The night shift settled in, SecureResponse's vendors continued their work, and the City of Millbrook moved forward - changed but undefeated by the crisis.

PART 2: TECHNICAL DEEP DIVE

Investigation Timeline:

2330-0000: Initial Detection

- Ransomware message discovered
- System lockouts identifie
- Initial service disruptions
- Emergency services impacted
- Backup systems verified compromise
- DIS Risk Solutions alerted
- Partner activation initiated

0000-0200: Response Coordination

- DIS Risk Solutions engaged
- TechDefend deployment
- CyberForensics activation
- SecureResponse preparation
- Coverage review initiated
- Documentation protocols established
- Emergency response coordinated

0200-0600: Full Investigation

- Complete system analysis
- Impact quantificatio
- Critical services assessment
- Recovery planning
- Partner coordination
- Coverage documentation
- Emergency protocols established

Technical Analysis:

1. Attack Vector Identificatio
Ransomware Characteristics:
- Multi-stage encryption
- System lockout mechanisms
- Backup deletion capabilities
- Administrative access exploitation
- Emergency service targeting

Access Methods:
- Remote desktop compromise
- Credential exploitation
- System vulnerabilities
- Network penetration
- Administrative escalation

2. Infrastructure Analysis
System Architecture:
- No network segmentation
- Limited backup isolation
- Single-factor authentication
- Connected critical systems
- Inadequate monitoring

Critical Services:
- Emergency Services CAD systems
- Water treatment controls
- Traffic management system
- Payment processing platforms
- Building access controls

3. Impact Assessment
Coverage Implications:
- Main policy limit inadequate
- Sub-limits quickly exceeded
- Retention immediately met
- Business interruption beyond coverage
- Notification costs exceeding limit

Operational Impact:
- Emergency dispatch compromised
- Infrastructure controls manual
- Payment systems offlin
- Communication systems limited
- Administrative functions impacted

4. Security Control Analysis
Missing Controls:
- Network segmentation
- Multi-factor authentication
- Backup isolation
- System monitoring
- Access management

Failed Safeguards:
- Backup verificatio
- Access controls
- System updates
- Security protocols
- Emergency procedures
5. Recovery Complexity
Technical Challenges:
- Critical service restoration
- System decontamination

- Data recovery
- Network rebuilding
- Security implementation

Implementation Constraints:
- Emergency service requirements
- Limited resources
- Time sensitivity
- System dependencies
- Public safety concerns

6. Forensic Investigation
Evidence Collection:
- System logs
- Network traffi
- Access records
- Backup status
- Security alerts

Analysis Findings:
- Attack methodology
- System vulnerabilities
- Impact scope
- Recovery requirements
- Future prevention

7. DIS Risk Solutions Coordination
Initial Response:
- Coverage activation (2330 hours)
- Partner team deployment
- Evidence preservation protocols
- Documentation requirements
- Claims process initiation

Coverage Management:
- Policy limit assessment ($500,000)
- Sub-limit tracking
- Retention documentation
- Cost allocation strategy
- Recovery planning coordination

Partner Integration:
TechDefend:
- Emergency response deployment
- System restoration planning
- Security implementation
- Recovery support coordination
- Future protection strategy

CyberForensics:
- Investigation management
- Evidence preservation
- Analysis coordination
- Documentation protocols
- Prevention recommendations

SecureResponse:
- Vendor network activation
- Recovery assistance
- System restoration support
- Implementation oversight
- Security enhancement planning

Documentation Requirements:
- Incident chronology
- Response actions
- Technical finding

- Recovery efforts
- Partner activities

Recovery Planning:
- Emergency service priorities
- System restoration sequence
- Security implementation timeline
- Partner coordination schedule
- Coverage utilization strategy

8. Solution Development
Technical Response:
- Emergency service restoration
- System security implementation
- Network reconstruction
- Monitoring deployment
- Access control enhancement

Implementation Strategy:
Phase 1 - Critical Services:
- Emergency response systems
- Infrastructure controls
- Communication restoration
- Security implementation
- Partner coordination

Phase 2 - Recovery:
- System reconstruction
- Security enhancement
- Process improvement
- Documentation completion
- Coverage alignment

Phase 3 - Prevention:
- Security implementation
- Process enhancement
- Training development
- Partner integration
- Coverage improvement

9. Risk Analysis
Coverage Assessment:
- Current limit: $500,000
- Retention: $50,000
- Business interruption sub-limit: $75,000
- Regulatory defense sub-limit: $100,000
- Reputational harm sub-limit: $25,000

Coverage Gaps:
- Inadequate primary limits
- Restrictive sub-limits
- Limited breach response
- Insufficient business interruptio
- Minimal regulatory defense

Future Requirements:
- Primary coverage: $5M+
- Appropriate sub-limits
- Pre-breach services
- Security partnerships
- Vendor network access

Security Enhancement:
- Network segmentation
- Multi-factor authentication
- Backup isolation

- System monitoring
- Access management

Long-term Protection:
- Enhanced coverage program
- Security improvement implementation
- Response protocol development
- Partner relationship management
- Regular testing and updates

PART 3: IMPLEMENTATION GUIDE

1. IMPACT ASSESSMENT

Financial Impact: Direct Costs: - Estimated total costs: $2.4M+ - Available coverage: $500K after retention - SecureResponse savings: ~$500K - Funding gap: $1.3M approximately

Insurance Implications: - Primary Coverage: $500K cyber liability policy - Retention: $50K per cyber incident - Sub-limits: • Business Interruption: $75K • Regulatory Defense: $100K • Reputational Harm: $25K - Coverage Triggers: Basic ransomware, data breach - Claims Process: BOR required for direct carrier engagement - Expected Coverage: Limited by sub-limits and retention

Systems Affected: Primary Systems: - Emergency Services Dispatch - Water Treatment Controls - Traffic Management - Payment Processing - Building Access

2. TECHNICAL RESPONSE

Immediate Actions (0-2 Hours): - Emergency service continuity protocols - BOR process initiation - TechDefend emergency deployment - CyberForensics engagement - SecureResponse preparation

Investigation Steps (2-6 Hours): - Initial cost assessment - Coverage verification - System impact analysis - Vendor network activation - Documentation protocols

Solution Development (6-24 Hours): - Temporary system deployment - Manual control implementation - Security measure integration - Cost containment activation - Response coordination

3. IMPLEMENTATION TIMELINE

Immediate (0-24 hours): Hour 0-2: - Initial assessment - Emergency response activation - BOR process initiation - Vendor engagement

Hour 2-6: - Coverage analysis - Cost assessment - System stabilization - Vendor deployment

Hour 6-24: - Emergency service restoration - Critical infrastructure security - Initial public communication - Documentation establishment

4. KEY TAKEAWAYS

Business Lessons: - Adequate coverage crucial for municipalities - Sub-limits significantly impact response options - Pre-breach services provide essential protection - Vendor network access reduces overall costs - Documentation critical for claims process

Technical Insights: - Emergency service continuity paramount - Manual control protocols essential - Temporary system deployment capability - Vendor coordination efficiency - Cost containment strategie

Process Improvements: - BOR procedures streamlined - Coverage verification protocols - Vendor network activation - Claims documentation systems - Cost allocation tracking

5. ROI ANALYSIS

Prevention Costs: - $5M Comprehensive Coverage: $75K annually - Pre-breach Services: $25K annually - Security Improvements: $250K annually - Training Programs: $50K annually Total Prevention Cost: $400K annually

Incident Costs: - Direct Response: $2.4M - Coverage Available: $500K - SecureResponse Savings: $500K - Emergency Funds: $1M Total Incident Cost: $2.4M+

Future Protection: - Risk Reduction: $2M annually - Coverage Benefits: $5M+ protection - Vendor Network Savings: 25-30% - Security Improvements: Ongoing value Total Value Proposition: $7M+ annually

6. ACTION CHECKLIST

Immediate Response (0-2 Hours): □ Contact insurance broker/carrier □ Initiate BOR process □ Engage emergency response vendors □ Activate manual protocols □ Begin documentation process

First 24 Hours: □ Process BOR with carrier □ Deploy SecureResponse vendors □ Establish cost tracking □ Implement temporary systems □ Coordinate public communications

Recovery Phase: □ Maximize coverage utilization □ Manage sub-limit allocations □ Document all expenses □ Track vendor deployments □ Monitor response costs

7. C-SUITE COMMUNICATION PROTOCOL

Executive Notification Sequence

City Manager (Andrea Sullivan) - Initial incident assessment - Emergency response activation - Council and public communications - Strategic decision authority - Final approval on major actions

Finance Director (Jennifer Koslowski) - DIS Risk Solutions coordination - Insurance coverage verification - Emergency fund allocation - Cost impact analysis - Claims documentation oversight

Public Works Director (David Reeves) - Infrastructure impact assessment - Critical system evaluation - Manual control implementation - Recovery timeline development - Resource allocation management

Emergency Management Coordinator (Tom Reilly) - Response team coordination - Resource deployment oversight - Inter-agency communications - Public safety management - Recovery operations direction

DIS Risk Solutions (Damian Davis) - Insurance carrier engagement - SecureResponse coordination - Vendor network activation - Strategic response guidance - Coverage maximization strategy

Communication Templates: - Initial Notification • Incident overview • Coverage status • Immediate actions taken • Required decisions

- Status Updates • Response progress • Vendor activities • Coverage utilization • Next steps

- Decision Requests • Options analysis • Cost implications • Coverage impact • Required actions

- Executive Summaries • Situation overview • Response effectiveness • Current status • Strategic implications

- Public Statements • Approved messaging • Service impact updates • Resident communications • Media response

Decision Matrix:

- Emergency Service Criteria • Impact thresholds • Response capabilities • Risk assessment • Public safety implications

- System Restoration Authority • Decision hierarchy • Vendor consultation • Recovery implications • Service continuity

- Resident Notification Triggers • Regulatory requirements • Legal obligations • Communication timing • Service disruption levels

- Media Response Guidelines • Message approval process • Spokesperson designation • Response timing • Public information flo

- Recovery Milestones • Service restoration • System verification • Operations resumption • Security enhancement

Chapter 6

IoT Infiltration

PART 1: NARRATIVE CASE STUDY

Company Profile: SmartTech Manufacturing
Annual Revenue: $145M
Industry: Smart Manufacturing (Industrial IoT)
Employees: 320 Client Base: Tier 2 automotive and industrial components manufacturers Market Position: Regional leader in smart manufacturing with innovative connected assembly systems
Geographic Presence: Main smart factory in Detroit with satellite facility in Tennessee

0215 Hours - SmartTech Manufacturing, Detroit Facility

Eric Rodriguez, third-shift Production Supervisor, was reviewing the overnight production metrics when the first anomaly appeared. Three robotic assembly stations suddenly adjusted their operational parameters, slowing their cycle time by 1.2 seconds.

"That's not right," he muttered, reaching for his phone to call Maya Patel, IoT Systems Specialist. The automated systems shouldn't be changing their timing without approval from Engineering.

0230 Hours - Production Floor

Maya arrived to find Eric staring at the production dashboard. "The robots are accepting commands from somewhere," she explained, scrolling through access logs. “But I don’t see any authorized changes in the system.”

“Could someone have hacked in?” Eric asked.

Maya’s face paled as she pulled up the device configuration panel. “Oh no. All these new IoT sensors we installed last quarter... they’re still using their default passwords. Every single one of them.”

0245 Hours - Initial Investigation

Steve Chang, Head of Operations Technology, arrived to find Maya frantically documenting device credentials.

“How many devices are we talking about?” he asked.

“At least 400 new sensors and control units,” Maya replied. “The vendor supplied them pre-configured for ‘easy setup.’ We changed the passwords on the main control systems, but the individual sensors...”

“Let me guess,” Steve interrupted. “Still set to admin/admin or the vendor defaults?”

Maya nodded grimly. “And they’re all listed in the vendor’s public documentation.”

0300 Hours - Security Assessment

The facility’s security team gathered in the control room: - Michael Sullivan - IT Security Manager - Dr. Rebecca Liu - Industrial Systems Engineer - Raj Kumar - Network Administrator - Angela Foster - Quality Control Specialist - Brian Mitchell - Maintenance Supervisor

“I’m calling DIS Risk Solutions,” Michael announced. “We just signed with them last month, and IndustrialGuard was scheduled to begin their IoT security implementation next week. We’re completely exposed.”

0315 Hours - DIS Risk Solutions Engagement "Damian Davis"

"Damian, it's Michael Sullivan at SmartTech Manufacturing. I apologize for the early hour, but we've got an emergency."

"No apology needed, Michael. What's happening?"

"We've discovered unauthorized access to our production systems. Someone's manipulating our IoT devices - the ones IndustrialGuard was supposed to start securing next week."

"Alright, Michael. Walk me through exactly what you're seeing," Damian said, fully alert now.

"We've got unauthorized access through default passwords on about 400 IoT devices. They're modifying production parameters, and we've got at least six hours of potentially compromised parts for Parker Automotive."

"This is serious, Michael. We're looking at multiple coverage triggers here - cyber, product liability, and possibly business interruption impacts," Damian responded. "Start documenting everything. I'll get IndustrialGuard's emergency response team out there immediately, and I'm bringing in CyberForensics for the investigation. Have you contacted Parker Automotive yet?"

0330 Hours - Response Coordination

"Not yet," Michael replied. "We wanted to understand the full scope first.

"Good thinking," Damian said. "Let's get IndustrialGuard and CyberForensics on-site before we make that call. We'll need solid documentation of the impact before engaging with Parker."

IndustrialGuard's emergency response team arrived, led by Lisa Chen, their Industrial Systems Specialist. After a quick briefing, she shook her head.

"Four hundred devices with default passwords... this is exactly what our security assessment would have caught next week," she said, pulling up a diagnostic tool. "First priority is stopping any ongoing unauthorized access. Then we'll need to document every modified parameter before we change anything."

Dr. Rebecca Liu pointed to her screen. "The changes are subtle. They're adjusting calibration parameters just enough to affect product quality without triggering major alarms."

"How many parts are affected?" Steve asked.

"Based on timestamps, potentially everything produced in the last six hours. That's about 3,200 components for Parker Automotive - they're our largest customer. They use these precision components in their brake assembly systems."

"Parker accounts for 40% of our production," Steve added grimly. "If these parts don't meet their quality specifications...

0345 Hours - Crisis Escalation

Steve reached for his phone to call Richard Harrison, Director of Manufacturing.

"Richard, we have a situation," Steve began. "Someone's accessed our production systems through unsecured IoT devices. DIS Risk Solutions has their response teams here, but we're looking at quality issues with Parker's brake components."

"Parker's brake assemblies?" Harrison's voice sharpened. "How many parts?"

"At least 3,200 units from the last six hours of production. And Damian Davis says we're looking at both cyber and product liability implications."

0400 Hours - Emergency Response

The control room was buzzing with activity as the team worked to stabilize the situation. Lisa Chen, leading IndustrialGuard's response team, reviewed the latest diagnostic data.

"We've isolated the compromised devices," Lisa announced. "But the changes to the production parameters are more extensive than we initially thought. We need to start mapping the full scope of the modifications."

Dr. Rebecca Liu, the Industrial Systems Engineer, nodded. "I've cross-referenced the affected parameters with the production logs. The attackers are targeting tolerances that directly impact safety-critical components."

"Parker Automotive's brake assemblies," Steve Chang muttered. "This is a nightmare scenario."

Angela Foster, the Quality Control Specialist, chimed in. "We've quarantined all affected components, but we'll need detailed testing protocols to identify which ones can be salvaged."

Damian Davis, still on the line with Michael Sullivan, provided guidance. "Michael, make sure every action is documented. From a coverage perspective, we need a clear timeline of events, response actions, and any potential impacts on Parker Automotive."

0430 Hours - Escalating the Investigation

The CyberForensics team, led remotely by Dr. Robert Foster, began analyzing the attack patterns.

"The changes are deliberate and precise," Dr. Foster explained over the video link. "This isn't random sabotage. Whoever did this understands both your production systems and Parker's quality control requirements."

Lisa Chen frowned. "That means they had prior knowledge of our processes. Either there's been a breach of internal information, or someone with industry expertise is behind this."

Dr. Foster nodded. "The forensic evidence suggests the latter. The attackers are systematically testing the limits of your quality thresholds. This points to industrial espionage."

Steve Chang's face darkened. "If they're targeting us, they could be targeting others in the automotive supply chain."

0500 Hours - Coordination with Parker Automotive

As the investigation deepened, Richard Harrison, Director of Manufacturing, joined the call. "We need to notify Parker Automotive," he said. "They're going to want answers, and fast."

Damian agreed. "Let's coordinate the message carefully. We need to provide transparency while ensuring the investigation isn't compromised. Michael, I recommend looping in Parker's engineering team to assess the impact on their assembly line."

By 0515 hours, Tom Zhang, Parker Automotive's Senior Safety Engineer, was on the line. "We've shut down our brake assembly lines until we can verify the integrity of the components," Zhang reported. "How soon can we get a detailed analysis of the affected parts?"

Angela Foster interjected. "We're working on enhanced testing protocols. We should have preliminary results within two hours."

Zhang's tone was firm. "Make it one hour. Our production schedule is already slipping."

0530 Hours - Initial Findings

Angela and Janet Lee, Parker's Quality Systems Manager, began analyzing the quarantined components.

"We've identified three distinct patterns in the parameter modific - tions," Angela explained. "Each one targets a different aspect of the brake component machining process."

Janet nodded. "These changes are subtle enough to bypass standard quality checks, but they could lead to catastrophic failures in high-stress conditions."

Dr. Foster added, "This level of precision suggests a highly skilled actor. We're looking at a coordinated effort to disrupt both your production and Parker's."

0600 Hours - Strategic Alignment

By the time the sun began to rise, the team had a clearer picture of the attack. Damian convened a strategy call with all stakeholders.

"Here's where we stand," Damian summarized. "We've contained the immediate threat, but the full scope of the impact is still unfolding. Our priorities are: securing the production systems, verifying the integrity of the affected components, and maintaining transparent communication with Parker."

Lisa Chen outlined the next steps. "IndustrialGuard will focus on securing the remaining IoT devices and implementing proper credentials. Angela and Janet will finalize the testing protocols, and Dr. Foster's team will continue the forensic investigation."

Damian concluded the call. "This is a challenging situation, but we've got the right team in place. Let's stay coordinated and keep moving forward."

0615 Hours - Expanded Response

"The parameter changes show a clear pattern," Dr. Robert Foster explained from the CyberForensics remote link. "They targeted specific tolerance adjustments that would be difficult to detect in standard quality checks."

Mark Stevens arrived, immediately pulling Harrison and Rachel Torres into a coverage discussion. "We need to document every decision point,"

Mark emphasized. “Especially regarding the quarantine of suspected parts and customer notification.

“Parker’s sending their engineering team,” Harrison updated the group. “Tom Zhang wants them here by 0700.”

0630 Hours - Strategy Alignment

Lisa Chen gathered the team to outline next steps. “IndustrialGuard will tackle this in phases:
1. Secure critical production devices
2. Document all parameter modification
3. Implement proper security protocols”

“From a coverage perspective,” Rachel added, “we need to maintain detailed logs of:
- Initial discovery timeline
- Response actions taken
- All customer communications
- Quality control measures”

0645 Hours - Quality Assessment

Angela Foster pulled up the latest analysis. “We’ve identified three di - tinct modification patterns in the brake component specifications. Each one subtle enough to pass individual checks, but potentially significant when combined.”

“Parker’s engineers will want to see this immediately,” Harrison said. “Tom Zhang specifically asked about the impact on their assembly line testing.”

0700 Hours - Parker Engineering Team Arrival

Tom Zhang arrived with his team, including:
- David Wu - Senior Safety Engineer

- Janet Lee - Quality Systems Manager
- Mike Rodriguez - Production Integration Specialist

"Our assembly line is on hold," Zhang announced. "We need answers fast."

Lisa Chen and Angela Foster led them to the quality control lab where the suspect components were quarantined. "We've mapped every parameter change," Angela explained, pulling up detailed specifications. "The modifications affected three key tolerance points in the brake component machining."

0715 Hours - Joint Analysis

"These changes are sophisticated," David Wu observed, examining the data. "They wouldn't trigger individual quality alerts, but in combination..."

"That's what concerns us," Dr. Robert Foster interjected from the video conference. "The pattern suggests detailed knowledge of both your quality control parameters and Parker's testing protocols."

Mark Stevens, who had been taking detailed notes, looked up. "Mr. Zhang, we'll need documentation of any production impacts at Parker for the coverage investigation."

0730 Hours - Scope Assessment

Rachel Torres joined remotely for the coverage discussion. "We're looking at multiple coverage triggers here," she explained. "Cyber incident, business interruption at both facilities, and potential product liability implications."

0745 Hours - Technical Analysis

"Parker's test data adds another layer of concern," Janet Lee reported, comparing specifications. "These modified parameters... they're precisely calculated to stay just within our acceptance thresholds."

Lisa Chen nodded grimly. "Which means whoever did this understands both SmartTech's manufacturing systems and Parker's quality requirements. This wasn't a random attack."

"That's significant from an investigation standpoint," Dr. Robert Foster added. "We're seeing evidence of industry-specific ta geting."

0800 Hours - Coverage Strategy

"Given the specialized nature of this attack," Damian advised, "we need to approach this carefully. Rachel, walk everyone through the coverage implications."

Rachel Torres shared her screen. "We're dealing with:
- Cyber incident coverage for the system compromise
- Business interruption at SmartTech
- Contingent business interruption for Parker
- Potential product liability implications"

"And regulatory reporting requirements," Mark Stevens added. "Given these are safety-critical components."

0815 Hours - Response Planning

Harrison gathered the joint team: "We need parallel tracks here:

1. Technical Response:
- Lisa's team securing IoT devices
- Angela and Janet coordinating quality review
- Dr. Foster's forensics investigation

2. Business Continuity:
- Mike Rodriguez working on Parker's production adjustments
- Alternative component sourcing
- Customer impact management

3. Coverage Documentation:
- Mark tracking all response costs
- Rachel managing coverage aspects
- Regulatory compliance review"

0900 Hours - Security Implementation

"I've got something," Dr. Robert Foster reported. "The access patterns suggest the attack originated from within your industry. They knew exactly when to modify parameters to align with Parker's testing schedule."

Lisa Chen looked up from her terminal. "Which means this could be happening at other facilities. Damian, should we notify..."

"Already on it," Damian interrupted. "We're reaching out to other clients in the automotive supply chain. Mark, add industrial espionage to the coverage review."

1000 Hours - Testing Implementation

"Here's what we know," Angela Foster began, pulling up the test results. "The parameter modifications follow three distinct patterns. We can clear components faster if we batch test by pattern type."

Janet Lee nodded. "I've mapped these patterns against Parker's assembly line requirements. Batches showing Pattern A have the highest risk profile for brake performance.

"Document every test result," Mark Stevens emphasized. "Especially any components we clear for production. Rachel needs this for the coverage documentation."

1100 Hours - Production Decision

Tom Zhang consulted with David Wu and Janet Lee. "We can't wait any longer. We need to notify our leadership about the production delay."

"Before you make that call," Rachel advised, "we should discuss how to frame this. There are coverage implications for both SmartTech and Parker depending on how this is characterized."

"Agreed," Harrison said. "We need to balance transparency with the ongoing investigation. Plus, we don't want to signal vulnerability to competitors."

1115 Hours - Strategy Alignment

The team gathered to prepare for the FBI's arrival:

"Dr. Foster, summarize your findings," Damian requested

"We're looking at a sophisticated campaign targeting automotive supply chain tolerances," Dr. Foster reported. "The attackers understand both manufacturing processes and quality control systems. This isn't random cybercrime - it's coordinated industrial espionage."
1200 Hours - Industry Briefing
Damian organized a conference call with the affected suppliers' insurance and security teams, while maintaining client confidentialit .

"We're dealing with a sophisticated actor targeting automotive manufacturing intellectual property," he explained. "Each affected facility shows the same pattern: IoT compromise followed by subtle manipulation of quality control parameters."

1215 Hours - Pattern Analysis

"The timing is significant," Dr. Robert Foster shared. "Each facility was compromised shortly after installing new IoT sensors. Someone's monitoring industrial equipment deployments in the automotive sector."

Special Agent Thompson nodded. "We're seeing a clear pattern. They wait for new IoT implementations, then strike before security protocols are fully established."

"That's going to matter for coverage," Rachel Torres added. "Especially for facilities still in their implementation window."

1230 Hours - Immediate Actions

Lisa Chen outlined the security response: "Every facility needs to:
1. Audit all IoT device credentials
2. Review quality control parameters
3. Check production tolerances
4. Document any subtle modifications
5. Preserve forensic evidence"

"And from a coverage standpoint," Mark Stevens added, "document everything. This is evolving from a cyber incident to a national security concern."

1245 Hours - Parker Update

Tom Zhang returned from a call with Parker's executive team. "They're shutting down three production lines. We need to know how long until we can resume component delivery."

"Angela, where are we with testing?" Harrison asked.

"We've cleared about 20% of the quarantined components," Angela Foster reported. "Janet's team has streamlined the testing protocol, but we're still finding subtle variations in Pattern A batches."

1300 Hours - Testing Protocol

"Pattern A variations are consistent with intelligence gathering," Dr. Robert Foster observed. "They're testing different tolerance limits, probably mapping our manufacturing capabilities."

Janet Lee agreed. "These aren't random modifications. Each variation explores a different aspect of our quality control thresholds."

"That's significant for the investigation," Special Agent Thompson noted. "This isn't just about disrupting production - it's systematic industrial espionage."

1315 Hours - Coverage Analysis

"The evidence of coordinated industrial espionage strengthens our coverage position," Rachel Torres explained. "Mark, make sure we're documenting:
- Pattern of sophisticated targeting
- Focus on intellectual property
- Industry-wide impact
- National security implications"

"Already compiling it," Mark Stevens responded. "The policy's cyber-espionage endorsement should respond differently than a standard breach."

1330 Hours - Production Impact

Mike Rodriguez updated Parker's situation: "Without cleared components, we're looking at:
- Three production lines down
- 47 employees idle
- Potential overtime costs for catch-up
- Supply chain ripple effects"

"Document all these impacts," Damian advised. "We're dealing with both direct and contingent business interruption claims."

1345 Hours - Industry Coordination

"We've established a secure channel for affected suppliers to share attack indicators," Lisa Chen announced. "Six facilities now confirming similar patterns."

Special Agent Thompson pulled up a map. "The pattern's clear - they're systematically targeting automotive supply chain manufacturers, focusing on those with new IoT implementations."

"This level of coordination suggests nation-state involvement," Damian noted. "Rachel, good thing we negotiated that affirmative coverage during the last renewal."

1400 Hours - Coverage Update

"Most cyber policies now exclude nation-state attacks," Rachel Torres explained. "But we specifically negotiated affirmative coverage for SmartTech, given the industrial espionage risks in automotive manufacturing."

"It wasn't an easy negotiation," Mark Stevens added. "But this is exactly the scenario we were worried about. The policy includes both cyber and intellectual property provisions for state-sponsored attacks, with no attribution requirement."

"That's going to be crucial," Damian noted. "Many affected suppliers are discovering they're excluded from coverage due to standard nation-state exclusions."

1415 Hours - Strategic Advantage

"That coverage negotiation is proving critical," Damian observed. "Other suppliers are facing these losses without insurance backing."

"Which affects the broader industry response," Special Agent Thompson noted. "Some companies are hesitant to share attack details, worried about uncovered losses and liability."

"We can be more transparent," Harrison said. "Knowing we have coverage lets us focus on proper response rather than liability concerns."

1430 Hours - Response Strategy

"The affirmative coverage changes our options," Rachel Torres explained. "We can:
- Implement full testing protocols
- Share attack indicators with authorities
- Engage specialized forensics
- Consider production alternatives

All without worrying about exclusions."

"That's significant," Lisa Chen added. "Some facilities are rushing production restarts because they can't afford extended interruption without coverage."

1445 Hours - Parker Discussion

"This affects how we proceed with Parker," Mark Stevens noted. "We can take the time to do this right, knowing the policy will respond to:
- Extended business interruption
- Forensic investigations
- Customer-related losses
- Potential future claims"

Tom Zhang looked relieved. "That gives us more options for managing the production delays."

1500 Hours - Response Planning

"Damian, Rachel, Mark - having the right coverage in place made a huge difference today. We could focus on doing things right instead of just doing them fast," Harrison acknowledged. "Now, let's focus on getting back to production. Where do we stand with testing?"

Angela Foster pulled up the latest test results. "We've cleared about 60% of the quarantined components using the enhanced protocol. Another four hours should complete the testing."

"Parker's immediate needs?" Harrison asked.

"I can work with that timeline," Tom Zhang responded. "We'll adjust shift schedules to handle the cleared components as they're released."

1615 Hours - Security Implementation

"IndustrialGuard's team has secured 80% of the IoT devices," Lisa Chen reported. "More importantly, we're implementing proper security protocols that should have been in place from the start."

"The attack patterns are clear now," Dr. Robert Foster added. "We can help prevent similar incidents across the industry."

1630 Hours - Final Assessment

Harrison gathered the team for a status review. The control room, chaotic fourteen hours ago, now hummed with organized purpose.

"When I walked in here at four this morning, we were facing a crisis that could have crippled two companies," Harrison began. "Instead, we're ending the day with:
- Identified and contained breach
- Established testing protocols
- Protected intellectual property
- Maintained customer transparency
- Supported federal investigation
- Implemented lasting security improvements"

"Most importantly," he added, looking around the room, "we've shown how to handle these incidents properly. Sometimes the right way is the harder way."

1645 Hours - Moving Forward

Lisa Chen outlined the final security implementations while Angela Foster and Janet Lee coordinated the remaining component testing.

"We'll have new IoT security protocols fully implemented by end of shift tomorrow," Lisa confirmed. "This includes everything we should have done during the initial installation."

"And Parker's production schedule?" Harrison asked.

"Back to normal by second shift tomorrow," Tom Zhang replied. "The cleared components are already moving through their testing protocol."

1700 Hours - Lessons Learned

As the day shift prepared to hand over to evening personnel, Harrison reflected on the past fourteen hours. The facility had faced a sophisticated attack targeting not just their systems, but the heart of their manufacturing capabilities. They'd emerged stronger, with improved security, validated testing protocols, and a deeper understanding of their vulnerabilities.

1715 Hours - Evening Transition

"One final thing," Harrison addressed the team. "Today wasn't just about responding to an attack. It was about proving that doing things the right way - thorough testing, proper security, full transparency with partners - that's what builds lasting trust."

Special Agent Thompson gathered her materials. "Your response will help protect others in the industry. That level of cooperation makes a real difference."

"The evening shift has been briefed," Lisa Chen reported. "They'll continue implementing the new security protocols while maintaining the enhanced monitoring."

1730 Hours - Final Briefing

Angela Foster and Janet Lee completed their handover to the evening quality team. "All test protocols are documented and in place. Every component gets full verification before release."

Tom Zhang nodded appreciatively. "Parker won't forget how this was handled. Transparency and thoroughness matter more than quick fixes."

1745 Hours - Day's End

As Harrison watched the day shift leaving, he thought about how differently this could have played out. A rushed response, cut corners, hidden problems - the usual temptations during a crisis. Instead, they'd chosen the harder but better path.

The facility's operations were returning to normal, but it wasn't the same normal as yesterday. It was better, stronger, more secure. Sometimes, he reflected, it takes a crisis to show you how to do things right.

1800 Hours - Shift Change

The evening shift settled in as Harrison made his final rounds. The production floor hummed with a different kind of efficiency now - more measured, more secure, more aware.

Through the control room window, he could see Lisa Chen's team continuing their methodical security implementation. On the testing floo , Angela Foster's protocols were being followed with newfound appreciation for precision. The Parker components moved through inspection under Janet Lee's enhanced verification process.

"Quite a difference from this morning," Damian observed, preparing to head out. "You know, most companies face these situations alone, scrambling for help after the fact."

Harrison nodded. "Today showed why preparation matters. Not just the insurance and security - but having the right partners, the right protocols, the right mindset."

"That's the real lesson here," Damian agreed. "Security isn't just about preventing attacks. It's about being ready to handle them properly when they come."

As the facility's lights dimmed to evening levels, the new IoT security protocols blinked steadily on the monitoring screens. SmartTech Manufacturing had faced a sophisticated attack and emerged not just intact, but transformed. In the end, Harrison reflected, that might prove to be the most valuable production of the day.

PART 2: TECHNICAL DEEP DIVE

Investigation Timeline:

2100-0215: Initial Compromise

- Default IoT credentials exploited
- Parameter modifications initiated
- Quality control thresholds altered
- Production specifications changed
- Attack patterns established
- DIS Risk Solutions alerted
- Partner activation initiated

0215-0400: Detection and Response

- Cycle time anomaly detected
- IoT access identified
- DIS Risk Solutions engaged
- IndustrialGuard deployed
- CyberForensics activated
- Coverage review initiated
- Documentation protocols established

0400-1200: Full Investigation

- Parameter changes documented
- Parker team engaged
- Quality testing initiated

- Coverage implications assessed
- Industry pattern identified
- Partner coordination
- Recovery planning initiated

Technical Analysis:

1. Attack Vector Identification

IoT Device Vulnerabilities:
- Default manufacturer credentials retained
- Published password documentation
- Unsecured management interfaces
- Direct internet accessibility
- Limited access logging

Access Methods:
- Standard device logins
- Web-based management portals
- Remote access protocols
- Maintenance interfaces
- Configuration utilities

2. Infrastructure Analysis

System Architecture:
- Unsegmented IoT network
- Direct internet connectivity
- Limited monitoring capabilities
- Inadequate access controls
- Insufficient logging

Production Impact:
- 400+ compromised devices
- 12 production lines affected
- 3,200 suspect components

- Modified quality parameters
- Altered calibration settings

3. Impact Assessment
Coverage Implications:
- Cyber incident triggers
- Product liability exposure
- Business interruption losses
- Contingent BI for Parker
- Nation-state attack coverage

Operational Impact:
- Production line stoppage
- Customer relationship management
- Supply chain disruption
- Reputation management
- Industry-wide implications

4. Security Control Analysis
Missing Controls:
- IoT password management
- Network segmentation
- Device monitoring
- Change detection
- Access logging

Failed Safeguards:
- Default credential policies
- Security implementation timing
- Network architecture
- Quality control thresholds
- Device management protocols

5. Recovery Complexity
Technical Challenges:
- Individual device reconfiguration
- Parameter verification requirements
- Quality control validation
- Production line integration
- Security protocol implementation

Implementation Constraints:
- Production timeline pressure
- Customer requirements
- Quality control standards
- System dependencies
- Industry regulations

6. Forensic Investigation
Evidence Collection:
- IoT device logs
- Parameter change history
- Production data
- Quality control records
- Access timestamps

Analysis Findings:
- Systematic parameter modifications
- Targeted quality thresholds
- Industry knowledge indicators
- Nation-state attack patterns
- Industrial espionage markers

7. DIS Risk Solutions Coordination
Initial Response:
- Coverage activation (0215 hours)
- Partner team deployment

- Evidence preservation protocols
- Documentation requirements
- Claims process initiation

Coverage Management:
- Policy review ($10M limit)
- Nation-state coverage confirmation
- Retention documentation ($250K)
- Cost allocation strategy
- Recovery planning coordination

Partner Integration:
IndustrialGuard:
- IoT security assessment
- Device reconfiguration
- Parameter verification
- Security implementation
- Monitoring deployment

CyberForensics:
- Investigation management
- Evidence preservation
- Parameter analysis
- Documentation protocols
- Prevention recommendations

Documentation Requirements:
- Incident chronology
- Response actions
- Technical findings
- Recovery efforts
- Partner activities

Recovery Planning:
- Production restoration priorities
- Quality control verification
- Security implementation timeline
- Partner coordination schedule
- Coverage utilization strategy

8. Solution Development
Technical Response:
- IoT device credential changes
- Network access restrictions
- Parameter verification protocols
- Quality control enhancement
- Production line security

Implementation Strategy:
Phase 1 - Immediate Response:
- Device security
- Parameter verification
- Production assessment
- Customer communication
- Partner coordination

Phase 2 - Recovery:
- System restoration
- Security enhancement
- Process improvement
- Documentation completion
- Coverage alignment

Phase 3 - Prevention:
- Security implementation
- Process enhancement
- Training development

- Partner integration
- Coverage improvement

9. Risk Analysis

Coverage Assessment:
- Primary Coverage: $10M
- Retention: $250K
- Nation-state coverage: Included
- Product liability coverage: Included
- Business interruption coverage: Included

Coverage Implications:
- Nation-state attack coverage
- Product liability implications
- Business interruption scope
- Supply chain impact
- Future protection requirements

Security Enhancement:
- IoT security baseline
- Device management protocols
- Network segmentation
- Access control systems
- Monitoring capabilities

Long-term Protection:
- Enhanced security program
- Continuous monitoring
- Regular assessments
- Partner integration
- Coverage maintenance

PART 3: IMPLEMENTATION GUIDE

1. IMPACT ASSESSMENT

Financial Impact: Direct Costs: - IoT security implementation: $850K - Production line stoppage: $1.2M - Quality control testing: $450K - Forensic investigation: $275K Total Direct Impact: $2.775M

Insurance Implications: - Primary Coverage: $10M cyber liability policy - Retention: $250K per cyber incident - Sub-limits: • Business Interruption: $5M • Product Liability: $5M • Contingent BI: $2.5M - Coverage Triggers: IoT compromise, production loss, product quality - Nation-state Attack: Affirmatively covered - Claims Process: Dual-track (cyber and product liability)

Systems Affected: Primary Systems: - 400+ IoT devices - 12 production lines - Quality control systems - Parameter management - Calibration controls

2. TECHNICAL RESPONSE

Immediate Actions (0-12 Hours): - IoT device access containment - Production line shutdown - Quality control isolation - Parameter verification initiation - Evidence preservation protocols

Investigation Steps (12-24 Hours): - Device inventory audit - Parameter modification mapping - Quality impact assessment - Production line evaluation - Customer impact analysis

Solution Development (24-48 Hours): - IoT security implementation - Network segmentation - Monitoring deployment - Testing protocol establishment - Documentation procedures

3. IMPLEMENTATION TIMELINE

Immediate (0-24 hours): Hour 0-6: - Initial containment - DIS Risk Solutions engagement - IndustrialGuard deployment - Parker notific - tion - Evidence collection

Hour 6-12: - Parameter verification - Quality testing initiation - Production assessment - Customer coordination - Coverage confirmatio

Hour 12-24: - Security implementation - Testing protocols - Production planning - Documentation development - Stakeholder communication

Extended Timeline:

Short-term (24-72 hours): Day 2: - Complete IoT device security - Verify all parameters - Resume critical production - Enhance monitoring - Document finding

Day 3: - Implement network segmentation - Expand testing protocols - Restore production capacity - Deploy security controls - Update procedures

Long-term (72+ hours): Week 1: - Full security implementation - Production normalization - Quality verification - Documentation completion - Process improvement

4. KEY TAKEAWAYS

Business Lessons: - IoT security fundamental to operations - Default credentials create critical risk - Quality control requires layered verific - tion - Customer transparency builds trust - Coverage preparation crucial

Technical Insights: - Device management essential - Network segmentation critical - Parameter monitoring vital - Access control fundamental - Documentation necessary

Process Improvements: - IoT security protocols - Device management procedures - Quality control processes - Testing methodologies - Incident response plans

5. ROI ANALYSIS

Prevention Costs: Initial Investment: - IoT security platform: $450K - Network segmentation: $275K - Monitoring systems: $225K - Staff training: $150K - Documentation systems: $100K Total Prevention Cost: $1.2M

Incident Costs: Direct Impact: - Production stoppage: $1.2M - Emergency response: $850K - Quality testing: $450K - Customer impact: $275K Less Insurance Recovery: ($2.525M after retention) Total Net Impact: $250K (retention)

Future Protection: Annual Savings: - Risk reduction: $1.5M - Efficiency gains: $750K - Quality improvements: $500K - Process optimization: $250K Total Annual Value: $3M

6. ACTION CHECKLIST

Immediate Response: □ Secure IoT devices □ Halt affected production □ Engage DIS Risk Solutions □ Document parameter changes □ Notify key stakeholders

Technical Implementation: □ Deploy security controls □ Verify device configurations □ Implement monitoring □ Test quality controls □ Document procedures

7. C-SUITE COMMUNICATION PROTOCOL

Executive Notification Sequence

Director of Manufacturing (Richard Harrison) - Initial incident assessment - Production impact evaluation - Resource allocation - Customer communication - Recovery oversight

Head of Operations Technology (Steve Chang) - Technical impact assessment - System modification approval - Resource coordination - Recovery timeline development - Security implementation

Quality Control Manager (Angela Foster) - Quality impact assessment - Testing protocol development - Customer requirements - Compliance verification - Production validatio

DIS Risk Solutions (Damian Davis) - Coverage coordination - Response management - Vendor activation - Strategic guidance - Claims oversight

Communication Templates:

Initial Notification: • Incident overview • Current status • Immediate actions • Required decisions • Next steps

Status Updates: • Response progress • Production impact • Customer status • Coverage status • Action items

Decision Matrix:

Production Halt Criteria: • Quality impact threshold • Safety implications • Customer requirements • Coverage considerations • Regulatory obligations

System Restoration Authority: • Security verification required • Quality control approval • Customer acceptance • Coverage confirmation • Documentation complete

Customer Notification Triggers: • Quality impact confirmed • Production delay >4 hours • Safety concerns identified • Regulatory requirements • Coverage implications

Response Escalation Guidelines: • Technical impact severity • Production stoppage duration • Customer impact level • Coverage implications • Regulatory requirements

Recovery Milestones: • IoT security implementation • Quality control verification • Production restoration • Customer approval • Documentation completion

Documentation Requirements:

Technical Documentation: • Parameter modifications • Security implementations • Quality test results • Production impacts • System changes

Coverage Documentation: • Incident timeline • Response actions • Cost tracking • Customer impact • Recovery efforts

Chapter 7

Crypto Chaos

PART 1: NARRATIVE CASE STUDY

Company Profile: CryptoNext Solutions
Annual Revenue: $12.5M (with $180M in managed digital assets)
Latest Valuation: $125M (Series B funding round)
Industry: Financial Technology (Cryptocurrency Exchange & DeFi Services)
Employees: 84
Client Base: 175,000 retail users and 22 institutional clients
Market Position: Emerging crypto platform known for innovative DeFi products and user-friendly trading interface
Geographic Presence: Headquartered in Miami with remote development teams

Funding History:
- Seed Round: $2.5M (valuation: $12M)
- Series A: $8M (valuation: $40M)
- Series B: $25M (valuation: $125M)
- Series C: In preparation

2245 Hours - CryptoNext Solutions, Miami Headquarters

Jake Sullivan, Lead Blockchain Developer, was reviewing smart contract deployment logs when his monitoring dashboard lit up. The automated alerts showed unusual token movements across multiple user wallets.

"Hey Kevin," he called to Kevin Park, DevSecOps Engineer, who was pulling another late night preparing for the Series C security audit. "Are we running any automated wallet rebalancing right now?"

Kevin looked up from his terminal, confused. "No, all automated operations are paused during the audit prep. What are you seeing?"

"Unusual token transfers... they're using our smart contract's batch transfer function, but these aren't scheduled operations." Jake pulled up the transaction logs, his face growing pale. "And they're all being approved by a valid admin key."

2300 Hours - Initial Assessment

Grace Liu, Head of Security, joined them virtually from her home office. Her video feed showed her already scanning through transaction data.

"Talk to me about the scope," she demanded, fingers flying across her keyboard. "And someone get DIS Risk Solutions on the line - this could trigger both our crypto asset and cyber coverage."

"Multiple wallets affected," Jake reported. "The transactions are using our BatchTransfer smart contract, but with maximum allowance settings we never authorized. Someone's found a way to manipulate the approval mechanism."

"How much exposure?" Grace's voice was tense.

Kevin pulled up the real-time blockchain explorer. "So far, about $8.5 million in various tokens. The transactions are still ongoing."

2315 Hours - Emergency Response

The emergency response team assembled on a secure video call:
- Daniel Zhao - CTO and Co-founder
- Grace Liu - Head of Security

- Chris Bennett - Smart Contract Specialist
- Lisa Parker - Compliance Office
- Andrew Foster - Legal Counsel
- Sophia Chen - Customer Operations Lead

Damian Davis from DIS Risk Solutions joined immediately. "Walk me through what you're seeing," he said, already patched in through their incident response line.

Chris shared his screen, displaying the smart contract analysis. "They're exploiting a vulnerability in our approval mechanism. The BatchTransfer contract isn't properly validating cumulative allowances across multiple transactions. They're using this to drain user wallets that have given any level of token approval to our platform."

"I'm activating SecureResponse's blockchain forensics team," Damian announced. "And CloudShield is already analyzing your network traffic patterns. Grace, have you initiated the incident response protocol we established during your coverage review?"

2330 Hours - Technical Discovery

"It gets worse," Kevin added, pulling up the deployment logs. "This vulnerability was introduced in our last smart contract update... three days ago. The one we rushed out for the Series C technical review."

Grace's face hardened. "The one that skipped the full security audit because we were behind schedule?"

"Rachel Torres from our claims team is joining," Damian added. "Mark Stevens will be on site within the hour. We need to document everything - this will trigger both the crypto asset and cyber coverage portions of your policy."

Daniel winced. The pressure to demonstrate new features for potential Series C investors had pushed them to accelerate their deployment timeline.

2345 Hours - Crisis Escalation

"We need to notify Victoria," Grace said, referring to Victoria Nash, CEO and Co-founder. "This isn't just a technical issue anymore. We're about to have 175,000 users discovering unauthorized transactions, right in the middle of our Series C due diligence."

"SecureResponse's blockchain team is seeing similar patterns across multiple DeFi platforms," Damian reported. "This could be part of a coordinated attack."

Daniel reached for his phone. "I'll call Victoria. Kevin, start preparing the smart contract freeze. Chris, we need a fix ready the moment we pause the contract. Sophia, draft user communications. Lisa, start documenting everything for the regulators."

0000 Hours - Executive Briefing

Victoria Nash joined the emergency call, her video feed showing she was still at the office reviewing Series C documents with potential investors. "Give me the worst of it," she demanded.

"Smart contract vulnerability in our latest update," Daniel explained. "Attackers are exploiting it to drain user wallets. We're looking at $8.5 million in unauthorized transfers so far, and it's still active."

"Christ," Victoria muttered. "Options?"

Grace laid them out: "One: Freeze the smart contract immediately. Stops the bleeding but locks everyone's assets. Two: Deploy emergency fix without proper testing. Risky. Three: Attempt to front-run the attackers with our own transactions to protect remaining assets."

"Your policy will respond better to decisive action that prevents further losses," Damian advised. "CloudShield can help validate the fix while SecureResponse continues tracing the unauthorized transactions."

0015 Hours - Risk Assessment

Lisa Parker pulled up the compliance dashboard. "We have regulatory obligations here. Multiple jurisdictions, various reporting timelines. And the Series C due diligence team will need to be notified.

"The investors are literally in the building," Victoria noted grimly. "Down on third floor with the auditors, reviewing our security protocols.

"Which we just compromised by rushing this deployment," Grace added quietly.

0030 Hours - Technical Analysis

Chris Bennett's analysis revealed the full scope of the vulnerability. "The BatchTransfer contract has a critical flaw in how it handles allowance validations," he explained, sharing his screen showing the problematic code. "When processing multiple transactions, it's not properly decreasing allowances after each transfer. One approval can be used multiple times."

"How did this get through review?" Grace demanded.

Kevin looked uncomfortable. "We... abbreviated the testing cycle. Management wanted the multi-transaction feature ready for the Series C demo tomorrow."

0045 Hours - Crisis Deepening

Sophia Chen's customer service dashboard was lighting up. "First users are noticing the unauthorized transactions. Social media's starting to pick up chatter. We've got about an hour before this goes viral in crypto circles."

Andrew Foster, reviewing the legal implications, spoke up. "We need to make a decision. Every minute we delay could affect our liability. And our Series C investors could argue we've materially misrepresented our security practices."

Mark Stevens joined the call. "From a coverage standpoint, your response time and decision-making process are crucial. We need to document every step."

0100 Hours - Decision Point

Victoria surveyed her team's faces on the video call. The weight of 175,000 users' trust – and the company's future – hung in the balance.

"Grace, time to freeze and fix?

"Contract freeze is ready to deploy. Chris has a patch prepared, but it needs testing. Minimum two hours to properly verify the fix.

"Daniel, technical implications of an immediate freeze?"

"All user transactions halt. DEX liquidity pools freeze. Automated trading bots fail. But we prevent further losses."

"Damian, coverage implications?"

"Your policy will respond better to decisive action that prevents further losses," Damian advised. "CloudShield can help validate the fix while SecureResponse continues tracing the unauthorized transactions."

Victoria took a deep breath. "Do it. Freeze the contract. Grace, supervise the fix. Daniel, help Chris with testing. Sophia, prepare user communications – be transparent, we own this mistake. Lisa, start regulatory notifications. Andrew, brief the Series C team – they deserve to know what they're buying into."

0115 Hours - Emergency Actions The team sprang into action:

- Smart contract freeze initiated
- Emergency notifications prepared
- Social media response drafted
- Regulatory filings begun
- Incident documentation started

Kevin's screen showed the final damage tally: $12.3 million in unauthorized transfers across 1,547 user wallets.

0130 Hours - Investor Impact

Victoria and Andrew headed to the third floor to brief the Series C investors and due diligence team. The potential $125M funding round – and the company's future – hung in the balance.

"We show them everything," Victoria decided. "The vulnerability, our response, the planned fix. Either they believe in our ability to handle a crisis, or they don't. But we do this with full transparency."

0145 Hours - Investor Briefing

The Series C due diligence team and lead investors sat stone-faced as Victoria and Andrew presented the situation. Among them:
- Thomas Reynolds - Lead Investment Partner, Blockchain Ventures
- Dr. Diana Mitchell - Technical Due Diligence Lead
- James Cooper - Cybersecurity Auditor
- Lauren Maxwell - Financial Analyst
- Richard Davidson - Legal Counsel

"A rushed deployment with a skipped security audit," Dr. Mitchell noted, reviewing the incident timeline. "During due diligence. That's... concerning."

Victoria nodded. "We made a critical mistake prioritizing feature deployment over security. We're owning that mistake and fixing it transparently."

0200 Hours - Technical Deep Dive

Back in the crisis room, Chris and Kevin were walking Grace through the fix while CloudShield s team validated each code change.

"We've added cumulative allowance tracking," Chris explained, highlighting the new code. "Each transaction in the batch now properly decrements the allowance and validates against the remaining total."

"Testing?" Grace demanded.

"Running attack simulations now," Kevin replied. "So far, twenty-seven test scenarios, all passing. But we need more coverage before deployment."

0215 Hours - User Impact Analysis

Sophia shared the growing impact metrics:
- 1,547 affected wallets
- $12.3M in unauthorized transfers
- 842 support tickets opened
- 3,200+ social media mentions
- 5 crypto news sites picking up the story

"CryptoWatch and BlockchainDaily are requesting comments," she added. "We need to get ahead of this narrative."

0230 Hours - Regulatory Response

Lisa Parker was coordinating with regulators across jurisdictions:
- SEC cryptocurrency division
- FinCEN compliance office
- State regulatory bodies
- International financial authorities
- Crypto exchange partners

"We're looking at multiple reporting requirements," she reported. "Each with different timelines and documentation needs. And we'll need to prove our response was timely and appropriate."

Rachel Torres spoke up from the DIS line. "We're documenting everything for the regulators. The coverage response demonstrates we had appropriate protections in place."

0245 Hours - Recovery Planning Daniel assembled the technical recovery roadmap:

1. Smart contract freeze (completed)
2. Vulnerability patching (in progress)
3. Security audit (expedited)
4. Phased reactivation
5. Asset recovery attempt

"The good news," he added, "is that all transactions are on-chain. SecureResponse's blockchain forensics team is already tracing every unauthorized transfer."

0300 Hours - Series C Discussion

Thomas Reynolds finally spoke after hours of observation. "You know what impresses me more than perfect security? How a team handles imperfect security. Walk me through your incident response again."

Victoria and Grace detailed their response timeline, decision points, and recovery plans.

"The vulnerability is bad," Reynolds acknowledged. "But your response..." he glanced at his team, "that's what we're actually investing in. Having DIS Risk Solutions and their partners already integrated shows maturity in your risk management."

0315 Hours - Communication Strategy

The team crafted their multi-level communication plan:

User Communication:
- Immediate notification email
- Social media updates
- Support ticket responses
- Community AMAs
- Recovery timeline

Investor Updates:
- Incident analysis
- Response documentation
- Security improvements
- Governance changes
- Future safeguards

0330 Hours - Path Forward

Victoria addressed her exhausted team. "We've got three priorities: Fix the technical issue, protect our users, and rebuild trust. Everything else is secondary."

Grace nodded. "CloudShield has validated the fix. We can deploy within the hour."

"And the Series C?" Daniel asked quietly.

Victoria managed a small smile. "Thomas Reynolds thinks our incident response actually demonstrated why we're worth investing in. But we're going to have some new security requirements in the term sheet."

0345 Hours - Recovery Initiation

The team began executing their recovery plan:
- Contract fix deployment prep
- Asset recovery strategy

- User compensation planning
- Security protocol overhaul
- Compliance enhancement

"Mark's documenting everything for the claim," Damian added. "And SecureResponse will continue monitoring the blockchain for any recovery opportunities."

"One more thing," Victoria added. "After this is resolved, we're implementing mandatory security reviews. No more rushed deployments, no matter what demo or deadline we're facing."

The team nodded grimly. Sometimes the most expensive lessons are the most valuable.

PART 2: TECHNICAL DEEP DIVE

Investigation Timeline:

2200-2245: Initial Compromise

- Smart contract vulnerability introduced
- Initial unauthorized transactions begin
- Token approvals exploited
- BatchTransfer function compromised
- Asset drainage initiated
- DIS Risk Solutions alerted
- Partner activation initiated

2245-2315: Detection and Analysis

- Anomalous transfers detected
- Initial scope assessment
- DIS Risk Solutions engaged
- CloudShield activated
- SecureResponse deployed
- Coverage review initiated
- Documentation protocols established

2315-0400: Full Investigation

- Complete vulnerability analysis
- Impact quantificatio
- Asset tracking initiated
- Smart contract audit
- Recovery planning
- Partner coordination
- Coverage documentation

Technical Analysis:

1. Attack Vector Identificatio
Smart Contract Vulnerability:
- Improper allowance validation
- Batch processing flaw
- Approval mechanism exploitation
- Permission reuse vulnerability
- Missing cumulative checks

Access Methods:
- BatchTransfer function calls
- Token approval exploitation
- Multiple wallet interactions
- Sequential transaction chains
- Automated execution scripts

2. Infrastructure Analysis
Contract Architecture:
- ERC-20 token interfaces
- Custom approval mechanisms
- Batch processing functions
- Permission management
- Transaction queuing

Affected Systems:
- Smart contract infrastructure
- Token approval registry
- Transaction processing queue
- User wallet interfaces
- Liquidity pools

3. Impact Assessment
Financial Exposure:
- $12.3M total unauthorized transfers
- 1,547 affected wallets
- Multiple token types impacted
- DEX liquidity affected
- Trading pairs compromised

Operational Impact:
- Platform functionality frozen
- Trading activities halted
- Liquidity pools locked
- User transactions blocked
- API services affected

4. Security Control Analysis
Missing Controls:
- Cumulative allowance tracking
- Transaction amount validation
- Multi-signature requirements
- Rate limiting mechanisms
- Approval expiration checks

Failed Safeguards:
- Code review process
- Security audit procedures
- Deployment protocols
- Testing requirements
- Change management

5. Recovery Complexity
Technical Challenges:
- Contract upgrade requirements
- State synchronization

- Balance reconciliation
- Transaction reversal complexity
- Cross-chain implications

Implementation Constraints:
- Immutable blockchain state
- Gas fee considerations
- Network congestion
- Cross-contract dependencies
- Time sensitivity

6. Forensic Investigation
Evidence Collection:
- Smart contract states
- Transaction histories
- Approval logs
- Wallet interactions
- Block explorer data

Analysis Findings:
- Attack methodology
- Exploitation pattern
- Transaction flo
- Token movements
- Wallet correlations

7. DIS Risk Solutions Coordination
Initial Response:
- Coverage activation protocols
- Partner team deployment
- Evidence preservation standards
- Documentation requirements
- Claims process initiation

Coverage Management:
- Dual policy response (crypto/cyber)
- Regulatory compliance support
- Client communication guidance
- Recovery strategy development
- Documentation protocols

Partner Integration:
CloudShield:
- Code validation processes
- Security implementation
- Deployment oversight
- Testing coordination
- Monitoring enhancement

SecureResponse:
- Blockchain forensics
- Transaction tracing
- Asset recovery planning
- Pattern analysis
- Industry correlation

Documentation Requirements:
- Incident chronology
- Response actions
- Technical finding
- Recovery efforts
- Partner activities

8. Solution Development
Technical Response:
- Smart contract patch
- Allowance tracking implementation
- Validation enhancement

- Security feature addition
- Monitoring improvement

Implementation Strategy:
Phase 1 - Immediate Response:
- Contract freeze
- Evidence preservation
- Partner activation
- Coverage confirmatio
- Initial communication

Phase 2 - Investigation:
- Forensic analysis
- Impact assessment
- Coverage review
- Documentation collection
- Compliance validation

Phase 3 - Recovery:
- Contract restoration
- Security enhancement
- Process improvement
- Coverage alignment
- Long-term monitoring

PART 3: IMPLEMENTATION GUIDE

1. IMPACT ASSESSMENT

Financial Impact: Direct Costs: - Unauthorized transfers: $12.3M - Emergency response: $850K - Security enhancement: $450K - Customer compensation: $275K - Partner activation: $175K Total Direct Impact: $14.05M

Insurance Implications: Primary Coverage: $10M structured as: • $5M Crypto Asset Liability Coverage • $5M Cyber Liability Coverage

Retention: $250K per incident • Applies to each and every claim • Annual aggregate retention: $500K • Retention applies to both crypto asset and cyber events • Time deductible: 8 hours for BI • Maintenance deductible: $100K for PCI

Coverage Triggers: • Digital asset theft • Smart contract failure • System compromise • Business interruption • Regulatory defense • Customer notificatio

Partner Integration: CloudShield: • Code validation services • Security implementation • Deployment oversight • Testing coordination • Monitoring enhancement

SecureResponse: • Blockchain forensics • Transaction tracing • Asset recovery planning • Pattern analysis • Industry correlation

Systems Affected: Primary Systems: - Smart contract infrastructure - Token approval registry - Trading engine - Wallet interfaces - Liquidity pools

Secondary Systems: - User authentication - Transaction monitoring - API services - Trading bots - Analytics platform

Business Disruption: Duration: - Critical phase: 8 hours - Total recovery: 72 hours

Impact Scope: - 175,000 users affected - 22 institutional clients impacted - All trading pairs frozen - Complete platform halt - Series C due diligence affected

2. TECHNICAL RESPONSE

Immediate Actions:
- Smart contract freeze
- DIS Risk Solutions engagement
- Partner team activation
- Platform trading halt
- User notificatio
- Evidence preservation
- Regulatory reporting

Investigation Steps:
- Contract audit
- Transaction analysis
- Impact assessment
- Vulnerability identificatio
- Coverage verificatio
- Recovery planning
- Documentation collection

Solution Development:
- Contract patch creation
- Security enhancement
- Testing protocol
- Deployment strategy
- Monitoring upgrade

- Partner integration
- Coverage alignment

3. IMPLEMENTATION TIMELINE

Immediate (0-24 hours):
Hour 0-4:
- Contract freeze implementation
- DIS Risk Solutions activation
- CloudShield deployment
- SecureResponse engagement
- Initial user communication
- Evidence preservation
- Trading halt confirmatio

Hour 4-8:
- Patch development
- Coverage confirmatio
- Regulatory notificatio
- Customer support activation
- Social media response
- Series C team briefin
- Partner coordination

Hour 8-12:
- Fix validation
- Impact assessment
- User notificatio
- Documentation collection
- Claims initiation
- Media response
- Investor updates

Hour 12-24:
- Security implementation
- Testing completion
- Platform preparation
- Recovery planning
- Coverage review
- Communication updates
- Process documentation

Short-term (24-72 hours):
Day 2:
- Contract reactivation
- Security enhancement
- User verificatio
- Trading restoration
- Coverage alignment
- Partner integration
- Documentation completion

Day 3:
- Full platform restoration
- Enhanced monitoring
- Process improvement
- User compensation
- Coverage finalizatio
- Partner assessment
- Long-term planning

Long-term (72+ hours):
Week 1:
- Security protocol enhancement
- Process documentation
- Staff training
- Partner integration

- Coverage review
- Regulatory compliance
- Customer trust rebuilding

4. KEY TAKEAWAYS

Business Lessons:
- Security audit importance
- Deployment process criticality
- Coverage preparation value
- Partner integration benefit
- User trust significanc
- Regulatory compliance necessity
- Investor communication priority

Technical Insights:
- Smart contract security fundamentals
- Testing protocol importance
- Deployment process rigor
- Monitoring system necessity
- Recovery plan criticality
- Partner coordination value
- Coverage integration benefit

Process Improvements:
- Mandatory security reviews
- Enhanced testing protocols
- Deployment checkpoints
- Communication procedures
- Compliance documentation
- Partner integration
- Coverage alignment

5. ROI ANALYSIS

Prevention Costs:
Initial Investment:
- Smart contract security: $450K
- Platform hardening: $275K
- Monitoring systems: $225K
- Staff training: $150K
- Documentation systems: $100K
Total Prevention Cost: $1.2M

Incident Costs:
Direct Impact:
- Unauthorized transfers: $12.3M
- Emergency response: $850K
- Customer compensation: $275K
- Recovery efforts: $450K
Less Insurance Recovery: ($11.05M after retention)
Total Net Impact: $2.825M

Future Protection:
Annual Savings:
- Risk reduction: $8M
- Efficiency gains: $1.2
- Prevention benefits: $2.5
- Resource optimization: $800K
Total Annual Value: $12.5M

6. ACTION CHECKLIST

Immediate Response:
- Contract freeze initiation
- DIS Risk Solutions notificatio
- Partner activation

- Platform shutdown
- User communication
- Evidence collection
- Regulatory notificatio

Assessment Tasks:
- Vulnerability analysis
- Impact evaluation
- Asset tracking
- Risk assessment
- Coverage review
- Compliance review
- Partner coordination

Implementation Steps:
- Patch deployment
- Security enhancement
- Process improvement
- Training execution
- Documentation update
- Coverage alignment
- Partner integration

7. C-SUITE COMMUNICATION PROTOCOL

Executive Notification Sequence

CEO and Co-founder (Victoria Nash)
- Initial incident assessment
- Investor relations management
- Strategic decision authority
- Public communications
- Stakeholder management

CTO and Co-founder (Daniel Zhao)
- Technical impact assessment
- Resource allocation
- System modification approva
- Recovery timeline development
- Security enhancement oversight

Head of Security (Grace Liu)
- Security response coordination
- Technical team management
- System restoration oversight
- Control implementation
- Future prevention planning

Compliance Officer (Lisa Parker
- Regulatory compliance management
- Documentation oversight
- Audit coordination
- Policy implementation
- Governance enhancement

DIS Risk Solutions (Damian Davis)
- Coverage coordination
- Response management
- Partner activation
- Strategic guidance
- Claims oversight

Communication Templates:

Initial Notification
- Incident overview
- Current status
- Immediate actions

- Required decisions
- Next steps

Status Updates:
- Response progress
- Asset impact status
- Customer status
- Coverage status
- Action items

Partner Updates:
- Technical finding
- Response actions
- Implementation status
- Recovery progress
- Required support

Decision Matrix:

Platform Shutdown Criteria:
- Asset loss threshold
- Security impact level
- Customer risk exposure
- Coverage implications
- Regulatory obligations

System Restoration Authority:
- Security verification require
- Partner validation complete
- Coverage confirmatio
- Documentation complete
- Regulatory compliance

Customer Notification Triggers:
- Asset impact confirme
- Platform disruption >1 hour
- Security concerns identifie
- Regulatory requirements
- Coverage implications

Response Escalation Guidelines:
- Technical impact severity
- Asset loss magnitude
- Customer impact level
- Coverage implications
- Regulatory requirements

Recovery Milestones:
- Smart contract security
- Platform restoration
- Customer asset verificatio
- Partner integration
- Documentation completion

Documentation Requirements:

Technical Documentation:
- Smart contract modification
- Security implementations
- Test results
- Platform impacts
- System changes

Coverage Documentation:
- Incident timeline
- Response actions
- Cost tracking

- Customer impact
- Recovery efforts

Partner Integration:
- CloudShield validation
- SecureResponse finding
- Implementation status
- Recovery support
- Ongoing monitoring

Chapter 8

AI Deception

PART 1: NARRATIVE CASE STUDY

Company Profile: NeuraTech Innovations
Annual Revenue: $28M
Industry: AI/ML Research & Development
Employees: 115
Client Base: 35 enterprise clients (primarily healthcare, finance, and manufacturing)
Market Position: Emerging leader in specialized AI model development and deployment
Geographic Presence: Headquarters in Boston with satellite R&D lab in Austin
Funding Status: Series B completed ($45M raised at $180M valuation)

1430 Hours - NeuraTech Innovations, Boston Research Center

Dr. Olivia Park, Lead AI Researcher, stared at her screen in disbelief. She was reviewing a competitor's recently released research paper when something caught her eye – the neural network architecture looked eerily familiar.

"Marcus," she called to Marcus Chen, Senior ML Engineer, "can you look at this? These attention mechanisms... they're identical to our proprietary healthcare model."

Marcus wheeled his chair over, frowning as he scanned the paper. "That's... impossible. These are our exact hyperparameter configur - tions. Even the dropout rates match."

"And look at the training results," Olivia pointed. "The error distribution patterns are nearly identical to what we see in our diagnostic models."

1445 Hours - Initial Analysis

Dr. William Bradford, Director of AI Research, joined them at Olivia's workstation. "Show me the similarities."

Olivia pulled up side-by-side comparisons: "Their model's architecture, training patterns, even the edge case handling – it's all matching our GenAI Healthcare Suite. This isn't convergent development; they've somehow accessed our model internals."

"Could they have reverse-engineered it?" Marcus asked.

"Not with this level of detail," William shook his head. "They'd need access to our training data, model weights, and architecture specific - tions. All of which are supposed to be secured in our isolated development environment."

1500 Hours - Security Alert

Sophia Anderson, Information Security Lead, arrived after Olivia's urgent message. Her face grew increasingly grim as they walked her through the evidence.

"I'm calling DIS Risk Solutions," she announced, already dialing. "This looks like a significant data breach. We need CyberGuard Solutions to analyze our development environment for unauthorized access immediately."

"The paper was published this morning," Olivia explained. "But look at their claimed development timeline – they supposedly built this in three months. It took us two years to optimize these parameters."

"And millions in compute resources," William added. "Not to mention our proprietary training datasets from five major healthcare providers. Someone has to have breached our security."

1515 Hours - Emergency Meeting

The crisis team assembled in the main conference room: - Dr. Katherine Morgan - Chief Technology Officer - Dr. William Bradford - Director of AI Research - Sophia Anderson - Information Security Lead - Andrew Wilson - Legal Counsel - Dr. Olivia Park - Lead AI Researcher - Marcus Chen - Senior ML Engineer - Jennifer Zhao - Compliance Manager

Damian Davis from DIS Risk Solutions joined via secure video link, along with Rachel Torres and Mark Stevens. "Walk me through what we know," Damian said, as CyberGuard Solutions' team began their remote connection to the development environment.

William projected the comparison analysis. "We've identified what appears to be a significant data breach of our development environment. The evidence suggests someone has extracted our AI model's core architecture and training data."

"DataDefend's forensics team is standing by," Rachel added. "We need to preserve everything to document the extent of the unauthorized access and data exfiltration.

1530 Hours - Technical Assessment

Marcus pulled up the development environment logs. "I've been reviewing access patterns to our AI development infrastructure. There's something odd about the data transfer logs from the past month."

Sophia leaned forward. "What kind of odd?"

"Small, periodic data extractions. Nothing that would trigger our usual alerts. But when you aggregate them..." He displayed a graph showing the cumulative data movement. "Someone's been slowly extracting our model data."

"CyberGuard's team is seeing the same patterns," Mark Stevens noted. "They're analyzing the extraction timestamps now. This looks like a sophisticated exfiltration strategy designed to avoid detection.

1545 Hours - Scope Analysis

Olivia's analysis revealed the extent of the data breach: - Model architecture files - Training data sets - Parameter configurations - Testing frameworks - Performance metrics

"The attacker has essentially extracted everything needed to replicate our system," she explained. "Including our proprietary healthcare diagnostic algorithms that took two years to develop."

Andrew Wilson grimaced. "The same algorithms we just licensed to three major healthcare systems for $45M."

"We need to treat this as a major cyber incident," Damian advised. "The unauthorized access and data exfiltration could trigger regulatory reporting requirements, especially given the healthcare data involved."

1600 Hours - Vulnerability Assessment

CyberGuard Solutions' team had identified the likely breach vector. "They exploited your continuous integration pipeline," their lead engineer reported through the video link. "Someone inserted code into your automated testing framework that was slowly exfiltrating model parameters during routine validation runs."

"How long?" Katherine asked, her voice tight.

"Based on the logs, at least six weeks. The code was disguised as a model optimization routine. It was even documenting improvements in your test metrics while stealing your data."

"DataDefend's team is starting their forensic analysis now," Damian added. "We need to establish a clear timeline of the breach and document all compromised assets."

1615 Hours - Impact Analysis

The team gathered around the conference room displays showing multiple analyses:

Business Impact: - Critical data breach - Development environment compromise - Client trust implications - Market position threatened - Regulatory compliance concerns

Jennifer Zhao consulted her compliance documentation. "Given the nature of the stolen data, we have regulatory obligations to notify both our healthcare partners and relevant authorities about the breach."

1630 Hours - Pattern Recognition

Marcus had been digging deeper into the development logs with CyberGuard's team. "Found something," he announced. "The exfiltr - tion code... it was committed during our last major push to improve model performance. When we brought in those contractors to help scale our training infrastructure."

Dr. Bradford's face darkened. "The contractors Quantum Minds recommended to us."

"They played us," Katherine realized. "They knew we were rushing to meet our licensing commitments. Offered help through a shell consulting company, then used it to breach our systems."

"This changes the scope of our cyber incident," Damian noted. "We're looking at a coordinated attack with insider involvement."

1645 Hours - Strategic Options

Andrew Wilson laid out their immediate priorities: - Document unauthorized access - Preserve forensic evidence - Notify affected parties - File regulatory reports - Consider legal remedies

"DataDefend needs to thoroughly document the breach timeline," Rachel emphasized. "Every unauthorized access, every data transfer. We need to understand the full scope of the compromise."

1700 Hours - Technical Response

Sophia proposed immediate actions: - Isolate development environment - Audit all recent code commits - Revoke contractor access - Update security protocols - Monitor model deployments

"CyberGuard's team can help implement these security measures," Mark added. "But we need to move quickly to prevent any further data exfiltration.

1715 Hours - Insurance Coordination

Rachel Torres finished preparing the incident notice to the carrier. "I've documented the initial findings, including the unauthorized access timeline and preliminary data exfiltration analysis. The carrier will want to know about the healthcare data implications."

"What's our coverage response looking like?" Katherine asked.

"The cyber policy should respond to the breach investigation costs, forensics, and regulatory compliance," Damian explained. "Including CyberGuard's work and DataDefend's analysis. But we need to document everything carefully, especially given the potential regulatory notifications we may need to make.

Rachel nodded. "I'll submit the notice to the carrier immediately via email and follow up with a phone call to their cyber claims hotline."

1730 Hours - Documentation Strategy

The team began cataloging the evidence: - System access logs - Data transfer records - Code commit history - Testing framework logs - Security alert timelines

"CyberGuard's team will help establish the technical timeline," Damian advised. "We need to understand how they bypassed our security controls and maintained persistent access."

1745 Hours - Crisis Response

Katherine assembled the response plan:

Technical Actions: - Complete security audit - New access controls - Enhanced monitoring - Contractor screening - System hardening

Response Steps: - Evidence preservation - Client notifications - Regulatory filings - Security enhancement - Monitoring implementation

1800 Hours - Board Notification

Katherine reached for her phone to call the board chair. "Before we do anything public, the board needs to know. This breach affects our entire market position."

"What do we tell our clients?" Jennifer asked.

"The truth," Katherine decided. "That we discovered and stopped a sophisticated cyber attack targeting our development environment. That we're working with DIS Risk Solutions and their partners to investigate the full scope of the breach and enhance our security."

1815 Hours - Path Forward

Dr. Bradford addressed the team. "While we handle the breach response, we need to focus on securing our development environment. They may have stolen our data, but we can prevent this from happening again."

Olivia nodded. "I've been thinking about implementing additional security layers in our development pipeline. CyberGuard's team has some interesting suggestions about containerization and access controls."

"And we can implement enhanced monitoring for any unusual data transfer patterns," Marcus added. "Make it harder for someone to slowly exfiltrate data without detection.

1830 Hours - Future Security

Sophia outlined her enhanced security framework, developed in consultation with CyberGuard Solutions: - Air-gapped development - Advanced access monitoring - Behavioral analysis - Zero-trust architecture - Continuous validation

"We're not just fixing a breach," she concluded. "We're rebuilding our security from the ground up."

"DataDefend will help document everything for the cyber claim," Rachel added. "The better we understand how this breach happened, the better we can prevent future incidents."

1845 Hours - Final Assessment

Katherine surveyed her team. "Today showed us that in AI development, security can't be an afterthought. It has to be built into everything we do."

"The breach response plan worked exactly as designed," Damian noted. "Quick detection, immediate partner engagement, and proper evidence preservation. Now we focus on recovery and prevention."

The team nodded in agreement. In the rapidly evolving world of AI research, security had to be as innovative as the technology it protected. Sometimes it took a breach to drive that lesson home.

PART 2: TECHNICAL DEEP DIVE

Investigation Timeline:

1430-1515: Initial Discovery

- Model similarity detected
- Architecture comparison initiated
- Parameter analysis begun
- Training pattern review
- DIS Risk Solutions alerted
- Partner activation initiated

1515-1700: Initial Response

- Security team activation
- DIS Risk Solutions engaged
- CyberGuard Solutions deployed
- DataDefend activated
- Log analysis initiated
- Code review started
- Access pattern analysis

1700-1845: Full Investigation

- Complete system analysis
- Development environment audit
- Contractor access review
- Evidence preservation
- Impact assessment
- Coverage documentation
- Partner coordination

Technical Analysis:

1. Attack Vector Identificatio
Development Environment Compromise:
- CI/CD pipeline exploitation
- Testing framework manipulation
- Model parameter extraction
- Training data access
- Architecture documentation theft

Access Methods:
- Embedded exfiltration cod
- Automated testing abuse
- Gradual data extraction
- Parameter harvesting
- Documentation scraping

2. Infrastructure Analysis
Development Environment:
- Jupyter notebook servers
- Training clusters
- Model serving infrastructure
- Version control systems
- CI/CD pipelines

Affected Systems:
- Model training infrastructure
- Testing frameworks
- Validation environments
- Documentation systems
- Deployment pipelines

3. Impact Assessment
Data Breach Scope:
- AI model architecture exposed
- Training datasets compromised
- Parameter configurations stole
- Testing frameworks accessed
- Performance metrics extracted

Business Impact:
- Development environment compromised
- Healthcare data exposed
- Client trust threatened
- Regulatory implications
- Market position impacted

4. Security Control Analysis
Missing Controls:
- Data exfiltration monitorin
- Contractor access limitations
- Code review protocols
- Change management procedures
- Access logging requirements

Failed Safeguards:
- Development environment security
- Access control systems
- Change validation
- Security monitoring
- Code review process

5. Recovery Complexity
Technical Challenges:
- Development environment restoration
- Access control reconfiguratio

- Security implementation
- Monitoring enhancement
- Partner integration

Implementation Constraints:
- Business continuity requirements
- Client obligations
- Regulatory compliance
- Resource limitations
- Time sensitivity

6. Forensic Investigation
Evidence Collection:
- System access logs
- Data transfer records
- Code commit history
- Testing framework logs
- Security alerts
- Contractor access data
- CI/CD pipeline records

Analysis Findings:
- Exfiltration methodolog
- Attack timeline
- Data movement patterns
- Code manipulation
- Access exploitation

7. DIS Risk Solutions Coordination
Initial Response:
- Coverage activation
- Partner team deployment
- Evidence preservation protocols

- Documentation requirements
- Claims process initiation

Coverage Management:
- Cyber policy review
- Breach response coordination
- Cost tracking implementation
- Documentation protocols
- Recovery planning

Partner Integration:
CyberGuard Solutions:
- Development environment analysis
- Security implementation
- Access control enhancement
- Monitoring deployment
- Recovery support

DataDefend:
- Forensic investigation
- Evidence preservation
- Breach analysis
- Documentation support
- Prevention recommendations

Documentation Requirements:
- Incident chronology
- Response actions
- Technical finding
- Recovery efforts
- Partner activities

8. Solution Development

Technical Response:

- Development environment security
- Access control enhancement
- Monitoring implementation
- Code review protocols
- Partner integration

Implementation Strategy:

Phase 1 - Immediate Response:

- Development environment isolation
- Access control implementation
- Evidence preservation
- Partner activation
- Initial security measures

Phase 2 - Investigation:

- Forensic analysis
- Impact assessment
- Coverage review
- Documentation collection
- Compliance validation

Phase 3 - Recovery:

- Security enhancement
- Process improvement
- Training development
- Partner integration
- Long-term monitoring

9. Risk Analysis

Coverage Assessment:

- Cyber policy response
- Breach investigation costs

- Forensics coverage
- Regulatory compliance
- Response coordination

Security Enhancement:
- Development environment protection
- Access control systems
- Monitoring capabilities
- Code review processes
- Contractor management

Future Requirements:
- Enhanced security protocols
- Continuous monitoring
- Regular assessments
- Partner integration
- Coverage maintenance

Long-term Protection:
- Security program enhancement
- Development environment hardening
- Access control improvement
- Partner coordination
- Coverage alignment

PART 3: IMPLEMENTATION GUIDE

1. IMPACT ASSESSMENT

Financial Impact: Direct Costs: - Emergency response: $850K - Security enhancement: $450K - Client notifications: $275K - Partner activation: $175K Total Direct Impact: $1.75M

Insurance Implications: Primary Coverage: $10M cyber liability policy

Retention: $250K per cyber incident • Applies to each and every claim • Annual aggregate retention: $500K • Time deductible: 12 hours for business interruption • Maintenance deductible: $100K for PCI

Coverage Triggers: • Data breach • System compromise • Business interruption • Regulatory defense • Customer notificatio

Partner Integration: CyberGuard Solutions: • Development environment analysis • Security implementation • Access control enhancement • Monitoring deployment • Recovery support

DataDefend: • Forensic investigation • Evidence preservation • Breach analysis • Documentation support • Prevention recommendations

Systems Affected: Primary Systems: - Development environment - Training infrastructure - Testing frameworks - CI/CD pipelines - Version control systems

Secondary Systems: - Documentation repositories - Collaboration tools - Monitoring systems - Access control - Deployment infrastructure

Business Disruption: Duration: - Critical phase: 24 hours - Total recovery: 14 days

Impact Scope: - 35 enterprise clients affected - Healthcare data compromised - Development environment breached - Security controls compromised - Regulatory implications triggered

2. TECHNICAL RESPONSE

Immediate Actions: - Development environment isolation - DIS Risk Solutions engagement - Partner team activation - Access control implementation - Evidence preservation - Contractor access revocation - System monitoring enhancement

Investigation Steps: - Forensic analysis initiation - Log review coordination - Access pattern analysis - Data exfiltration assessment - Breach scope determination - Coverage verification - Documentation collection

Solution Development: - Security control enhancement - Access management improvement - Monitoring implementation - Partner integration - Documentation protocols

3. IMPLEMENTATION TIMELINE

Immediate (0-24 hours): Hour 0-4: - Breach confirmation - DIS Risk Solutions activation - CyberGuard Solutions deployment - DataDefend engagement - Initial containment - Evidence preservation - Access control implementation

Hour 4-8: - Forensic analysis - Coverage confirmat on - Client communication prep - Security enhancement - Partner coordination - Documentation initiation - Response planning

Hour 8-12: - System analysis - Impact assessment - Regulatory review - Client notification - Security implementation - Documentation collection - Recovery planning

Hour 12-24: - Complete containment - Enhanced monitoring - Access control verification - Partner integration - Documentation completion - Recovery initiation - Communication updates

Short-term (24-72 hours): Day 2: - Security enhancement - System hardening - Client engagement - Partner coordination - Documentation review

Day 3: - Process improvement - Training initiation - Security validation - Partner assessment - Recovery continuation

Long-term (72+ hours): Week 1: - Security protocol enhancement - Process documentation - Staff training - Partner integration - Coverage review

4. KEY TAKEAWAYS

Business Lessons: - Development environment security criticality - Contractor access management importance - Partner integration benefits - Client trust preservation - Regulatory compliance necessity - Coverage preparation value - Documentation importance

Technical Insights: - Access control fundamentals - Monitoring system necessity - Partner coordination value - Documentation requirements - Security implementation priorities

Process Improvements: - Mandatory security reviews - Enhanced access controls - Contractor vetting process - Documentation protocols - Partner integration procedures

5. ROI ANALYSIS

Prevention Costs: Initial Investment: - Security enhancement: $450K - Monitoring systems: $275K - Access controls: $225K - Staff training: $150K - Documentation systems: $100K Total Prevention Cost: $1.2M

Incident Costs: Direct Impact: - Emergency response: $850K - Client notifications: $275K - Recovery efforts: $450K - Partner activation: $175K Less Insurance Recovery: ($1.5M after retention) Total Net Impact: $250K

Future Protection: Annual Savings: - Risk reduction: $2M - Efficiency gains: $500K - Prevention benefits: $750K - Resource optimization: $250K Total Annual Value: $3.5M

6. ACTION CHECKLIST

Immediate Response: □ Development environment isolation □ DIS Risk Solutions notification □ Partner team activation □ Evidence preservation □ Access control implementation □ System monitoring □ Client communication preparation

Assessment Tasks: □ Breach scope analysis □ Impact evaluation □ System assessment □ Coverage review □ Regulatory requirements □ Client implications □ Partner coordination

Implementation Steps: □ Security enhancement deployment □ Access control improvement □ Monitoring implementation □ Training execution □ Documentation update □ Partner integration □ Recovery validation

7. C-SUITE COMMUNICATION PROTOCOL

Executive Notification Sequence

Chief Technology Officer (Dr. Katherine Morgan) - Initial incident assessment - Technical impact evaluation - Resource allocation - Recovery oversight - Partner coordination

Director of AI Research (Dr. William Bradford) - Development impact assessment - Research team coordination - Technical recovery - Security implementation - Future prevention

Information Security Lead (Sophia Anderson) - Security response coordination - Technical team management - System restoration oversight - Control implementation - Partner integration

Compliance Manager (Jennifer Zhao) - Regulatory compliance management - Documentation oversight - Client obligation review - Policy implementation - Governance enhancement

DIS Risk Solutions (Damian Davis) - Coverage coordination - Response management - Partner activation - Strategic guidance - Claims oversight

Communication Templates:

Initial Notification: • Incident overview • Current status • Immediate actions • Required decisions • Next steps

Status Updates: • Response progress • System status • Client impact • Coverage status • Action items

Decision Matrix:

Development Environment Authority: • Security impact threshold • Client risk exposure • Coverage implications • Regulatory obligations • Partner recommendations

System Restoration Authority: • Security verification required • Partner validation complete • Coverage confirmation • Documentation complete • Regulatory compliance

Client Notification Triggers: • Data impact confirmed • System disruption >4 hours • Security concerns identified • Regulatory requirements • Coverage implications

Response Escalation Guidelines: • Technical impact severity • Client impact level • Coverage implications • Regulatory requirements • Partner recommendations

Recovery Milestones: • Environment security • System restoration • Client notification • Partner integration • Documentation completio

Documentation Requirements:

Technical Documentation: • System modifications • Security implementations • Test results • Environment impacts • Partner activities

Coverage Documentation: • Incident timeline • Response actions • Cost tracking • Client impact • Recovery efforts

SECTION III

ENTERPRISE AND CONSUMER INDUSTRIES

Chapter 9

Mobile Mayhem

PART 1: NARRATIVE CASE STUDY

Company Profile: Local Chic Boutique
Annual Revenue: $4.2M
Industry: Retail (Fashion & Accessories)
Employees: 32 (across 3 locations)
Client Base:
- Loyalty app: 3,200 active users
- Social media followers: 12,000
- Regular customers: ~2,000
- Average transaction: $85
Market Position: Growing local boutique chain known for personalized shopping experience
Geographic Presence: Three locations in Atlanta metro area
Technology:
- Mobile POS systems (12 devices)
- Customer loyalty app (3,200 active users)
- Online ordering with in-store pickup
- Instagram/social commerce integration
- Third-party payment processor integration

1645 Hours - Local Chic Boutique, Buckhead Location

Amanda Brooks, Store Manager, was reconciling the day's sales when something caught her eye. Several transactions showed unusual payment processing locations – charges being processed through servers in Eastern Europe instead of their regular payment processor.

"Hey Mike," she called to Mike Turner, the owner who was helping on the floor during the holiday rush. "Can you look at something weird in the payment system?"

Mike walked over, already exhausted from the busy shopping day. "What's up?"

"These transactions... they're routing strange. And look at these amounts – they're all just under our $500 authorization threshold."

1700 Hours - Initial Discovery

Mike pulled up the store's payment processor dashboard on his laptop. "That can't be right. We're seeing three times the normal transaction volume, but the bank deposits don't match."

"Could it be a glitch?" Amanda asked, watching as Mike scrolled through the transactions.

"Wait," Mike paused, "when did we last update the POS software on the mobile devices?"

Amanda's face fell. "I... don't know. The vendor set them up last year, and we just kind of... use them?"

1715 Hours - Pattern Recognition

Mike called Jessica Yang, the manager at their Midtown location. "Jessica, can you check something for me? Look at your payment routing details for today's transactions."

A moment of silence, then: "Oh god, Mike. Some of these are processing through... Romania? And Russia? That's not right, is it?"

"Check the transaction amounts," Mike instructed, his stomach sinking. "How many are between $450 and $500?"

"At least twenty... no, thirty of them. Should I shut down the mobile POS systems?"

1730 Hours - Crisis Assessment

The managers from all three locations joined an emergency video call: - Mike Turner - Owner - Amanda Brooks - Buckhead Manager - Jessica Yang - Midtown Manager - Ryan Martinez - Decatur Manager - Eric Sullivan - Part-time IT Support

"Talk to me about our exposure," Mike demanded.

Eric, who helped with IT issues on weekends around his regular job, looked grim. "The mobile POS devices are still running last year's software. No security updates. And... I think everyone's using the same admin password. The one that came with the devices."

"The default password?" Mike's voice rose. "For all twelve devices?"

"It was easier to remember," Amanda admitted quietly.

1745 Hours - Initial Response

"Okay, first things first," Eric said, pulling up the POS system documentation on his tablet. "We need to shut down all mobile payment devices until we can assess the damage."

"Shut down?" Ryan protested. "It's holiday season! We can't process sales without them."

Mike rubbed his temples. "Better no sales than fraudulent ones. Amanda, call our payment processor's security line. Jessica, Ryan – shut down all mobile POS devices at your locations. Eric, what else?"

"We need to check every transaction from... when did you first notice the irregular routing, Amanda?"

"Around 2PM, but who knows how long it was happening before I noticed."

1800 Hours – Scope Assessment

The team regrouped after the initial shutdown: - 127 suspicious transactions identified - $58,450 in questionable charges - 12 compromised POS devices - 3 locations affected - Unknown number of exposed cards

"The processor's security team is reviewing it now," Amanda reported. "They're saying the routing redirect suggests our POS devices were compromised by malware."

"Malware?" Mike looked at Eric. "How?"

"Remember that 'helpful' email about a POS system update last week? The one that looked like it was from our vendor?"

1815 Hours - Vendor Contact

Mike finally reached their POS vendo 's after-hours support.

"Sir, when was the last authorized update to your system?" the support representative asked.

"Apparently never," Mike replied, his voice tight. "We're still running whatever version was installed during setup."

"That would be version 6.2... sir, we're on version 8.5 now. There have been multiple critical security updates since then."

1830 Hours - Customer Impact

Jessica's voice was strained on the conference call. "We've got customers asking why our POS is down. Some are getting declined transaction notifications from their banks. Social media is starting to light up.

"And tomorrow's our biggest sale day of the season," Ryan added. "We've been promoting it for weeks."

1845 Hours - Insurance Reality Check

Mike was on the phone with his business insurance agent, pacing the back office

"No, Jim, not property theft - cyber theft. Digital. The payment systems..." He paused, listening. "What do you mean it's not covered under general liability?"

Amanda watched Mike's face darken as he listened.

"Look Mike," Jim said, clearly uncomfortable, "I'll be straight with you. Cyber liability and cybersecurity aren't my areas of expertise. But I know someone who specializes in this exact situation. Let me give you Damian Davis's direct line at DIS Risk Solutions. He helps small businesses with cyber incidents like this all the time."

Mike scribbled down the number. "Thanks, Jim. At least that's something."

1900 Hours - Initial Contact

"DIS Risk Solutions, this is Damian Davis."

"Mr. Davis, this is Mike Turner from Local Chic Boutique in Atlanta. Jim Robertson gave me your number. We've got a situation with our payment systems, and Jim said you might be able to help."

"Tell me what you're seeing, Mike," Damian replied, his tone shifting from formal to focused.

As Mike described the suspicious transactions and compromised POS systems, Damian asked pointed questions about the timeline, scope, and current containment efforts.

"Okay, I understand the situation," Damian said. "You've done the right thing by shutting down the devices. I'd like to bring in our incident response team - we have partners who specialize in retail POS breaches. Can you gather your team for an emergency call in ten minutes?"

Mike made a decision. "Amanda, draft a social media post. Be honest - tell them we've identifie a security issue and are temporarily processing credit cards manually while we update our systems. Jessica, Ryan - dig out those old manual credit card imprinters from the storage rooms."

1915 Hours - Security Assessment

Eric had been analyzing the POS system logs. "It looks like they used the default admin password to install a card skimming malware. Every time a card was swiped, it sent the data to their servers before processing the legitimate transaction."

"But why didn't anyone notice the weird routing?" Ryan asked.

"Because they only diverted every fourth or fifth transaction," Eric explained. "Just enough to avoid immediate detection. They were playing the long game until something triggered them to accelerate today."

1900 Hours - Response Planning

Mike gathered the team to develop their response plan:

Immediate Actions: - Continue manual card processing - Contact affected customers - File police report - Document all findings - Preserve evidence

Next Steps: - System updates required - New security protocols needed - Staff training essential - Customer communication plan - Recovery timeline

"What about our insurance?" Jessica asked.

Mike's face fell. "We have basic business insurance, but I don't know if it covers cyber incidents. I never thought we were big enough to need it."

1930 Hours - Expert Engagement

"We need help," Eric admitted. "This is beyond my expertise. We need a real cybersecurity firm to clean the systems and document the breach properly."

Mike nodded grimly. "Get me some names. And costs." He looked at the mounting expenses in his notebook: lost sales, system updates, security consultants, potential liability...

"The holiday sale can wait," he decided. "We do this right, or we don't do it at all."

1945 Hours - DIS Engagement

Damian Davis joined their emergency conference call, along with Rachel Torres from DIS Risk Solutions.

"I've briefed Rachel on the situation," Damian began. "Given what you've described, we need to move quickly on several fronts. TechDefend, our partner for small business incident response, can have a team on site at your Buckhead location within the hour. They specialize in retail POS systems."

"And the costs?" Mike asked hesitantly.

"Let's focus on containing the incident first," Damian advised. "TechDefend works on a fixed-rate model for small businesses, and SecureResponse, our forensics partner, can scale their involvement based on what we find. Rachel will help coordinate everything.

"We'll also need to think about customer notification requirements," Rachel added. "Georgia has specific laws about credit card breaches. But first, let s get the technical team in place."

2000 Hours - Partner Deployment

The TechDefend team arrived at the Buckhead location, led by their senior engineer, Marcus Chen. Within minutes, they had set up a mobile incident response center in the store's back office

"First priority is preserving evidence while containing the breach," Marcus explained, his team already working on the POS systems. "SecureResponse will handle the deeper forensics, but we need to make sure we're documenting everything properly from the start."

2015 Hours - Response Coordination

"We've seen this pattern before," Marcus explained, showing Mike and Damian the initial findings on his laptop. "It's a known exploit targeting outdated POS software, but the attackers have modified it specifically for small retailers during the holiday season."

Rachel Torres was coordinating with SecureResponse over the conference line. "Their forensics team can start remote analysis now, using TechDefend's secure connection. We'll want them on site tomorrow for a full investigation."

"And costs?" Mike asked again, more urgently this time.

"TechDefend's small business incident response package is $15,000," Damian explained. "That covers the immediate response, containment, and basic remediation. SecureResponse's forensics work will depend on the scope, but typically ranges from $20,000 to $35,000 for this type of breach."

Mike winced at the numbers.

"I know it sounds high," Damian acknowledged, "but trying to handle this without proper expertise usually costs far more in the long run. And once we get through this, we need to talk about preventing it from happening again."

2030 Hours - Technical Assessment

Marcus's team had made their first breakthrough. "Good news and bad news," he reported. "Good news is we've identified the malware and can remove it. Bad news is it's been present for at least two weeks, not just today."

"Two weeks?" Mike's voice cracked.

"The acceleration in fraudulent transactions today was probably triggered by our detection," Marcus explained. "They knew they'd been found, so they tried to grab as much as they could before being shut down."

"Rachel, what does this mean for customer notification?" Damian asked.

"With a two-week exposure window, we need to notify anyone who used a credit card at any location during that period," she replied. "SecureResponse can help create a notification plan that complies with state requirements."

2045 Hours - Moving Forward

"Let's talk next steps," Damian said. "You need more than just incident response - you need a sustainable security program. Have you considered our subscription service?"

Mike looked up from the mounting cost estimates. "What's that?"

"It's designed for businesses like yours," Damian explained. "Instead of paying everything out of pocket during a crisis, you get ongoing security support, incident response coverage, and access to our partner network, all for a predictable monthly fee."

"The subscription includes quarterly POS security assessments from TechDefend, staff training, and comprehensive incident response services through SecureResponse," Rachel added. "Plus, we help you find the right cyber insurance coverage."

2100 Hours - Immediate Priorities

Marcus from TechDefend had established their action plan:

- Isolate and preserve compromised POS devices
- Deploy loaner systems with current security patches
- Begin malware removal and system cleaning
- Implement proper access controls
- Set up enhanced monitoring

“We can have you back to secure card processing by tomorrow afternoon,” Marcus said. “But you’ll need to maintain proper security measures going forward. That’s where our ongoing support really helps.”

“The subscription would have covered all of this?” Mike asked, looking at the growing list of emergency expenses.

“Everything except the cyber insurance retention,” Damian confirmed. “And more importantly, it might have prevented it entirely through regular security checks.”

2115 Hours - Partnership Discussion

“Here’s what I propose,” Damian said. “Let TechDefend and SecureResponse handle the immediate crisis. Once we’ve contained this incident, we can discuss a long-term security program that fits your budget.”

Mike nodded, watching Marcus’s team work. “I never thought a small boutique would be a target. Now I realize we can’t afford not to have proper security.”

“That’s exactly why we developed these solutions,” Rachel explained. “Small businesses need the same level of protection as large corporations, just scaled appropriately.”

2130 Hours - Next Steps

The team reviewed their action items:

Immediate (Tonight):
- TechDefend continuing emergency response
- Evidence preservation ongoing
- Temporary security measures in place
- Staff instructions for tomorrow
- Customer communication drafted

Tomorrow:
- SecureResponse team arriving on site
- Full forensic investigation
- Customer notification planning
- Security program discussion
- Long-term solution development

2145 Hours - Looking Forward

"I should have taken this seriously sooner," Mike said, after most of the team had left. "The POS vendor warned us about updates. Our bank offered security services. We just didn't think it applied to us."

"That's a common misconception," Damian replied. "But you're taking the right steps now. With TechDefend and SecureResponse, plus a proper security program going forward, you'll be in a much stronger position."

2200 Hours - Final Assessment

"One more thing," Rachel said, reviewing her notes. "Given the credit card exposure, we should start preparing for regulatory requirements. SecureResponse will help with the notification process, but you'll want to consider cyber insurance coverage moving forward."

"I thought the subscription covered everything?" Mike asked.

“The subscription covers incident response services and ongoing security support,” Damian explained. “But cyber insurance is separate - it helps with the financial impact of breaches, regulatory fines, and potential lawsuits. They work together: the subscription helps prevent incidents and provides immediate response, while insurance handles the financial consequences if something does happen.

2215 Hours - Path Forward

As TechDefend’s team continued their work, Mike sat down with Damian and Rachel to outline immediate next steps:

Tonight:
- Complete initial containment
- Preserve evidence
- Document all finding
- Prepare for tomorrow

Tomorrow:
- SecureResponse forensics team arrival
- Customer notification plannin
- Staff briefing and trainin
- Security program discussion
- Insurance coverage review

“We’ll get through this,” Damian assured him. “And when we’re done, you’ll have the security program you need, not just the one you think you can afford.”

Mike looked at his three stores’ worth of compromised POS systems. “Sometimes the most expensive choice is thinking you’re saving money by skipping security.”

2230 Hours - Final Steps

Marcus approached with an update from TechDefend's initial assessment. "We've contained the immediate threat and preserved the evidence. SecureResponse's team will want to see this in the morning, but we've stopped any ongoing data exfiltration.

"What about tomorrow's operations?" Mike asked.

"You can process cards manually for now," Marcus advised. "We'll have secure temporary POS systems in place by tomorrow afternoon. But long-term, you'll need a complete security overhaul."

2245 Hours - Moving Forward

As the team prepared to wrap up for the night, Damian outlined what the next few days would look like:

"TechDefend will handle the immediate technical response. SecureResponse will manage the forensics and help with customer notifications. Rachel will coordinate everything and help you navigate the regulatory requirements. Once we're through the crisis phase, we'll sit down and build a proper security program that protects all three locations."

Mike nodded, exhausted but relieved to have a plan. "And the subscription service will help prevent this from happening again?"

"That's the goal," Rachel replied. "Regular security assessments, staff training, incident response coverage - everything you need to protect your business properly."

2300 Hours - Lessons Learned

As they prepared to leave, Mike looked around his flagship store. "You know what's ironic? We spend thousands on security cameras and alarm systems to prevent shoplifting, but we never thought about protecting our customers' payment data."

"Physical security versus cyber security," Damian noted. "Most small businesses focus on what they can see. But in today's world, digital assets need just as much protection."

"Well, that changes tomorrow," Mike said firml . "We're doing this right from now on."

The team nodded in agreement. Sometimes it takes a crisis to reveal what's truly important - and what's truly at risk.

PART 2: TECHNICAL DEEP DIVE

Investigation Timeline:

1400-1645: Pre-Detection Phase

- Malware installation via default credentials
- Initial card data exfiltratio
- Transaction routing manipulation
- Automated data harvesting
- Selective transaction targeting

1645-1800: Initial Response

- Anomaly detection in payment routing
- POS system assessment
- Emergency device shutdown
- Management team mobilization
- TechDefend deployment initiated
- DIS Risk Solutions engagement

1800-2200: Full Investigation

- Transaction pattern analysis
- System log review
- Malware identification and isolatio
- Impact scope assessment
- Evidence preservation
- SecureResponse forensics activation

Technical Analysis:

1. Attack Vector Identificatio

POS System Vulnerabilities:
- Default admin credentials unchanged
- Outdated software (Version 6.2 vs. 8.5)
- Unencrypted local data storage

- Weak authentication protocols
- Missing security patches
- Uniform access credentials across devices

Access Methods:
- Default password exploitation
- Social engineering via fake vendor email
- Malware deployment through compromised access
- Transaction interception and rerouting
- Remote command execution
- Automated data exfiltratio

2. Infrastructure Analysis

Payment Environment:
- Mobile POS terminals (12 devices)
- Payment processing gateway
- Transaction routing system
- Local data storage
- Network infrastructure
- Third-party payment processor integration

Affected Systems:
- Payment processing infrastructure
- Transaction logging systems
- Customer data storage
- Receipt generation
- Loyalty program database
- Inventory management integration

3. Impact Assessment

Payment Data Exposure:
- 127 confirmed compromised transaction
- $58,450 in fraudulent charges

- 12 affected POS devices
- Two-week exposure window
- Multiple location impact
- Unknown total card data exposure

Business Impact:
- Operations disruption
- Revenue loss ($4,000+ per hour)
- Customer trust damage
- Brand reputation harm
- Regulatory exposure
- Holiday season disruption

4. Security Control Analysis

Missing Controls:
- Password management protocols
- Update management system
- Security monitoring tools
- Device management policies
- Access control standards
- Incident response plan

Failed Safeguards:
- Default configuration retentio
- Basic authentication only
- Minimal system logging
- Limited transaction monitoring
- Inadequate staff training
- No security update protocol

5. Recovery Complexity

Technical Challenges:
- Device remediation requirements
- System update implementation
- Security control deployment
- Data recovery processes
- Evidence preservation needs
- PCI compliance restoration

Implementation Constraints:
- Limited IT resources
- Budget restrictions
- Staff expertise gaps
- Operational continuity needs
- Time pressure (holiday season)
- Multi-location coordination

6. Forensic Investigation

Evidence Collection:
- Transaction logs
- System configuration
- Access records
- Malware samples
- Network traffic dat
- POS device images
- Email communication records

Analysis Findings:
- Attack methodology identificatio
- Compromise timeline reconstruction
- Data loss scope assessment
- System vulnerability mapping

- Control failure documentation
- Exfiltration pattern analysi

7. DIS Risk Solutions Coordination

Initial Response:
- Emergency response activation
- TechDefend deployment
- SecureResponse engagement
- Evidence preservation protocols
- Documentation requirements
- Client communication support

Partner Integration:
TechDefend:
- Immediate incident response
- POS system analysis
- Security implementation
- System remediation
- Ongoing monitoring setup

SecureResponse:
- Forensic investigation
- Evidence preservation
- Breach scope analysis
- Compliance documentation
- Recovery recommendations

Documentation Requirements:
- Incident chronology
- Response actions
- Technical finding
- Recovery efforts

- Partner activities
- Compliance documentation

8. Solution Development

Technical Response:
- POS system updates
- Security control implementation
- Monitoring enhancement
- Access control deployment
- Encryption implementation
- Staff training development

Implementation Strategy:
Phase 1 - Immediate Response:
- System shutdown and isolation
- Evidence preservation
- Manual processing implementation
- Initial security measures
- Customer communication

Phase 2 - Investigation:
- Forensic analysis
- Impact assessment
- Compliance review
- Documentation collection
- Partner coordination

Phase 3 - Recovery:
- Security enhancement
- Process improvement
- Staff training
- Long-term monitoring
- Compliance maintenance

9. Risk Analysis

Coverage Assessment:
- Current coverage gaps
- Incident response costs
- Forensics expenses
- Regulatory requirements
- Business interruption impact
- Future coverage needs

Security Enhancement:
- POS system protection
- Access control implementation
- Monitoring capabilities
- Staff training programs
- Vendor management
- Update protocols

Future Requirements:
- Enhanced security measures
- Continuous monitoring
- Regular assessments
- Partner integration
- Coverage maintenance
- Compliance validation

Long-term Protection:
- Security program development
- POS environment hardening
- Access control enhancement
- Partner coordination
- Coverage alignment
- Regular security audits

PART 3: IMPLEMENTATION GUIDE

1. IMPACT ASSESSMENT

Financial Impact: Direct Costs: - Emergency response: $38,500 - POS system replacement: $12,000 - Customer notifications: $2,500 - Credit monitoring: $15,000 - Staff training: $3,500 Total Direct Impact: $71,500

Insurance Implications: Primary Coverage: Basic business liability only - No cyber coverage - No incident response coverage - No regulatory defense coverage - No customer notification coverage - No business interruption coverage

Coverage Gaps: - Cyber incident response - POS system compromise - Customer data breach - Business interruption - Regulatory compliance

Partner Integration: TechDefend: - POS system analysis - Security implementation - System remediation - Monitoring deployment - Recovery support

SecureResponse: - Forensic investigation - Evidence preservation - Breach documentation - Compliance guidance - Recovery planning

Systems Affected: Primary Systems: - Mobile POS devices (12) - Payment processing - Transaction routing - Card data storage - Customer database

Secondary Systems: - Loyalty program - Inventory management - Receipt generation - Email marketing - Social media integration

Business Disruption: Duration: - Critical phase: 24 hours - Total recovery: 7 days

Impact Scope: - 3 retail locations affected - 32 employees impacted - 2,000+ customers potentially exposed - Holiday season disrupted - Brand reputation damaged

2. TECHNICAL RESPONSE

Immediate Actions: - POS system shutdown - DIS Risk Solutions engagement - TechDefend deployment - Manual processing implementation - Evidence preservation - Customer notification preparation - Staff communication

Investigation Steps: - Transaction analysis - System assessment - Impact evaluation - Customer data review - Regulatory compliance check - Documentation collection - Partner coordination

Solution Development: - Security implementation - System updates - Process improvement - Training development - Documentation creation

3. IMPLEMENTATION TIMELINE

Immediate (0-24 hours): Hour 0-6: - System shutdown - DIS Risk Solutions activation - TechDefend deployment - Evidence preservation - Initial containment - Staff notification - Manual processing setu

Hour 6-12: - SecureResponse engagement - Forensic analysis - Impact assessment - Customer communication prep - Security enhancement - Documentation initiation - Response planning

Hour 12-18: - Complete containment - Customer notification - Security implementation - Documentation collection - Partner coordination - Staff training - Recovery planning

Hour 18-24: - System analysis - Enhanced monitoring - Access control implementation - Partner integration - Documentation completion - Recovery initiation - Communication updates

Short-term (1-7 days): Day 1-2: - System updates - Security enhancement - Staff training - Customer support - Documentation review

Day 3-4: - Security implementation - Process improvement - Training continuation - Customer updates - Recovery progress

Day 5-7: - Final security validation - Process documentation - Staff certification - Customer follow-up - Recovery completio

4. KEY TAKEAWAYS

Business Lessons: - Size doesn't ensure safety - Basic security essential - Insurance critical - Training necessary - Documentation important

Technical Insights: - Default passwords dangerous - Updates critical - Monitoring essential - Documentation necessary - Training fundamental

Process Improvements: - Security protocols - Update procedures - Access controls - Training programs - Incident response

5. ROI ANALYSIS

Prevention Costs: Technology Investment: $12,000 Staff Training: $3,500 Process Implementation: $4,500 Ongoing Maintenance: $2,400/year Total Prevention Cost: $22,400

Incident Costs: Direct Response: $38,500 Business Impact: $58,450 Recovery Efforts: $48,000 Long-term Effects: Under assessment Total Incident Cost: $144,950+

Future Savings: Risk Reduction: $75,000 annually Efficiency Gains: $12,000 annually Prevention Benefits: $25,000 annually Resource Optimization: $8,000 annually Total Projected Savings: $120,000 annually

6. ACTION CHECKLIST

Immediate Response: System shutdown Evidence collection Customer notification Manual processing setup Incident documentatio

Assessment Tasks: Impact analysis System review Customer assessment Risk evaluation Compliance check

Implementation Steps: Security deployment System updates Process improvement Training execution Documentation update

7. C-SUITE COMMUNICATION PROTOCOL

Executive Notification Sequence

Owner (Mike Turner): - Initial incident assessment - Response coordination - Resource allocation - Customer communication - Recovery oversight

Store Managers: Buckhead Location (Amanda Brooks): - Location response coordination - Staff management - Customer interaction - Implementation oversight - Documentation management

Midtown Location (Jessica Yang): - Location security implementation - Staff coordination - Customer management - Process execution - Training oversight

Decatur Location (Ryan Martinez): - Location recovery management - Staff supervision - Customer service - Process implementation - Documentation coordination

IT Support (Eric Sullivan): - Technical response coordination - System restoration - Security implementation - Update management - Control deployment

DIS Risk Solutions (Damian Davis): - Response management - Partner coordination - Coverage guidance - Strategic planning - Recovery oversight

Communication Templates:

Initial Notification: • Incident overview • Current status • Immediate actions • Required decisions • Next steps

Status Updates: • Response progress • System status • Customer impact • Partner status • Action items

Decision Matrix:

System Shutdown Authority: • Transaction anomaly detection • Fraud pattern identification • Security breach confirmation • Partner recommendation • Customer risk exposure

Recovery Authorization: • Security verification complete • Partner validation obtained • System testing successful • Documentation complete • Staff training completed

Customer Notification Triggers: • Data breach confirmed • System compromise >4 hours • Fraud patterns detected • Regulatory requirements • Partner recommendations

Response Escalation Guidelines: • Transaction impact severity • Customer data exposure • Location disruption level • Partner recommendations • Recovery timeline impact

Recovery Milestones: • System security • POS restoration • Customer notification • Partner integration • Documentation completio

Documentation Requirements:

Technical Documentation: • System modifications • Security implementations • Test results • POS configurations • Partner activitie

Response Documentation: • Incident timeline • Action items • Cost tracking • Customer impact • Recovery efforts

Chapter 10

Cloud Configuration Crisis

PART 1: NARRATIVE CASE STUDY

Company Profile: CloudFlow Solutions
Annual Revenue: $180K (pre-Series A)
Industry: Software as a Service (Project Management Platform)
Employees: 4 total - Co-founders: • Ryan Matthews - CEO/Product • Marcus Wei - CTO/Engineering - Team: • Ben Foster - Full-stack Developer • Sophie Taylor - Part-time Customer Success/Marketing
Client Base: - 125 active users - 15 paying business customers - Rest on free tier/beta
Market Position: Early-stage SaaS startup in project management space
Geographic Presence: All remote team
Funding: - $300K angel investment - Currently raising seed round
Technology Stack: - AWS infrastructure - Basic CI/CD pipeline - Limited security oversight - Rapid deployment focus - Bootstrap mentality

0845 Hours - CloudFlow Solutions (Virtual Office)

Marcus Wei, CTO and co-founder, was reviewing the morning's AWS billing alert when something caught his eye. The data transfer costs had spiked overnight - nearly 100 times their normal volume.

"Hey Ryan," he messaged his co-founder on Slack. "You didn't happen to run any large data exports last night, did you?"

Ryan Matthews, CEO, replied instantly: “No... why?”

“Because someone did. A lot of them. And this is exactly what CloudShield warned us about in last week’s security assessment.”

0900 Hours - Initial Discovery

Marcus dove into the AWS console while on a video call with Ryan. “I’m seeing massive data transfers from our primary S3 bucket. It looks like... oh no.”

“What?”

“Remember last week when we quickly spun up that demo environment for the investor pitch? I think we left the bucket permissions set to public. CloudShield’s monitoring system just sent an alert.”

Ryan’s face drained of color. “The bucket with all our customer project data?”

“Yeah. And someone found it. I’m calling James from CloudShield now.”

0915 Hours - Emergency Response

The entire team joined an emergency Zoom call: - Ryan Matthews - Looking shell-shocked - Marcus Wei - Frantically checking logs - Ben Foster - Already reviewing the codebase - Sophie Taylor - Monitoring customer channels - James Chen - CloudShield Technical Lead

“Talk to me about exposure,” Ryan demanded.

James shared his screen, showing the AWS CloudWatch logs. “Our monitoring picked up the anomaly at 0230 hours. The bucket was publicly accessible for six days. Based on the access patterns, someone ran automated scanning tools and found it last night. They pulled everything.”

“I thought the monitoring was supposed to prevent this,” Ryan said.

"We just completed your initial security assessment last week," James reminded him. "The full implementation of our security controls isn't complete yet. This is exactly why Damian at DIS Risk Solutions recommended immediate deployment."

0930 Hours - Impact Assessment

Marcus pulled up their customer database. "We're looking at potential exposure of: - Project timelines - Task assignments - Internal comments - File attachments - Client communications"

"Any payment data?" Ryan asked hopefully.

"No, that's on Stripe. But there's enough sensitive internal business data here to..." Marcus trailed off.

"To kill us," Ryan finished. "Right as we're trying to close our seed round."

James was already making calls. "I'm activating SecureResponse for forensics. This needs immediate containment."

0945 Hours - Reality Check

"I thought we were too small for anyone to care about," Ryan said, running his hands through his hair. "We're barely making $15K MRR. Who would even bother attacking us?"

"That's exactly why Damian pushed so hard for the SecureResponse subscription," James replied. "Small companies are prime targets because they often have minimal security. You're lucky we at least got the monitoring in place last week."

"But we're just a startup," Ryan protested. "We were going to implement everything gradually..."

"Which is why we recommended SecureResponse," a new voice joined the call. Rachel Torres from DIS Risk Solutions had connected. "It gives you enterprise-level protection scaled for startups. Right now, let's focus on containment. The incident response team is standing by."

1000 Hours - Customer Impact

Sophie's Slack message cut through their discussion: "Guys, we have a problem. One of our customers - Thompson Manufacturing - is asking why their internal project data is showing up on a public website."

"Which customer is that?" Ryan asked, dreading the answer.

"Our biggest one. $2,500 MRR. They're using CloudFlow to manage their upcoming product launch."

Rachel took charge. "James, get your CloudShield team to start the exposure analysis. I'll have SecureResponse begin data mapping. We need to know exactly what was exposed and when."

1015 Hours - Initial Response

The team reviewed their situation: - Unknown number of exposed customers - SecureResponse subscription just initiated - CloudShield monitoring partially implemented - Limited security documentation - Incident response plan in development

"At least we got the SecureResponse subscription in place," Marcus said. "Damian warned us this could happen."

"The subscription means we have coverage for the incident response," Rachel confirmed. "But we need to move fast to minimize the damage."

1030 Hours - Growing Concern

"How do we handle customer communications?" Sophie asked. "Our entire customer support process is just me working part-time."

"SecureResponse will help with the notification process," Rachel explained. "They have templates and procedures for exactly this situation. James, what's CloudShield's initial assessment?"

James was analyzing the logs. "We've identified the initial access point and timeline. The automated scanning tools found the misconfiguration shortly after it was created. We're building a complete access log now."

1045 Hours - Response Coordination

Ryan pulled up their startup's finances: - Bank Balance: $42,000 - Monthly Burn: $28,000 - Runway: 1.5 months - Emergency Fund: $0

"Thank god we listened to Damian about the SecureResponse subscription," Ryan said quietly. "These response costs would have bankrupted us."

"That's why we structure the subscription for startups," Rachel explained. "The incident response costs are covered, and CloudShield's monitoring should prevent this from happening again once fully implemented."

"The seed investors..." Marcus started.

"Will want to know we have a professional incident response team handling this," Rachel finished. "That's a lot better than trying to handle it alone."

1100 Hours - Customer Management

Sophie's voice was tense on the Zoom call. "Thompson Manufacturing's CTO is demanding a call. Three other customers have emailed asking about data security. And... someone just posted about us on Twitter."

"Let me handle the Thompson call," Rachel offered. "We'll demonstrate that you have enterprise-grade incident response through SecureResponse. James, can you join to outline CloudShield's security implementation plan?"

"Already preparing the technical briefing," James confirmed. "We'll show them the security controls being implemented."

1115 Hours - Exposure Analysis

Ben shared CloudShield's initial assessment: "The exposed bucket contained: - Internal project timelines - Confidential product launches - Private team discussions - Strategic planning documents - Competitor analysis"

"Everything our customers trusted us with," Ryan said.

"Which is why we're going to handle this professionally," Rachel assured him. "SecureResponse has managed similar incidents for companies your size. We have proven protocols for this exact scenario."

1130 Hours - Professional Response

Marcus was reviewing the incident response dashboard SecureResponse had set up. "Look at this - real-time tracking of affected data, automated customer impact analysis, compliance requirements by state..."

"This is what enterprise-grade incident response looks like," Rachel explained. "The subscription gives you access to the same tools and expertise that large companies use."

James from CloudShield added, "Once we complete the security implementation, you'll have similar capabilities for prevention. The monitoring would have caught this misconfiguration before it became an issue."

1145 Hours - Customer Communication

Sophie returned from the Thompson Manufacturing call, where Rachel and James had led the discussion. "They're not pulling their business. The CTO said having SecureResponse and CloudShield involved gives him confidence we're taking security seriousl ."

"Professional incident response makes a difference," Rachel noted. "It shows you're prepared, even if you're small."

"We have two more enterprise calls this afternoon," Sophie added. "Having you both on the calls will help."

1200 Hours - Path Forward

The team reviewed SecureResponse's incident management plan:

Immediate Actions: - Complete exposure analysis - Implement CloudShield security controls - Execute customer notification plan - Document incident timeline - Preserve evidence

Next Steps: - Full security implementation - Enhanced monitoring deployment - Staff security training - Process documentation - Customer trust rebuilding

1215 Hours - Security Implementation

"Here's what we're doing," James from CloudShield explained, sharing his screen. "We're implementing our full security stack now, not gradually as originally planned. Rachel, your team good with that?"

"SecureResponse agrees," Rachel nodded. "The incident response gives us a perfect baseline for implementation. We'll document everything for the seed investors too - show them you're handling security properly now."

Ryan watched the activity dashboard. "All these security features we thought we'd implement 'eventually'..."

"Are exactly what you need from day one," James finished. "Size doesn't matter to attackers. Security readiness does."

1230 Hours - Resource Coordination

The team reviewed their available resources: - SecureResponse incident management team - CloudShield security implementation - DIS Risk Solutions coordination - Basic AWS tools - Limited internal staff

"The subscription model makes sense now," Ryan said, watching the professional response unfold. "We could never have managed this alone."

"That's the point," Rachel explained. "You get enterprise-level security and incident response, scaled and priced for startups. The alternative..."

"Would have been trying to handle a data breach with four people and no experience," Marcus finished griml .

1245 Hours - Recovery Planning

James outlined CloudShield's implementation schedule: - Immediate security controls - Enhanced monitoring - Access management - Configuration validation - Ongoing assessmen

"Meanwhile," Rachel added, "SecureResponse will: - Complete the forensics - Handle customer notifications - Document everything - Manage compliance requirements - Build your incident response plan"

1300 Hours - Investor Management

Rachel was preparing Ryan for the emergency investor call. "Focus on three things: One, you have professional incident response through SecureResponse. Two, CloudShield is implementing comprehensive security. Three, you're handling this like an enterprise, not a startup."

"The investors were worried about our security readiness," Ryan remembered. "This isn't exactly what I had in mind for proving we take it seriously."

"Actually," Rachel said, "showing them how you handle a crisis with professional support might be more convincing than any pitch deck."

1315 Hours - Cost Analysis

Marcus reviewed the incident costs covered by their SecureResponse subscription: - Emergency response - Forensic investigation - Customer notifications - Compliance management - Recovery suppor

"And if we hadn't had the subscription?" he asked.

"You'd be looking at around $75,000 minimum," Rachel replied. "Most startups never recover from that kind of unexpected cost."

1330 Hours - Technical Progress

James from CloudShield shared an update: "We've contained the exposure, implemented initial security controls, and set up enhanced monitoring. The SecureResponse team has mapped 85% of potentially exposed data."

"The automated scanning was actually a blessing in disguise," Rachel added. "If a targeted attacker had found this first...

"Let's not think about that," Ryan said. "Let's focus on making sure it never happens again."

1345 Hours - Path Forward

The team gathered to review their recovery plan:

Immediate Actions: - Complete CloudShield security implementation - Follow SecureResponse incident playbook - Document all exposed data - Continue customer communications - Preserve evidence

Next Steps: - Enhance security monitoring - Complete staff training - Establish security policies - Regular security assessments - Build customer trust

"It's basically rebuilding our security foundation," Marcus observed.

"With professional help this time," Rachel added. "That's what the SecureResponse subscription provides."

1400 Hours - Investor Call

The emergency investor call went better than expected. Ryan presented their response: - Professional incident management through SecureResponse - Comprehensive security implementation by CloudShield - Clear incident response protocols - Customer communication strategy - Long-term security roadmap

"You're handling this better than some large companies," the lead investor noted. "Having DIS Risk Solutions and their partners involved makes a big difference."

1415 Hours - Learning Experience

As they wrapped up the day's emergency response, Ryan addressed the team: "We made a classic startup mistake. We thought being small meant security could wait."

"But you made a smart decision getting the SecureResponse subscription," Rachel noted. "Professional incident response and CloudShield's security implementation will help rebuild customer trust."

"And next time?" Marcus asked.

James smiled. "With our monitoring in place, there won't be a 'next time' like this. That's a promise."

1430 Hours - Moving Forward

Ryan looked at their updated pitch deck, now with an entire slide dedicated to their security program: - SecureResponse subscription - CloudShield security implementation - Professional incident response - Regular security assessments - Continuous monitoring

"You know what's ironic?" he said. "The security program we thought we couldn't afford turned out to be the thing we couldn't afford to skip."

The team nodded in agreement. In the startup world, sometimes the most expensive decision is thinking security can wait until tomorrow.

PART 2: TECHNICAL DEEP DIVE

Investigation Timeline:

0230-0845: Pre-Detection Phase

- Automated scanning tools active
- Public bucket access exploited
- Data exfiltration bega
- CloudShield monitoring alerts triggered
- Cost anomaly detected
- Access logs generated

0845-1000: Initial Response

- Alert verificatio
- CloudShield team activation
- SecureResponse engagement
- DIS Risk Solutions notificatio
- System assessment
- Log analysis initiated
- Team mobilization

1000-1430: Full Investigation

- CloudShield security analysis
- SecureResponse forensics
- Exposure scope mapping
- Customer data review
- Access pattern analysis
- Cost impact assessment
- Recovery planning

Technical Analysis:

1. Attack Vector Identificatio
Cloud Misconfigurations
- Public S3 bucket permissions
- Default security settings
- Missing access controls
- Incomplete monitoring
- Limited logging capabilities
- Configuration drif

Access Methods:
- Automated scanning tools
- Direct bucket access
- Public file listing
- Bulk data downloads
- Sequential access patterns
- Automated exfiltratio

2. Infrastructure Analysis
Cloud Environment:
- AWS S3 storage
- Basic EC2 instances
- Default VPC settings
- Minimal IAM roles
- Standard logging
- CloudShield monitoring integration
- SecureResponse incident tools

Affected Systems:
- Primary data storage
- Customer file upload
- Project metadata
- User content

- System backups
- Configuration managemen
- Access controls

3. Impact Assessment

Data Exposure:
- 15 business customers affected
- 125 active users impacted
- 6 days of public access
- Multiple data types exposed
- Unknown download volume
- Customer project data compromised
- Internal documentation exposed

Business Impact:
- Customer data compromised
- Trust relationships damaged
- Revenue stream threatened
- Reputation harmed
- Investment round jeopardized
- Security credibility questioned
- Customer confidence impacte

4. Security Control Analysis
Missing Controls:
- S3 bucket policies
- Access monitoring
- Security scanning
- Configuration review
- Change management
- Deployment validation
- Security testing

Failed Safeguards:
- Default settings used
- Partial monitoring implementation
- Limited access controls
- Basic logging only
- Minimal oversight
- Configuration managemen
- Change control

5. Recovery Complexity

Technical Challenges:
- CloudShield implementation acceleration
- SecureResponse integration
- Resource constraints
- Tool deployment
- Documentation gaps
- Process absence
- Configuration managemen

Implementation Constraints:
- Budget limitations
- Time pressure
- Staffing shortage
- Knowledge gaps
- Customer demands
- Investor expectations
- Operational continuity

6. Forensic Investigation

Evidence Collection:
- AWS CloudTrail logs
- S3 access logs

- CloudShield monitoring data
- SecureResponse forensics
- Billing records
- Configuration histor
- User activity data

Analysis Findings:
- Attack timeline reconstruction
- Access pattern identificatio
- Data movement tracking
- Tool signature analysis
- Impact scope determination
- Vulnerability mapping
- Control failure analysis

7. DIS Risk Solutions Coordination

Initial Response:
- SecureResponse activation
- CloudShield deployment
- Evidence preservation
- Documentation requirements
- Customer communication
- Investor management
- Recovery planning

Partner Integration:
CloudShield:
- Security implementation
- Monitoring deployment
- Access control enhancement
- Configuration managemen
- Ongoing protection

SecureResponse:
- Incident management
- Forensic investigation
- Customer notificatio
- Compliance guidance
- Recovery support

8. Solution Development

Technical Response:
- CloudShield security stack deployment
- SecureResponse incident management
- S3 bucket security hardening
- Access control implementation
- Monitoring enhancement
- Logging improvement
- Configuration managemen

Implementation Strategy:
Phase 1 - Immediate Response:
- Access restriction
- Evidence preservation
- CloudShield activation
- SecureResponse deployment
- Initial containment
- Customer communication
- Documentation initiation

Phase 2 - Investigation:
- Forensic analysis
- Impact assessment
- Data mapping
- Customer notificatio

- Compliance review
- Evidence collection
- Documentation completion

Phase 3 - Recovery:
- Security enhancement
- Process improvement
- Training development
- Partner integration
- Long-term monitoring
- Documentation update
- Trust rebuilding

9. Risk Analysis

Coverage Assessment:
- SecureResponse subscription benefit
- CloudShield protection scope
- Incident response coverage
- Recovery support
- Customer notificatio
- Compliance management
- Future protection

Security Enhancement:
- Cloud security hardening
- Access control implementation
- Monitoring capabilities
- Configuration managemen
- Staff training
- Process development
- Partner integration

Future Requirements:
- Enhanced security measures
- Continuous monitoring
- Regular assessments
- Partner coordination
- Coverage maintenance
- Process refinemen
- Security validation

Long-term Protection:
- Security program development
- Cloud environment hardening
- Access control enhancement
- Partner integration
- Coverage alignment
- Regular testing
- Continuous improvement

PART 3: IMPLEMENTATION GUIDE

1. IMPACT ASSESSMENT

Financial Impact: Direct Costs: - Emergency response: $25,000 (covered by SecureResponse) - Security implementation: $15,000 (CloudShield deployment) - Customer notifications: $5,000 - Documentation: $3,500 - Staff training: $2,500 Total Direct Impact: $51,000

Insurance Implications: Primary Coverage: SecureResponse subscription - Incident response coverage - Customer notification support - Forensic investigation - Compliance guidance - Recovery assistance

Partner Integration: CloudShield: - Security implementation - Monitoring deployment - Access control enhancement - Configuration management - Ongoing protection

SecureResponse: - Incident management - Forensic investigation - Customer notification - Compliance guidance - Recovery suppor

Systems Affected: Primary Systems: - AWS S3 storage - Customer data repository - Project management platform - File storage system - Metadata database

Secondary Systems: - User authentication - Access controls - Logging systems - Monitoring tools - Backup systems

Business Disruption: Duration: - Critical phase: 24 hours - Total recovery: 14 days

Impact Scope: - 15 business customers affected - 125 active users impacted - Core product compromised - Seed round threatened - Brand reputation damaged

2. TECHNICAL RESPONSE

Immediate Actions: - S3 bucket access restriction - CloudShield security deployment - SecureResponse activation - Evidence preservation - Customer notification - Documentation initiation - Team coordination

Investigation Steps: - Access log review - Impact assessment - Customer data audit - Compliance check - Exposure analysis - Partner coordination - Recovery planning

Solution Development: - CloudShield implementation - Security control deployment - Process improvement - Training development - Documentation creation - Monitoring enhancement - Partner integration

3. IMPLEMENTATION TIMELINE

Immediate (0-24 hours): Hour 0-6: - Access restriction - CloudShield activation - SecureResponse engagement - Evidence preservation - Initial containment - Team notification - Customer communicatio

Hour 6-12: - Security implementation - Forensic analysis - Impact assessment - Documentation initiation - Partner coordination - Response planning - Status updates

Hour 12-24: - Complete containment - Enhanced monitoring - Access control implementation - Customer notification - Documentation completion - Recovery initiation - Communication updates

Short-term (1-7 days): Day 1-2: - CloudShield security deployment - Process development - Staff training - Customer support - Documentation review

Day 3-7: - Security validation - Process refinement - Training continuation - Customer updates - Recovery completion

Long-term (8-30 days): Week 2: - Security enhancement - Process documentation - Staff certification - Customer follow-up - Partner integration

Week 3-4: - Program optimization - Security validation - Process refinement - Documentation update - Continuous improvement

4. KEY TAKEAWAYS

Business Lessons: - Early security implementation critical - Professional support essential - Partner integration valuable - Documentation fundamental - Training imperative - Process development crucial - Customer trust paramount

Technical Insights: - Cloud security fundamentals - Configuration management - Access control requirements - Monitoring essentials - Partner capabilities - Response protocols - Recovery procedures

Process Improvements: - Security protocols - Change management - Access controls - Training programs - Partner integration - Documentation standards - Incident response

5. ROI ANALYSIS

Prevention Costs: Initial Investment: - CloudShield implementation: $15,000 - Security controls: $10,000 - Staff training: $2,500 - Documentation: $3,500 - Process development: $5,000 Total Prevention Cost: $36,000

Incident Costs: Direct Response: - Emergency response: $25,000 - Customer notifications: $5,000 - Recovery efforts: $12,000 - Documentation: $3,500 Less SecureResponse Coverage: ($25,000) Total Net Impact: $20,500

Future Protection: Annual Savings: - Risk reduction: $50,000 - Efficiency gains: $15,000 - Prevention benefits: $25,000 - Resource optimization: $10,000 Total Annual Value: $100,000

6. ACTION CHECKLIST

Immediate Response: □ Access restriction □ CloudShield activation □ SecureResponse engagement □ Evidence preservation □ Customer notification □ Documentation initiation □ Team coordination

Assessment Tasks: □ Impact analysis □ System review □ Customer assessment □ Partner coordination □ Compliance check □ Documentation review □ Recovery planning

Implementation Steps: □ Security deployment □ Process development □ Training execution □ Documentation update □ Partner integration □ Monitoring enhancement □ Recovery validation

7. C-SUITE COMMUNICATION PROTOCOL

Executive Notification Sequence

CEO/Product (Ryan Matthews): - Initial incident assessment - Customer communication - Investor relations - Resource allocation - Recovery oversight

CTO/Engineering (Marcus Wei): - Technical response coordination - CloudShield integration - Security implementation - Recovery planning - Infrastructure protection

Development Team (Ben Foster): - System analysis - Technical implementation - Security deployment - Code review - Infrastructure security

Customer Success (Sophie Taylor): - Customer communication - Status updates - Feedback management - Documentation - Trust rebuilding

DIS Risk Solutions (Damian Davis/Rachel Torres): - SecureResponse coordination - Partner management - Strategic guidance - Recovery oversight - Future protection

Communication Templates:

Initial Notification: • Incident overview • Current status • Immediate actions • Required decisions • Next steps

Status Updates: • Response progress • System status • Customer impact • Partner activities • Action items

Decision Matrix:

System Authority: • Security impact threshold • Customer risk exposure • Partner recommendation • Recovery implications • Business continuity

Recovery Authorization: • Security verification complete • Partner validation obtained • System testing successful • Documentation complete • Customer notification finish

Response Escalation Guidelines: • Technical impact severity • Customer data exposure • Partner recommendations • Recovery timeline impact • Business continuity risk

Recovery Milestones: • Security implementation • System restoration • Customer notification • Partner integration • Documentation completion

Documentation Requirements:

Technical Documentation: • System modifications • Security implementations • Partner activities • Test results • Recovery procedures

Response Documentation: • Incident timeline • Action items • Cost tracking • Customer impact • Recovery efforts

Chapter 11

Third-Party Threat

PART 1: NARRATIVE CASE STUDY

Company Profile: Hamilton Design Partners
Annual Revenue: $50M Industry: Professional Services (Architecture & Design)
Employees: 175
Client Base: - Commercial real estate developers - Municipal governments - Healthcare facilities - Educational institutions - Corporate campuses
Market Position: Regional leader in sustainable commercial architecture
Geographic Presence: Headquartered in Boston with offices in NYC and Providence
Technology Stack: - AutoCAD/Revit design software - Cloud-based rendering services - Project management platforms - Third-party visualization tools - Contractor collaboration portals

0930 Hours - Hamilton Design Partners, Boston Office

Patricia Morrison, Director of IT Operations, was reviewing the morning security report from HealthGuard IT when she noticed something odd. Their third-party rendering service, ArchRender Pro, was accessing project files outside of normal rendering jobs

"That's strange," she muttered, pulling up the access logs. The service was downloading complete project folders, including specifications, client communications, and preliminary designs – far more than needed for rendering. She immediately pinged Marcus Chen, their HealthGuard IT account manager.

0945 Hours - Initial Discovery

Patricia called David Parker, Head of Digital Design, while waiting for Marcus's response. "David, are your teams running any bulk renders today?"

"No, we're still in the design phase for most projects. Renders aren't scheduled until next week. Why?"

"Because ArchRender Pro has pulled over 300GB of project data in the last hour. HealthGuard IT's monitoring system just flagged it as anomalous behavior."

"That's... not possible. We don't even have that many projects in rendering phase."

"I'm calling Damian at DIS Risk Solutions," Patricia decided. "This could trigger our cyber policy."

1000 Hours - Emergency Assessment

The senior team assembled in the main conference room: - James Hamilton - Managing Partner - Patricia Morrison - Director of IT Operations - David Parker - Head of Digital Design - Jennifer Wu - Legal Counsel - Andrew Collins - Client Relations Director - Marcus Chen - HealthGuard IT (on video) - Damian Davis - DIS Risk Solutions (on video)

"Talk to me about exposure," James demanded, his architect's precision evident even in crisis.

Marcus shared his screen. "Our monitoring shows ArchRender Pro has accessed files from multiple projects, including: - New downtown medical center - University science building - Tech company headquarters - Government office complex - Mixed-use development

"Those are all under NDAs," Jennifer interjected. "Some with seven-figure penalties.

"Patricia, I'm activating CyberForensics," Damian said. "They're our designated forensics partner under your cyber policy. Rachel Torres will handle the insurance notification.

1015 Hours - Scope Analysis

David pulled up their project management system. "It's worse than just the renders. They've accessed: - Building specifications - Security system layouts - Infrastructure designs - Cost estimates - Client requirements"

"And because we trusted them as a vendor," Patricia added, "their service account had high-level access. HealthGuard IT flagged this as a potential risk in our last quarterly review."

Marcus nodded. "We recommended implementing stricter vendor controls, but the project deadlines took priority."

1030 Hours - Vendor Response

The team's call with ArchRender Pro's support desk wasn't encouraging.

"We're investigating," the support manager said. "But our preliminary finding is that our system was compromised two weeks ago. Several of our enterprise clients are affected."

"Two weeks?" James's voice was tight. "And we're just hearing about this now?"

Rachel Torres from DIS Risk Solutions joined the call. "I've notified the carrier of the incident. CyberForensics team is en route to begin their investigation."

1045 Hours - Client Impact

Andrew looked up from his laptop. "The medical center client is already calling. Their security team spotted our building plans on a dark web forum. Complete structural designs, including secure areas."

"Perfect," James said grimly. "A $40 million project at risk because we trusted a vendor's security."

Marcus from HealthGuard IT pulled up their security dashboard. "We're seeing increased scanning activity against your other vendor connections. We should review all third-party access immediately."

1100 Hours - Expanding Crisis

"We need to contact all affected clients," Andrew said, already drafting communications. "But what do we tell them?"

"The truth," James decided. "That our trusted vendor was compromised, and their project data may be exposed."

"And then watch them all sue us," Jennifer added. "Our contracts promise 'industry standard security measures' for their intellectual property."

Dr. Sarah Chen from CyberForensics joined the call. "We'll need complete access to your vendor management systems and all ArchRender Pro communications. The sooner we establish the timeline, the better."

1115 Hours - Vendor Assessment

Patricia pulled up ArchRender Pro's security documentation: - Last security audit: 18 months ago - Basic encryption standards - Minimal access controls - Limited monitoring - No breach notification protoco

"We never asked for this information before partnering with them," she realized. "We just signed their standard agreement."

Marcus from HealthGuard IT shared his screen. "This is exactly why we recommended our vendor risk assessment program last quarter. We're seeing similar patterns across their other integration points."

1130 Hours - Project Impact

The team reviewed their active projects: - 12 major developments affected - 8 government contracts compromised - 15 commercial projects exposed - 4 healthcare facilities impacted - Multiple NDAs violated

"Some of these are secure facilities," David noted. "Hospitals, government buildings, tech companies... they all had specific security requirements."

"Requirements we promised to meet," Jennifer reminded them. "Through our entire supply chain."

Dr. Chen from CyberForensics interjected, "We're seeing evidence that ArchRender Pro's compromise may have started even earlier than they're admitting. Our initial forensics suggests at least three weeks of suspicious activity."

1145 Hours - Damage Assessment

Andrew's client impact analysis was grim: - Medical center threatening contract termination - Government projects under review - Three clients demanding immediate answers - Multiple potential lawsuits - Reputation damage spreading

"The medical center contract alone is worth $40 million," James said. "And their lawyer is already talking about negligent vendor management."

"HealthGuard IT can provide documentation of our security recommendations," Marcus offered. "Including the vendor risk assessment we proposed."

1200 Hours - Industry Ripples

Patricia's phone buzzed with an industry alert. "ArchRender Pro just sent a mass notification. They're confirming a breach affecting 'select enterprise customers.'"

"Select enterprise customers?" James scoffed. "They're trying to minimize it."

"It's already on industry forums," David added, scanning his phone. "Other firms are checking their renders. This could affect half the major architectural firms in the countr ."

Marcus from HealthGuard IT was already implementing additional monitoring. "We're seeing increased attempts to access your systems through other vendor connections. We're locking down non-essential third-party access."

1215 Hours - Security Reality

The team reviewed their vendor management program: - No formal security assessments - Basic service level agreements - Standard NDAs only - Minimal monitoring - Trust-based access

"We have over 30 third-party vendors with various levels of access to our systems," Patricia reported. "How many others did we just... trust?"

"CyberForensics is building a complete vendor access map," Dr. Chen said. "We need to understand the full scope of potential exposure points."

1230 Hours - Regulatory Concerns

Jennifer was reviewing their obligations. "Some of these government projects fall under federal regulations. We're required to ensure our entire supply chain meets their security standards."

"Did we document any security reviews?" James asked.

"We documented that we trusted industry-standard vendors," Jennifer replied dryly. "I don't think that's going to be enough."

"HealthGuard IT can help implement a compliant vendor management program," Marcus offered. "We already have the framework in place from our other architectural clients."

1245 Hours - Moving Forward

The team outlined their immediate response plan:

Technical Response: - HealthGuard IT implementing enhanced monitoring - CyberForensics conducting detailed investigation - Vendor access restrictions in place - System-wide security review initiated - Access logs under analysis

Client Management: - Project impact assessment - Communication strategy - Security enhancement plan - Compliance documentation - Remediation timeline

1300 Hours - Response Coordination

"Here's where we stand," Marcus from HealthGuard IT reported. "We've: - Restricted all vendor access points - Enhanced monitoring across all systems - Implemented emergency access controls - Started comprehensive log analysis - Deployed additional security measures"

Dr. Chen added, "CyberForensics has begun forensic imaging of affected systems. We're prioritizing the medical center project data to understand the full scope of exposure."

1315 Hours - Moving Forward

The team drafted their response plan:

Immediate Actions: - Revoke ArchRender Pro access - Notify all affected clients - Document exposure scope - Continue forensic investigation - Begin vendor audit

Next Steps: - New vendor security protocols - Supply chain assessment - Access control overhaul - Monitoring enhancement - Compliance documentation

1330 Hours - Hard Lessons

"You know what's ironic?" David said, looking at their vendor list. "We spend months vetting vendors on their design capabilities, their pricing, their industry reputation..."

"But five minutes on security," Patricia finished. "Just checking the box that they're 'industry standard.'"

"That's why we recommend continuous vendor monitoring," Marcus noted. "Security isn't a one-time assessment."

1345 Hours - Industry Wake-Up

James was reviewing an urgent message from their professional association. Other firms were reporting similar exposures. The industry's casual approach to vendor security was having consequences.

"We're not the only ones who trusted blindly," he said. "But we might be one of the first to pay the price.

Dr. Chen shared preliminary findings. "The attack pattern suggests this was a targeted campaign against architectural firms. Your industry's intellectual property is becoming increasingly valuable to threat actors."

1400 Hours - Path Forward

The team gathered for one final planning session. James addressed them:

"We built our reputation on attention to detail - every line, every measurement, every specificati n perfect. But we overlooked the security of the tools we used to create them."

Patricia nodded. "We treated vendor security like a checkbox instead of a critical design element."

"Moving forward," Marcus added, "HealthGuard IT will help implement a comprehensive vendor risk management program. We'll integrate it with your existing design review process."

"And CyberForensics will provide a complete incident analysis," Dr. Chen concluded. "Including recommendations for preventing similar incidents across your vendor ecosystem."

The team nodded in agreement. In architecture, as in security, assuming something is sound without verification isn't professional practice - it's professional negligence.

PART 2: TECHNICAL DEEP DIVE

1. Investigation Timeline:

0900-0930: Pre-Detection Phase

- HealthGuard IT monitoring alerts triggered
- Anomalous data transfers detected
- Access pattern changes identifie
- System alerts generated
- Log entries recorded
- Resource utilization spikes noted

0930-1030: Initial Response

- HealthGuard IT team activation
- Alert verification complete
- DIS Risk Solutions notifie
- CyberForensics engagement initiated
- Team mobilization
- Preliminary assessment
- Initial containment measures

1030-1400: Full Investigation

- CyberForensics analysis underway
- HealthGuard IT security review
- Scope analysis completed
- Project data review
- Access audit performed
- Client notification proces
- Recovery planning initiated

2. Technical Analysis:

Attack Vector Identificatio
Vendor Vulnerabilities:
- Excessive access privileges
- Unmonitored data transfers
- Default security settings
- Limited access controls
- Inadequate monitoring
- Missing security protocols
- Insufficient access loggin

Access Methods:
- Legitimate vendor credentials
- Authorized system access
- Standard API calls
- Normal file transfer
- Trusted connections
- Automated data extraction
- Batch processing abuse

3. Infrastructure Analysis

Service Integration:
- Cloud rendering platform
- File sharing systems
- Project management tools
- Collaboration software
- Design applications
- HealthGuard IT monitoring
- CyberForensics tools

Affected Systems:
- Design file storag
- Project databases
- Client communications
- Specifications repositor
- Collaboration platforms
- Access control systems
- Security monitoring tools

4. Impact Assessment

Data Exposure:
- Architectural designs
- Building specification
- Security layouts
- Client communications
- Project timelines
- Infrastructure plans
- Cost estimates

Business Impact:
- $40M medical center contract at risk
- 8 government projects compromised
- 15 commercial projects exposed
- 4 healthcare facilities affected
- Multiple NDA violations
- Client trust damaged
- Industry reputation impacted

5. Security Control Analysis

Missing Controls:
- Vendor security assessments
- Access monitoring

- Data transfer limits
- Security requirements
- Compliance verificatio
- Change management
- Incident response procedures

Failed Safeguards:
- Basic vendor vetting
- Standard NDAs
- Trust-based access
- Minimal monitoring
- Limited auditing
- Inadequate logging
- Default configuration

6. Recovery Complexity

Technical Challenges:
- Multiple vendor integrations
- Complex access patterns
- Data sovereignty issues
- Compliance requirements
- Client specification
- System dependencies
- Access control implementation

Implementation Constraints:
- Limited IT resources
- Time pressure
- Client demands
- Regulatory requirements
- Industry standards
- Operational continuity
- Project deadlines

7. Forensic Investigation

Evidence Collection:
- HealthGuard IT monitoring data
- CyberForensics analysis
- Access logs
- Data transfer records
- System configuration
- Vendor communications
- Client documentation

Analysis Findings:
- Breach timeline reconstruction
- Access pattern identificatio
- Data movement tracking
- Tool signature analysis
- Impact scope determination
- Vulnerability mapping
- Control failure analysis

8. DIS Risk Solutions Coordination

Initial Response:
- Incident verificatio
- Partner activation
- Evidence preservation
- Documentation requirements
- Client communication
- Carrier notificatio
- Recovery planning

Partner Integration:

HealthGuard IT:
- Security monitoring
- Access control
- System hardening
- Vendor management
- Ongoing protection

CyberForensics:
- Incident investigation
- Evidence collection
- Timeline analysis
- Impact assessment
- Recovery guidance

9. Solution Development

Technical Response:
- HealthGuard IT security implementation
- CyberForensics investigation
- Vendor access review
- Security enhancement
- Monitoring improvement
- Access control upgrade
- Documentation development

Implementation Strategy:

Phase 1 - Immediate Response:
- Access restriction
- Evidence preservation
- Partner activation
- Initial containment

- Client notificatio
- Documentation initiation
- Team coordination

Phase 2 - Investigation:
- Forensic analysis
- Impact assessment
- Data mapping
- Vendor review
- Compliance check
- Evidence collection
- Documentation completion

Phase 3 - Recovery:
- Security enhancement
- Process improvement
- Training development
- Partner integration
- Long-term monitoring
- Documentation update
- Trust rebuilding

10. Risk Analysis

Coverage Assessment:
- Cyber policy response
- Incident investigation
- Client notificatio
- Regulatory compliance
- Legal support
- Business interruption
- Future protection

Security Enhancement:
- Vendor security controls
- Access management
- Monitoring capabilities
- Configuration standard
- Staff training
- Process development
- Partner integration

Future Requirements:
- Enhanced security measures
- Continuous monitoring
- Regular assessments
- Partner coordination
- Coverage maintenance
- Process refinemen
- Security validation

Long-term Protection:
- Security program development
- Vendor management enhancement
- Access control improvement
- Partner integration
- Coverage alignment
- Regular testing
- Continuous improvement

PART 3: IMPLEMENTATION GUIDE

1. IMPACT ASSESSMENT

Financial Impact: Direct Costs: - $40M medical center contract at risk - $2.5M response costs - $750,000 CyberForensics investigation - $250,000 HealthGuard IT emergency measures Indirect Costs: - Potential Future Losses: $85M+ in contracts - Recovery Costs: $1.2M estimated - Enhanced Security Implementation: $500,000

Insurance Implications: - Primary Coverage: $5M cyber liability policy through DIS Risk Solutions - Retention/Deductible: $50K per cyber incident - Coverage Triggers: • Data breach • System compromise • Third-party security incident • Business interruption • Cyber extortion - Notification Timeline: • 24 hours for initial incident report • 48 hours for detailed assessment • 72 hours for remediation plan - Claims Process: • DIS Risk Solutions coordination • CyberForensics investigation • HealthGuard IT documentation - Expected Coverage: • Incident response costs • Forensic investigation • Client notifications • Legal defense • Business interruption - Additional Notes: • Professional liability policy coordination • Vendor liability assessment • Regulatory compliance support

Systems Affected: Primary Systems: - Design file storage - Project databases - Rendering systems - Client portals - Collaboration platforms - HealthGuard IT monitoring - Access control systems

Secondary Systems: - Email communications - Document management - Version control - Backup systems - Security monitoring - Vendor integration points - Logging systems

Business Interruption: Duration: - Critical phase: 72 hours - Investigation phase: 14 days - Total recovery: 45 days Impact Scope: - 39 projects affected - 175 employees impacted - 30+ vendors to review - Multiple clients affected - Industry reputation damaged

2. TECHNICAL RESPONSE

Immediate Actions: - HealthGuard IT emergency protocols - CyberForensics activation - Vendor access suspension - Evidence preservation - Client data assessment - DIS Risk Solutions notificatio

Investigation Steps: - CyberForensics analysis - HealthGuard IT log review - Data exposure mapping - Vendor security assessment - Compliance verification - Impact evaluatio

Solution Development: - Enhanced monitoring implementation - Vendor security framework - Access control matrix - Documentation protocols - Compliance measures - Integration security controls

3. IMPLEMENTATION TIMELINE

Immediate (0-72 hours): Hour 1-12: - HealthGuard IT emergency response - CyberForensics deployment - Initial containment measures Hour 12-24: - Preliminary assessment - Insurance notification - Critical client communication Hour 24-48: - Detailed investigation - Vendor access review - Security enhancement initiation Hour 48-72: - Framework development - Client briefings - Documentation compilation

Short-term (1-14 days): Day 1-3: - Complete security assessment - Vendor risk evaluation - Client impact analysis Day 4-7: - Security framework implementation - Process restructuring - Training initiation Day 8-14: - Enhanced monitoring deployment - Documentation completion - Client trust rebuilding

Long-term (15-45 days): Week 3-4: - Comprehensive security implementation - Vendor re-assessment - Process refinement Week 5-6: - Training completion - Documentation finalization - Client relationship restoration

4. KEY TAKEAWAYS

Business Lessons: - Vendor security verification critical - Continuous monitoring essential - Professional partnerships valuable - Documentation crucial - Insurance coverage vital

Technical Insights: - HealthGuard IT monitoring fundamental - CyberForensics expertise essential - Access control critical - Vendor assessment necessary - Integration security crucial

Process Improvements: - Vendor assessment protocols - Security requirements - Access management - Monitoring systems - Documentation standards - Partner integration

5. ROI ANALYSIS

Prevention Costs: HealthGuard IT Services: $300,000/year Security Implementation: $250,000 Staff Training: $75,000 Process Development: $125,000 Ongoing Maintenance: $25,000/month Total Prevention Cost: $950,000

Incident Costs: Direct Response: $750,000 CyberForensics Investigation: $500,000 Business Impact: $40M at risk Recovery Efforts: $2.5M Long-term Effects: $85M+ potential Total Incident Cost: $128.75M+

Future Savings: Risk Reduction: $2.5M annually Efficiency Gains: $750,000 annually Prevention Benefits: $1M annually Resource Optimization: $500,000 annually Total Projected Savings: $4.75M annually

6. ACTION CHECKLIST

Immediate Response: □ HealthGuard IT activation □ CyberForensics engagement □ DIS Risk Solutions notification □ Vendor access review □ Evidence preservation □ Client communication

Assessment Tasks: □ Impact analysis □ Vendor evaluation □ Client assessment □ Risk review □ Compliance check □ Security audit

Implementation Steps: □ Framework deployment □ Process implementation □ Training execution □ Documentation completion □ Monitoring setup □ Partner integration

7. C-SUITE COMMUNICATION PROTOCOL

Executive Notification Sequence

Managing Partner (James Hamilton) - Initial incident assessment - Strategic direction - Resource allocation - Client relationships - Recovery oversight

Director of IT Operations (Patricia Morrison) - Technical response coordination - HealthGuard IT liaison - Security implementation - Vendor management - Infrastructure protection

Head of Digital Design (David Parker) - Project impact assessment - Design system security - Technical coordination - Resource management - Implementation oversight

Legal Counsel (Jennifer Wu) - Regulatory compliance - Client obligations - Contract review - Documentation oversight - Legal response

Client Relations Director (Andrew Collins) - Client communication - Stakeholder management - Reputation protection - Status updates - Trust restoration

Partner Communication:

HealthGuard IT (Marcus Chen) - Security monitoring - Technical response - System protection - Vendor assessment - Implementation support

CyberForensics (Dr. Sarah Chen) - Investigation management - Evidence collection - Analysis coordination - Recovery guidance - Future prevention

DIS Risk Solutions (Damian Davis) - Insurance coordination - Claims management - Coverage optimization - Risk assessment - Long-term protection

Communication Templates: - Initial Notification - Status Updates - Client Briefings - Vendor Communications - Team Updates - Partner Coordination

Decision Matrix: - Incident Classification Criteria - Response Escalation Guidelines - Vendor Access Authority - Client Notification Triggers - Recovery Milestones - Reinstatement Criteria

Chapter 12

The Integrated Defense

PART 1A: NARRATIVE CASE STUDY

Company Profile: Summit Resorts & Casino Group Annual Revenue: $7.2B Industry: Integrated Resort & Casino Operations Properties: 8 luxury resort/casino complexes Employees: 15,000 (across all properties)

Operations: - Casino Gaming Operations - Hotel/Guest Services - Entertainment Venues - Restaurant/Food Services (20+ venues per property) - Event/Conference Centers - Spa/Recreation Facilities - High-End Retail - VIP Services

Digital Footprint: - Casino Management Systems - Gaming Floor Operations - High-Roller Database - Mobile Check-in/Guest Services - Payment Processing Systems - Guest WiFi Networks - Building Automation - Surveillance Systems - Loyalty Program (2M+ members) - Third-party Integration - Online Booking Platforms - Player Tracking Systems

2100 Hours - Summit Las Vegas, Security Operations Center

Daniel Crawford, Director of Cybersecurity Operations, was monitoring the SOC dashboard during the resort's biggest weekend of the year. The championship fight was starting in two hours, the casino floor was packed, and all 3,000 rooms were booked.

That's when multiple alerts started triggering simultaneously.

"Sir," called Lauren Bishop, SOC Team Lead. "We're seeing anomalies across different systems: - Casino floor gaming terminals showing connection errors - Hotel room key system reporting validation issues - Payment processing delays at restaurants - Building automation system acting erratic - Surveillance cameras dropping offline in sections

Daniel's blood ran cold. One system having issues was a problem. Multiple systems showing anomalies during their highest-revenue weekend? That was an attack. He immediately activated their incident response plan, which included an automatic notification to Damian Davis at DIS Risk Solutions, their cyber insurance partner.

2115 Hours - Initial Response

The crisis team assembled in the SOC: - Daniel Crawford - Cybersecurity Operations - Lauren Bishop - SOC Lead - Robert Mitchell - Casino Operations Director - Victoria Hayes - Hotel Manager - Marcus Wong - IT Infrastructure - Amanda Pierce - Risk Management - Damian Davis - DIS Risk Solutions (via secure video) - Rachel Torres - DIS Risk Solutions Claims Specialist (via secure video)

"Give me the scope," Robert demanded, watching his casino floor monitors.

"It's not just one system," Lauren reported. "We're seeing coordinated probes across our entire infrastructure. Someone's testing our defenses. All of them. At once."

"I'm activating CyberGuard Solutions," Damian announced. "They're our designated incident response partner under your policy. DataDefend's forensics team is also being deployed."

2130 Hours - Threat Assessment

"They picked their timing well," Victoria noted grimly. "Championship fight night. Every room booked. Casino at peak capacity. Restaurants full. And..." she checked her watch, "ninety minutes until the main event starts."

Marcus pulled up the infrastructure map. "We're seeing attacks against: - Gaming floor network - Hotel management systems - Payment processing - Building controls - Security cameras - Guest databases"

"And our high-roller data?" Robert asked.

"That's the thing," Lauren interjected. "The attacks are probing but not penetrating. Like they're mapping our defenses."

Rachel Torres from DIS Risk Solutions was already coordinating with their partners: "CyberGuard Solutions is deploying their casino-specific incident response team. They've handled similar attacks at other properties."

2145 Hours - Escalating Situation

Amanda's phone buzzed. "Gaming Commission is asking why our automated reporting feed stopped. We have 15 minutes to restore it or they'll require a floor shutdown.

"We've got bigger problems," Marcus said. "Temperature controls in the main casino are failing. It's going to get hot in there fast."

"And the championship fight starts in an hour," Robert added. "With 20,000 people in the arena."

Mark Stevens, DIS Risk Solutions' Risk Analyst, joined the call: "Based on the attack pattern, this could trigger multiple coverage sections under your policy. We need to document everything for potential business interruption claims."

2150 Hours - Insurance Notification

"I'm sending formal notice to all carriers on your insurance tower," Rachel Torres announced. "With potential exposure across multiple properties and systems, we need to send notice to the entire $1B cyber insurance program."

"Given the scale," she continued. "They'll definitely want insight on potential business interruption exposure from the fight night revenue.

"Good call," Damian agreed. "Mark, start documenting revenue projections for tonight. The carriers will need baseline numbers for any business interruption calculations."

2200 Hours - Pattern Recognition

Daniel studied the attack patterns. "This isn't random. Look at the sequence: 1. Probe gaming systems during peak play 2. Test hotel controls during full occupancy 3. Disrupt climate when crowds are highest 4. Target surveillance during maximum capacity"

"They're stress-testing our systems," Lauren realized. "Finding our breaking points."

"Or creating chaos," Victoria suggested. "What better time to hit a casino than when everything's already stretched to the limit?"

Damian from DIS Risk Solutions added, "We're seeing similar patterns at other properties in our portfolio. This could be part of a coordinated attack on the gaming industry. I'm activating our multi-property response protocol."

PART 1B: NARRATIVE CASE STUDY

2215 Hours - Industry Experience

"CyberGuard Solutions' team is connecting now," Damian reported. "They've handled casino attacks across multiple jurisdictions. Dr. Sarah Chen, their lead investigator, will coordinate with your team."

Dr. Chen's face appeared on screen. "We're seeing signs of sophisticated pre-planning. The attackers knew exactly when to probe each system for maximum impact."

"And maximum leverage," Mark Stevens added. "Fight nights are your highest revenue periods. The potential business impact makes this a prime target."

2230 Hours - Global Response

Daniel initiated an emergency call with counterparts at other major properties: Platinum Dragon Resort (Macau) Sovereign Crown Resort (Melbourne) Azure Lotus Casino (Singapore) Coral Crest Resort (Bahamas)

"We're all seeing the same pattern," Platinum Dragon's CISO confirmed. "Sophisticated attacks during peak operations, targeting player rating systems and high-roller data."

"First time we've seen coordination like this," Azure Lotus's security director added. "Usually it's individual properties, individual crews..."

2245 Hours - Pattern Analysis

Lauren mapped the attack timeline across properties: Summit Las Vegas: Fight night Platinum Dragon: Tournament final Sovereign Crown: Race day Azure Lotus: Holiday weekend Coral Crest: Celebrity event

"Each property was targeted during signature events," she explained. "Not just peak times, but events drawing specific high-value guests.

"They're after the whales," Robert realized. "High-net-worth players who move between properties."

2300 Hours - Threat Evolution

"The attackers are getting more sophisticated," Dr. Chen reported. "They're: Cross-referencing guest lists between properties Mapping high-roller travel patterns Correlating player rating data Analyzing credit line histories Building comprehensive profiles

"They're not just after tonight's data," Damian observed. "They're building a blueprint of the entire VIP gaming ecosystem."

2315 Hours - Industry Vulnerability

The international call continued as each property reported findings

Platinum Dragon: "Our player rating systems showed subtle modific - tions going back three weeks."

Sovereign Crown: "Credit algorithms were tweaked to gradually increase limits."

Azure Lotus: "Comp calculations were modified to inflate player values."

Coral Crest: "High-roller database shows unauthorized access patterns."

Rachel Torres was documenting everything. "This level of coordination changes the exposure calculation completely. We're looking at potential impact across multiple properties, jurisdictions, and regulatory frameworks."

2330 Hours - Coordinated Defense

The properties agreed on joint protective measures:

Summit Las Vegas (Daniel): "We're implementing a unified defense protocol: Standardized monitoring Shared threat indicators Real-time alerts Coordinated response Joint investigation"

"CyberGuard Solutions will coordinate security measures across all properties," Damian added. "DataDefend's forensics team will handle the technical investigation."

2345 Hours - High-Stakes Reality

Amanda returned with updated exposure analysis: Combined player values: $500B+ Annual comp potential: $75B Credit lines: $250B Guest data value: Incalculable Industry reputation: Priceless

Mark Stevens was already calculating potential coverage implications. "With these numbers, we need to consider triggering multiple coverage sections across different properties."

0000 Hours - Industry Evolution

Lauren identified a critical pattern: "Each property's individual security worked as designed. It's the interconnected systems that were vulnerable: Inter-property comp programs Shared player ratings Cross-property credit VIP transfer protocols Global loyalty benefits

"The very features that make us competitive," Victoria observed, "also make us vulnerable."

"This is why we recommended the integrated security assessment last quarter," Damian noted. "These connection points need enterprise-level protection."

0015 Hours - Paradigm Shift

"The industry's changing," Daniel addressed the international team. "We built these connected systems to serve our global players, but we're still protecting them like individual properties."

Robert nodded. "Our highest-value players expect to: Move seamlessly between properties Access credit globally Transfer comps internationally Receive consistent recognition Experience unified service

"And the attackers," Dr. Chen added, "are using these connections against us."

0030 Hours - Future Framework

The properties began outlining a new Industry approach, with DIS Risk Solutions facilitating the collaboration:

Summit Las Vegas proposed: International security standards Unified monitoring systems Shared threat intelligence Joint response protocols Coordinated investigations

"We need to think about coverage that spans properties and jurisdictions," Rachel noted. "The traditional property-by-property approach doesn't fit this new realit ."

0045 Hours – Industry Transformation

"This isn't just about tonight," Daniel explained to the group. "This is about recognizing that we're no longer just individual properties. We're a connected global industry."

Victoria agreed. "Our guests move seamlessly between properties. Our security needs to do the same."

"But with one critical difference," Mark Stevens added. "Unlike our guests, our security can't have any gaps between properties. The coverage needs to be as integrated as the operations."

0100 Hours - New Dawn

As the Las Vegas strip's lights continued to shine, the team began implementing their new integrated strategy:

Physical Security Integration: Synchronized surveillance Coordinated floor operations Unified access controls Joint security protocols Shared threat responses

Digital Defense Coordination: Real-time system monitoring Cross-property alerts Integrated data protection Unified authentication Global threat detection

"This is the future of gaming industry security," Damian concluded. "Individual excellence, collectively coordinated."

0115 Hours - Risk Assessment

"Let's quantify what we've learned," Rachel Torres suggested. "Each property's exposure is now directly linked to the others."

Mark Stevens shared his analysis: Traditional risks: Individual property losses New reality: Cascading impacts across properties Old model: Property-specific coverage Current need: Enterprise-wide protection Future requirement: Industry-wide coordination

0130 Hours - Regulatory Landscape

Amanda coordinated with gaming authorities across jurisdictions while Damian facilitated multi-state insurance compliance.

"The regulators are watching closely," Amanda reported. "They're particularly interested in: Cross-border data flows Player protection measures Financial system integrity Compliance coordination International cooperation"

0145 Hours - Strategic Implementation

Dr. Chen from CyberGuard Solutions outlined their enhanced protection strategy: Real-time threat sharing between properties Unified incident response procedures Coordinated containment measures Integrated investigation protocols Synchronized recovery processes

"We're creating a security ecosystem," Daniel noted, "that matches our operational ecosystem."

0200 Hours - Industry Standards

The international team began formalizing their approach:

Technical Integration: Shared monitoring platforms Common security protocols Unified access controls Standardized alerts Integrated response systems

Operational Coordination: Cross-property communications Joint security operations Synchronized responses Unified protocols Shared intelligence

0300 Hours - Protection Framework

"Here's what we've built tonight," Daniel addressed the team, as Damian nodded in agreement:

Immediate Protection: Active threat monitoring Real-time response capabilities Cross-property coordination Integrated defense measures Unified security protocol

Long-term Security: Industry-wide standards Shared best practices Coordinated responses International cooperation Integrated protection

0400 Hours - Future Vision

The team reviewed their transformed security landscape:

Operational Changes: From isolated to integrated security From property-specific to enterprise-wide protection From reactive to proactive defense From individual to coordinated response From local to global security

"This is more than just a technical solution," Damian observed. "It's a complete paradigm shift in how we approach gaming industry security."

0500 Hours - New Beginning

As the first light began to appear over the desert horizon, the team had established a new security framework:

Immediate Implementation: Integrated monitoring across all properties Coordinated response protocols Unified security standards Cross-property protection Global threat detection

"Tonight changed everything," Daniel concluded, looking at the assembled faces on his screen. "We came in thinking like individual properties..."

"And emerged as a unified force," Damian finished. "This is how we protect the future of gaming - together."

PART 1C: NARRATIVE CASE STUDY

0515 Hours - Industry Innovation

Daniel addressed the international team: "Tonight showed us something crucial. The old model of individual property security is obsolete. Our attackers are coordinated - we need to be too."

"This is why enterprise-level protection is so critical," Damian added. "The gaming industry needs coverage that matches its operational complexity."

The properties agreed on immediate actions: - Creating an industry-wide SOC - Establishing shared security standards - Developing unified response protocols - Building integrated monitoring systems - Implementing cross-property authentication

0530 Hours - Regulatory Evolution

Amanda reported from her regulatory discussions: "Gaming authorities are already adapting: - New inter-jurisdiction frameworks - Combined investigation protocols - Shared compliance standards - Unified reporting requirements - International cooperation agreements"

"They see it too," Robert noted. "The industry's evolution demands regulatory evolution."

Rachel Torres was already working on documentation. "We'll need to adjust coverage structures to match these new regulatory frameworks."

0545 Hours - Recovery Phase

As the Las Vegas strip continued to glitter in the pre-dawn darkness, the team assessed their position:

Immediate Containment: - Attack patterns identified and blocked - Player rating systems verified - Credit algorithms restored - Comp calculations corrected - VIP data secured

Long-term Impact: - No guest data compromised - Gaming integrity maintained - Financial systems protected - Regulatory compliance preserved - Industry reputation intact

"CyberGuard Solutions' coordinated response made the difference," Damian observed. "This is why we partner with enterprise-level security providers."

0600 Hours - Lessons Learned

In the still-dark SOC, the international team conducted their final briefing

Daniel: "This attack targeted our industry's greatest strength - our interconnectedness. But that same interconnectedness is now becoming our best defense."

Lauren: "We've identified over 200 attack vectors that crossed property boundaries. Traditional property-by-property security would have missed most of them."

Mark Stevens: "And the coverage implications are clear - we need to structure protection that crosses those same boundaries."

0615 Hours - Industry Transformation

Under the artificial daylight of the casino floo , the properties formalized their new alliance:

Summit Las Vegas would lead: - Technology integration - Security standardization - Response coordination - Threat intelligence - Training development

"DIS Risk Solutions will help structure the insurance framework," Damian explained. "We'll create coverage that supports this new integrated approach."

0630 Hours - New Beginning

As the night shift dealers began their final hands and early morning staff started arriving, Daniel gathered his team for a final assessment

"Tonight changed everything," he said, watching the casino's 24/7 operation continue seamlessly, guests completely unaware of the battle that had been fought. "We're not just protecting buildings anymore. We're protecting an ecosystem."

"And insuring it accordingly," Rachel added. "The coverage needs to be as seamless as the operations."

0645 Hours - Morning Operations

The casino floor remained busy with late-night players and early morning arrivals, the controlled chaos of a major resort property masking the night's events.

Victoria reviewed the guest impact: "Not a single complaint about systems issues. The manual protocols worked perfectly."

"Because everyone did their part," Robert added, watching his pit crews smoothly handling the shift change. "From housekeeping to high-limit hosts, everyone executed their role in the response plan."

"This is why we emphasize integrated training," Damian noted. "Security, operations, and risk management all have to work together."

0700 Hours - Shift Change

As the morning shift arrived, Daniel briefed the incoming security team: - New monitoring protocols - Enhanced verification procedures - Cross-property alerts - Integrated response plans - Updated threat indicators

"We're not just passing on information," he explained. "We're passing on a new security paradigm."

Mark Stevens added, "The coverage framework will reflect these new protocols. Protection has to evolve with the threat landscape."

0715 Hours - Future Framework

The team gathered for their final meeting before handover

Amanda outlined the new reality: "We operate in: - Multiple jurisdictions – Different time zones – Various cultures – Diverse markets – Connected systems

But now we protect them as one."

"And insure them as one," Rachel emphasized. "No more gaps between properties or jurisdictions."

0730 Hours – Industry Standard

Lauren pulled up the new unified security dashboard, showing real-time data from all properties: - Player verification status - System integrity checks - Cross-property alerts - Integrated monitoring - Global threat indicators

"This is what integrated defense looks like," she explained. "Every property, every system, every threat - visible and manageable from any security operations center."

"And fully supported by your coverage," Damian added. "The insurance now matches the integration."

0745 Hours - Breakfast Meeting

In a private dining room overlooking the still-bustling casino floo , the executive team gathered to brief the CEO, Katherine Morrison, who had flown in overnight

"Walk me through what we learned," she said, as Robert pulled up the final numbers: - Gaming revenue: Unaffected - Guest experience:

Maintained - Systems integrity: Preserved - Data security: Protected - Industry impact: Transformative

"DIS Risk Solutions' enterprise approach proved crucial," Daniel noted. "Having the right partners made all the difference."

0800 Hours - Executive Insight

Katherine absorbed the briefing. "So they tried to use our greatest strength - our interconnected operations - as a weakness?"

"Yes," Daniel confirmed. "But instead, it became the catalyst for something bigger. The industry's first truly integrated defense system.

"Which we needed anyway," Rachel added. "Our coverage strategy has been pointing toward this for months. The attack just accelerated the timeline."

0815 Hours - Future Vision

Katherine outlined the group's new direction: "We're going to: - Lead industry security standards - Pioneer integrated defense - Set compliance benchmarks - Define best practices - Shape regulatory framework"

"Because someone has to," Damian noted. "And we just proved it works."

0830 Hours - Industry Leadership

The team reviewed commitments from other major properties worldwide: - Technology sharing agreements - Joint response protocols - Unified security standards - Shared threat intelligence - Combined training programs

"The industry was ready for this," Robert observed. "They were just waiting for someone to take the first step.

"And now we have a framework to support it," Mark Stevens added. "Both operationally and from a risk management perspective."

0845 Hours - Regulatory Impact

Amanda returned from a call with the Gaming Commission. "They're impressed. Not just with our response, but with the industry-wide initiative. They're talking about: - New security standards - Cross-jurisdiction protocols - International cooperation - Unified compliance frameworks - Integrated monitoring requirements"

"For once," Daniel noted, "we're ahead of the regulations instead of reacting to them."

"That's what enterprise-level protection looks like," Damian agreed. "Proactive, not reactive."

0900 Hours - Morning Review

As the morning sun finally began to peek through the desert haze, Katherine led the final assessment

Immediate Outcomes: - Attack thwarted - Systems secured - Data protected - Operations maintained - Guest experience preserved

Long-term Impact: - Industry transformation - Enhanced cooperation - Unified standards - Integrated defense - Global protectio

"This becomes a model for domestic gaming operations," Rachel noted. "We'll work with each property to align coverage with their specific regulatory requirements."

0915 Hours - Paradigm Shift

Robert watched the morning players filling the casino floo . "You know what's remarkable? None of our guests know what happened last night."

"That's the point," Victoria replied. "True security is invisible to those we protect."

"But now it's visible to those who would threaten us," Lauren added, monitoring the new integrated security dashboard. "Every property working in coordination, while respecting their local requirements."

0930 Hours - Future Framework

Katherine gathered the team for their final insights

"Last night proved something crucial," she began. "In today's connected world, isolation is not security - it's vulnerability. We succeed or fail as an ecosystem."

Daniel pulled up the new security metrics: - Real-time cross-property monitoring - Integrated threat detection - Unified response protocols - Synchronized security operations - Global incident management

"Each property maintains its sovereignty," Damian added, "while benefiting from collective defense.

0945 Hours - Industry Evolution

Amanda shared feedback from other properties: "They're all seeing what we saw: - Individual security isn't enough - Threats cross boundaries - Attackers exploit gaps - Integration is essential - Unity is strength"

"The old model of property-by-property security," Robert observed, "died last night."

Mark Stevens nodded. "While maintaining compliance with each jurisdiction's unique requirements."

1000 Hours - Moving Forward

The team outlined their next steps:

Immediate Implementation: - Deploy integrated monitoring - Establish unified protocols - Launch joint training - Coordinate responses - Share intelligence

Long-term Development: - Build common standards where possible - Create shared platforms within regulatory bounds - Develop regional frameworks - Establish best practices - Lead domestic regulatory evolution

1015 Hours - Cultural Shift

Katherine addressed the expanded team, now including representatives from IT, Operations, and Guest Services:

"For years, we've competed on everything - amenities, rewards, experiences. But security? That's where we collaborate, while respecting each property's unique market and regulatory requirements."

Victoria nodded. "Our guests choose properties based on luxury and service..."

"But they trust us all equally with their data, their privacy, their security," Daniel completed.

1030 Hours - Operational Integration

The new normal was taking shape:

Gaming Floor: - Enhanced monitoring - Integrated verification - Cross-property tracking - Unified player protection - Synchronized securit

Hotel Operations: - Coordinated systems - Shared security protocols - Unified guest protection - Integrated monitoring - Combined threat response

"Each property maintains its unique identity," Damian observed, "while participating in collective defense appropriate to their jurisdiction."

1045 Hours - Industry Standard

Lauren demonstrated the new integrated command center: "Each property can now: - Share threat intelligence in real-time - Coordinate response efforts - Monitor cross-property patterns - Track suspicious activities - Deploy unified defenses

"Making us stronger together," Robert noted, "while maintaining our unique identities and regulatory compliance."

"The coverage adapts to each property's specific needs," Rachel added, "while supporting the broader security framework."

1100 Hours - Final Assessment

As the morning wore on, Katherine made her closing observations:

"Last night, we faced a choice - continue operating as isolated properties or evolve into something stronger. We chose evolution. And in doing so, we didn't just protect our assets..."

"We transformed our approach to security," Daniel finished

"While creating a model that respects each property's unique requirements," Damian concluded.

The team looked out over the bustling casino floo , where guests continued their games, unaware that the very nature of their protection had fundamentally changed overnight.

In the world of integrated resorts, the game had changed. Security was no longer about walls and boundaries - it was about connections and cooperation, thoughtfully implemented across diverse regulatory landscapes. The future wasn't about standing alone - it was about standing together, each property maintaining its sovereignty while contributing to collective defense.

PART 2: TECHNICAL DEEP DIVE

1. Investigation Timeline:

2000-2100: Pre-Detection Phase

- CyberGuard Solutions monitoring alerts triggered
- Cross-property anomalies detected
- Player rating system irregularities identifie
- Gaming floor alerts generate
- Access pattern changes recorded
- Resource utilization spikes noted

2100-2200: Initial Response

- CyberGuard Solutions team activation
- Alert verification complete
- DIS Risk Solutions notifie
- DataDefend engagement initiated
- Team mobilization
- Preliminary assessment
- Initial containment measures

2200-1100: Full Investigation

- DataDefend analysis underway
- CyberGuard Solutions security review
- Scope analysis completed
- Cross-property data review
- Access audit performed
- Regulatory notification proces
- Recovery planning initiated

2. Technical Analysis:

Attack Vector Identification System Vulnerabilities:
- Cross-property integration points
- Inter-casino communication channels
- Shared player databases
- Connected loyalty systems
- Unified payment processin
- Default security settings
- Insufficient access loggin

Access Methods:
- Legitimate system credentials
- Authorized API access
- Standard data transfers
- Normal payment processing
- Trusted connections
- Automated player tracking
- Batch processing systems

3. Infrastructure Analysis

Service Integration:
- Casino Management Systems
- Player Rating Platforms
- Payment Processing Networks
- Loyalty Program Infrastructure
- Gaming Floor Systems
- CyberGuard Solutions monitoring
- DataDefend tools

Affected Systems:
- High-roller databases
- Credit management systems

- Player tracking platforms
- Payment processing networks
- Surveillance systems
- Access control systems
- Security monitoring tools

4. Impact Assessment

Data Exposure:
- Player profile
- Gaming histories
- Credit information
- VIP data
- Transaction records
- Security protocols
- Compliance documentation

Business Impact:
- Fight night revenue at risk ($100M+)
- Multiple properties compromised
- International operations affected
- Cross-border compliance issues
- Regulatory requirements violated
- Guest trust damaged
- Industry reputation impacted

5. Security Control Analysis

Missing Controls:
- Cross-property monitoring
- Integrated alerting
- Unified respons
- Coordinated defense
- Joint protocols

- International standards
- Incident response procedures

Failed Safeguards:
- Individual property security
- Isolated monitoring
- Local response plans
- Property-specific control
- Standalone systems
- Basic integration
- Default configuration

6. Recovery Complexity

Technical Challenges:
- Multi-property coordination
- Cross-system integration
- International compliance
- Regulatory requirements
- Cultural considerations
- Time zone management
- Access control implementation

Implementation Constraints:
- Different jurisdictions
- Various regulations
- Multiple languages
- Diverse standards
- Cultural variations
- Operational continuity
- Gaming compliance requirements

7. Forensic Investigation

Evidence Collection:
- CyberGuard Solutions monitoring data
- DataDefend analysis
- Access logs
- Player transaction records
- System configuration
- Cross-property communications
- Regulatory documentation

Analysis Findings:
- Attack timeline reconstruction
- Pattern identificatio
- Data movement tracking
- System vulnerability mapping
- Impact scope determination
- Compliance verificatio
- Control failure analysis

8. DIS Risk Solutions Coordination

Initial Response:
- Incident verificatio
- Partner activation
- Evidence preservation
- Documentation requirements
- Regulatory notificatio
- Carrier notificatio
- Recovery planning

Partner Integration:

CyberGuard Solutions:
- Security monitoring
- Access control
- System hardening
- Cross-property management
- Ongoing protection

DataDefend:
- Incident investigation
- Evidence collection
- Timeline analysis
- Impact assessment
- Recovery guidance

9. Solution Development

Technical Response:
- CyberGuard Solutions security implementation
- DataDefend investigation
- Cross-property access review
- Security enhancement
- Monitoring improvement
- Integration upgrade
- Documentation development

Implementation Strategy:

Phase 1 - Immediate Response:
- Access restriction
- Evidence preservation
- Partner activation
- Initial containment

- Regulatory notificatio
- Documentation initiation
- Team coordination

Phase 2 - Investigation:
- Forensic analysis
- Impact assessment
- Data mapping
- Property review
- Compliance check
- Evidence collection
- Documentation completion

Phase 3 - Recovery:
- Security enhancement
- Process improvement
- Training development
- Partner integration
- Long-term monitoring
- Documentation update
- Trust rebuilding

10. Risk Analysis

Coverage Assessment:
- Cyber policy response
- Multi-property investigation
- Regulatory notificatio
- Compliance verificatio
- Legal support
- Business interruption
- Future protection

Security Enhancement:
- Cross-property security controls
- Access management
- Monitoring capabilities
- Integration standards
- Staff training
- Process development
- Partner integration

Future Requirements:
- Enhanced security measures
- Continuous monitoring
- Regular assessments
- Partner coordination
- Coverage maintenance
- Process refinemen
- Compliance validation

Long-term Protection:
- Security program development
- Cross-property management
- Access control improvement
- Partner integration
- Coverage alignment
- Regular testing
- Continuous improvement

PART 3: IMPLEMENTATION GUIDE

1. IMPACT ASSESSMENT

Financial Impact: Direct Costs: - $100M+ fight night revenue at risk - $5M emergency response costs - $1.5M DataDefend investigation - $750,000 CyberGuard Solutions emergency measures

Indirect Costs: - Potential Future Losses: $500M+ in gaming revenue - Recovery Costs: $15M estimated - Enhanced Security Implementation: $25M

Insurance Implications: Primary Coverage: $1B cyber insurance tower structured as: • Primary Layer: $25M Carrier A: 100% ($25M)

• First Excess: $50M xs $25M Carrier B: 30% ($15M) Carrier C: 25% ($12.5M) Carrier D: 25% ($12.5M) Carrier E: 20% ($10M)

• Second Excess: $50M xs $75M Carrier F: 30% ($15M) Carrier G: 25% ($12.5M) Carrier H: 25% ($12.5M) Carrier I: 20% ($10M)

• Third Excess: $50M xs $125M Carrier J: 35% ($17.5M) Carrier K: 35% ($17.5M) Carrier L: 30% ($15M)

• Fourth Excess: $50M xs $175M Carrier M: 40% ($20M) Carrier N: 35% ($17.5M) Carrier O: 25% ($12.5M)

• Fifth through Twentieth Excess: Each $50M part of $825M xs $175M [Additional carrier participations structured similarly]

Retention/Deductible: $10M per cyber incident • Applies to each and every claim • Annual aggregate retention: $20M • Retention applies across all properties • Time deductible: 24 hours for BI • Maintenance deductible: $1.5M for PCI

- Coverage Triggers: • Multi-property breach • System compromise • Data theft • Business interruption • Regulatory action - Notification Timeline: 12 hours for cyber incidents - Claims Process: Dedicated gaming cyber claims unit with international capabilities - Expected Coverage: • Global incident response • Multi-jurisdiction business interruption • System recovery across properties • International legal defense • Regulatory compliance in all jurisdictions - Additional Coverage Features: • Multi-property aggregate protection • International jurisdiction coverage • Regulatory defense worldwide • Reputation harm coverage • Crisis management expenses

Systems Affected: Primary Systems: - Casino Management - Player Rating - Credit Systems - Payment Processing - Surveillance Networks

Secondary Systems: - Loyalty Programs - Hotel Operations - Food & Beverage - Entertainment Venues - Retail Operations

Business Interruption: Duration: - Critical phase: 14 hours - Total recovery: 30 days

Impact Scope: - 8 properties affected - 15,000 employees impacted - 2M+ loyalty members - Multiple jurisdictions - International operations

2. TECHNICAL RESPONSE

Immediate Actions: - Cross-property system isolation - International team activation - Multi-jurisdiction notification - Evidence preservation across venues - Global incident documentation

Investigation Steps: - Coordinated log review - Multi-property system assessment - International data analysis - Cross-border compliance check - Comprehensive impact evaluation

Solution Development: - Global security framework - International monitoring system - Cross-property protocols - Multi-jurisdiction compliance - Unified response procedure

3. IMPLEMENTATION TIMELINE

Immediate (0-24 hours): Hour 1-6: Global coordination initiation Hour 6-12: Multi-property containment Hour 12-18: International communication Hour 18-24: Cross-border response

Short-term (1-7 days): Day 1-2: Global security implementation Day 3-4: International process alignment Day 5-7: Cross-property training Daily: Multi-jurisdiction updates

Long-term (8-30 days): Week 2: International framework deployment Week 3: Global process refinement Week 4: Cross-border documentation Milestones: International validation

4. KEY TAKEAWAYS

Business Lessons: - International coordination essential - Cross-property integration critical - Global standards necessary - Multi-jurisdiction compliance crucial - Unified response vita

Technical Insights: - Integrated monitoring fundamental - Cross-property coordination essential - International standards critical - Global visibility necessary - Unified controls crucia

Process Improvements: - International security protocols - Cross-property procedures - Global response framework - Multi-jurisdiction compliance - Unified training standard

5. ROI ANALYSIS

Prevention Costs: Technology Investment: $75M Staff Training: $15M Process Implementation: $25M Ongoing Maintenance: $10M/month Total Prevention Cost: $235M annually

Incident Costs: Direct Response: $150M Business Impact: $500M potential Recovery Efforts: $75M Long-term Effects: $1B+ potential Total Incident Cost: $1.725B+ potential

Future Savings: Risk Reduction: $300M annually Efficiency Gains: $50M annually Prevention Benefits: $100M annually Resource Optimization: $75M annually Total Projected Savings: $525M annually

6. ACTION CHECKLIST

Immediate Response: □ Global system assessment □ International team activation □ Cross-property notification □ Multi-jurisdiction evidence collection □ Comprehensive documentation

Assessment Tasks: □ International impact analysis □ Cross-property evaluation □ Global risk assessment □ Multi-jurisdiction review □ Comprehensive compliance check

Implementation Steps: □ Global framework deployment □ International process implementation □ Cross-property training execution □ Multi-jurisdiction documentation □ Unified monitoring setu

7. C-SUITE COMMUNICATION PROTOCOL

Executive Notification Sequence

CEO (Katherine Morrison) - Global incident assessment - Strategic direction - Resource allocation - Property relationships - Recovery oversight

Director of Cybersecurity Operations (Daniel Crawford) - Technical response coordination - CyberGuard Solutions liaison - Security implementation - Cross-property management - Infrastructure protection

Casino Operations Director (Robert Mitchell) - Gaming operations assessment - System integrity verification - Technical coordination - Resource management - Implementation oversight

Legal Counsel (Sarah Chen) - Regulatory compliance - Gaming commission obligations - Multi-jurisdiction review - Documentation oversight - Legal response

Risk Management Director (Amanda Pierce) - Stakeholder communication - Property coordination - Reputation protection - Status updates - Trust maintenance

Partner Communication:

CyberGuard Solutions (Dr. James Chen) - Security monitoring - Technical response - System protection - Property assessment - Implementation support

DataDefend (Dr. Sarah Chen) - Investigation management - Evidence collection - Analysis coordination - Recovery guidance - Future prevention

DIS Risk Solutions (Damian Davis) - Insurance coordination - Claims management - Coverage optimization - Risk assessment - Long-term protection

Communication Templates: - Initial Notification - Status Updates - Property Briefings - Regulatory Communications - Team Updates - Partner Coordination

Decision Matrix: Authority Levels: - Global System Shutdown: CEO/ COO only - Regional Shutdown: Regional VP - Property Shutdown: Property President - System Isolation: CISO/CIO - Department Isolation: Department Head

Notification Triggers: - Multiple Property Impact: Immediate CEO notification - Single Property Major Impact: Regional VP then CEO - Cross-Border Impact: International compliance team - Regulatory Impact: Gaming compliance team - Industry Impact: Industry relations team

Response Escalation: Level 1: Property Level - Local incident response - Property security team - Local compliance - Property management - Local authorities

Level 2: Regional Level - Regional coordination - Multiple properties - Regional compliance - Regional management - Regional authorities

Level 3: International Level - Global coordination - All properties - International compliance - Executive management - Multiple jurisdictions

Recovery Milestones: Phase 1: Immediate Stability - System containment - Threat elimination - Data protection - Operation continuity - Guest service maintenance

Phase 2: Enhanced Security - Cross-property protocols - International standards - Unified monitoring - Global compliance - Industry leadership

Phase 3: Future Prevention - Industry standards development - Global security framework - International cooperation - Cross-border protocols - Unified defense syste

CONCLUSION: THE SECURITY-FIRST ENTERPRISE

Evolution of Threats (2025 and Beyond)

As we've seen through our journey across twelve industries and their cybersecurity challenges, the threat landscape has fundamentally changed. No longer do organizations face isolated incidents targeting specific vulnerabilities. Instead, modern cyber threats are sophisticated, interconnected, and industry-spanning campaigns that exploit the very interconnectedness of our digital economy.

From Chapter 1's examination of zero-day vulnerabilities in financial services to Chapter 12's integrated attack on gaming operations, we've witnessed an evolution in both attack sophistication and defensive requirements:

Historical Progression:
- Single-point vulnerabilities became system-wide exposures
- Local attacks evolved into supply chain compromises
- Individual targets transformed into industry-wide campaigns
- Technical exploits expanded to include human elements
- Isolated incidents grew into coordinated attacks

Emerging Threats:

1. AI-Enhanced Attacks
- Automated vulnerability discovery
- Behavioral pattern exploitation
- Adaptive attack methods
- Intelligent evasion techniques
- Machine learning manipulation

2. Quantum Computing Implications
- Encryption vulnerability
- Authentication risks
- Key distribution challenges
- Algorithm obsolescence
- Security protocol adaptation

3. Supply Chain Complexity
- Vendor network exploitation
- Third-party system compromise
- Integration point vulnerabilities
- Cross-company exposures
- International supply risks

Technology Evolution:

- Integrated monitoring systems require enterprise-wide coordination
- AI-driven threat detection demands organization-wide validation
- Real-time response systems need global synchronization
- Zero-trust architecture requires unified implementatio
- Automated defenses must coordinate across business units

Cross-Industry Collaboration:

- Integrated defense frameworks require industry-wide adoption
- Real-time threat sharing demands standardized protocols
- Insurance coverage needs cross-industry coordination

- Risk transfer strategies require market-wide collaboration
- Collective defense depends on unified response capabilitie

Building Resilient Organizations:
- Security architecture must support organizational agility
- Response capabilities require enterprise-wide integration
- Business continuity demands unified security framework
- Stakeholder confidence builds through consistent performanc
- Industry leadership requires continuous security innovation

Future-Proofing Security:
- Technology adoption requires enterprise-wide security validation
- Threat intelligence needs cross-sector sharing mechanisms
- Security frameworks must scale with organizational growth
- Response capabilities demand continuous enhancement
- Organizational resilience depends on unified security maturit

Regulatory Landscape:
- Global compliance requirements demand integrated approaches
- Privacy regulations require enterprise-wide solutions
- Industry standards need continuous organizational adaptation
- International cooperation shapes unified security requirement
- Regulatory frameworks must enable business innovation

The Path Forward:
- Security investments must align with enterprise strategy
- Risk management requires organizational integration
- Incident response needs enterprise-wide coordination
- Stakeholder trust demands consistent performance
- Market leadership requires security excellence

Final Insights:
- Security success depends on enterprise-wide commitment
- Business resilience requires unified security integratio

- Technology adoption demands comprehensive risk evaluation
- Risk management needs organizational coordination
- Market leadership requires security excellence across operations

Closing Thoughts:

The cybersecurity challenges faced across these twelve industries demonstrate that security is no longer a technical issue but a fundamental business imperative. Organizations that embrace an enterprise-wide security-first approach position themselves not just for survival but for market leadership in an increasingly connected world. The future belongs to those who recognize that security excellence drives business success.

As we've seen through our examination of various industries - from financial services to gaming, from healthcare to manufacturing - the fundamentals of security excellence remain consistent even as their applications vary. The organizations that thrive will be those that understand security as both a strategic imperative and a competitive differentiator.

The lessons learned across these sectors point to an inescapable conclusion: security cannot be an afterthought or a siloed solution. It must be woven into the very fabric of organizational strategy, culture, and operations. As technology continues to evolve and threats become more sophisticated, this integration becomes not just important but essential for survival.

Looking ahead, we see a business landscape where security excellence differentiates leaders from followers. Organizations that master the principles outlined in these chapters - from proactive monitoring to integrated defense, from supply chain security to human factor consideration - will find themselves better positioned to face whatever challenges emerge.

The future of business is inextricably linked with the future of security. As we've demonstrated throughout this book, organizations that recognize and act on this reality will be the ones that thrive in an increasingly connected and complex world. The question is no longer whether to prioritize security, but how to make it an integral part of every business decision and process.

In the end, security excellence is not just about protecting assets - it's about enabling business success, fostering innovation, and building lasting trust. The organizations that understand and embrace this principle will be the ones that lead their industries into the future.

This is the essence of the security-first enterprise: an organization that recognizes security not as a cost center or a constraint, but as a fundamental enabler of business success and sustainable growth. As we look to the future, this understanding will separate the organizations that merely survive from those that truly thrive.

FOREWORD (Technical)

As we navigate an era marked by rapid digital transformation, the attack surface of modern systems has expanded exponentially. In this context, *The Zero Day Files: Cybersecurity Unveiled* stands out as a timely and technically rigorous examination of one of the most persistent and insidious threats in the cyber domain—zero-day vulnerabilities.

This book doesn't merely introduce readers to zero-day exploits; it deconstructs them—analyzing their lifecycle, their market dynamics within the exploit economy, and their strategic utility in both cybercrime and nation-state operations. From sophisticated intrusion sets to advanced persistent threats (APTs), the author dissects real-world scenarios with clarity, offering technical granularity without compromising narrative flo .

What makes this work invaluable is its grounding in practical relevance. Concepts such as privilege escalation, code obfuscation, polymorphic malware, supply chain compromises, and lateral movement techniques are not presented in isolation. Instead, they are contextualized within broader threat intelligence frameworks and modern cybersecurity defense models like Zero Trust Architecture and MITRE ATT&CK.

The book also explores the operational challenges of vulnerability management, the latency of patch cycles, and the critical role of threat hunting and behavior analytics in detecting anomalous activities in real time. Readers will gain a greater appreciation for the strategic value of zero-day intelligence and its implications for incident response, risk assessment, and enterprise security posture.

Whether you're a security engineer, red team operator, SOC analyst, or CISO, The Zero Day Files offers insights that transcend theory and align with the operational realities of defending dynamic and complex infrastructures. It is both a technical deep-dive and a strategic resource for professionals committed to staying ahead of adversaries in an asymmetric digital battlefield

In an age where every system is a potential target and every second counts, the stakes have never been higher. Prepare to engage with the underlying architecture of cyber conflict—and arm yourself with the actionable knowledge needed to defend against evolving threats with precision and foresight.

Armie Shah
Vice President (VP) of Cybersecurity Operations

APPENDIX A

SECURITY IMPLEMENTATION GUIDE 1. Framework Components

1) STRATEGIC RISK & THREAT ASSESSMENT GUIDE

Executive Overview: Understanding and evaluating security risks requires balancing likelihood against business impact. This guide provides a structured approach for both business leaders and technical teams to assess, communicate, and act on security threats.

Key Decision Points: - How likely is the threat to materialize? - What's the potential business impact? - What level of response is required? - Which resources should be allocated?

THREAT ASSESSMENT MATRIX:

IMPACT (x)	Negligible (1)	Minor (2)	Moderate (3)	Major (4)	Catastroph-ic (5)
LIKELI-HOOD (y)					
Almost Certain (5)	MEDIUM	HIGH	HIGH	CRITICAL	CRITICAL
Likely (4)	LOW	MEDIUM	HIGH	HIGH	CRITICAL
Possible (3)	LOW	MEDIUM	MEDIUM	HIGH	HIGH
Unlikely (2)	LOW	LOW	MEDIUM	MEDIUM	HIGH
Rare (1)	LOW	LOW	LOW	MEDIUM	MEDIUM

Business Context:

LIKELIHOOD DEFINITIONS:
Business View: - Almost Certain: Expected multiple times per year - Likely: Expected annually - Possible: May occur within 1-2 years - Unlikely: May occur within 2-5 years - Rare: May occur every 5+ years

Technical View:
- Almost Certain: Active exploitation in wild, known threat actors - Likely: Published exploits, increasing attack trends - Possible: Known vulnerability, limited exploitation - Unlikely: Theoretical vulnerability, no known exploits - Rare: Complex attack chain, requires significant resources

IMPACT DEFINITIONS: Business View: - Catastrophic: Severe business disruption, major financial loss - Major: Significant disruption, substantial financial impact - Moderate: Limited disruption, moderate financial impact - Minor: Minor disruption, limited financial impact - Negligible: Minimal disruption, negligible financial impac

Technical View: - Catastrophic: System-wide compromise, data breach, service failure - Major: Multiple system compromise, significant data exposure - Moderate: Single system compromise, limited data exposure - Minor: System affected but contained, no data exposure - Negligible: System affected, no operational impact

Risk Level Responses:

CRITICAL: Business Response: - Immediate executive notification - Emergency resource allocation - Crisis management activation - Stakeholder communication

Technical Response: - Immediate containment measures - Incident response team activation - Real-time threat hunting - Forensic investigation initiation

HIGH: Business Response: - Priority executive review - Dedicated resource allocation - Accelerated remediation - Regular stakeholder updates

Technical Response: - Enhanced monitoring - Rapid patch deployment - Security control validation - Threat intelligence correlation

MEDIUM: Business Response: - Management notification - Planned resource allocation - Standard remediation - Regular reporting

Technical Response: - Standard monitoring - Scheduled patching - Regular security reviews - Baseline analysis

LOW: Business Response: - Team awareness - Normal operations - Standard procedures - Routine reporting

Technical Response: - Basic monitoring - Regular maintenance - Standard controls - Baseline security

Real-World Examples:

1. API Vulnerability (Chapter 1) Business Impact: - $2.3M potential exposure - 1,547 client accounts affected - Trading platform disruption

Technical Details: - Zero-day API authentication bypass - Real-time transaction manipulation - Multi-stage attack pattern

2. Supply Chain Compromise (Chapter 2) Business Impact: - 3,200 defective components - Multiple manufacturers affected - Production line shutdown

Technical Details: - Compromised vendor update system - Modified calibration parameters - Persistent unauthorized access

3. Healthcare Data Breach (Chapter 3) Business Impact: - 5,000+ patient records exposed - Regulatory compliance violation - Clinical operations affected

Technical Details: - Advanced spear-phishing campaign - Credential harvesting - Lateral movement across systems

Implementation Guidelines:

For Business Leaders: 1. Risk Assessment - Review business impact definitions - Consider industry-specific factors - Evaluate regulatory requirements - Assess reputational impact

2. Resource Allocation - Align budget with risk levels - Prioritize critical and high risks - Plan for medium-term improvements - Maintain baseline security

3. Communication Strategy - Define escalation procedures - Establish reporting frameworks - Maintain stakeholder engagement - Document decision rationale

For Technical Teams: 1. Threat Analysis - Monitor threat intelligence - Evaluate technical indicators - Assess control effectiveness - Document attack patterns

2. Control Implementation - Deploy security measures - Validate effectiveness - Monitor performance - Update as needed

3. Technical Response - Define containment procedures - Establish investigation protocols - Implement recovery processes - Document technical details

Business Planning:

Business Focus: - Quarterly risk reviews - Annual strategy updates - Post-incident analysis - Industry benchmark comparison

Technical Focus: - Monthly control reviews - Security testing - Threat hunting - Technical debt management

Success Metrics:

Business Metrics: - Risk reduction rate - Incident impact trends - Response time improvement - Resource utilization

Technical Metrics: - Vulnerability management - Control effectiveness - Detection capability - Response efficienc

2) SECURITY CONTROL CHECKLIST

Executive Overview: A comprehensive security program requires multiple layers of controls. This checklist provides both business leaders and technical teams with essential security controls across key categories, with examples from real incidents covered in previous chapters.

1. Technical Controls

Business View:

□ System Access & Authentication - Who can access what
□ Data Protection & Privacy - How sensitive information is secured
□ Network Security - How systems are protected
□ Endpoint Protection - How devices are secured
□ Cloud Security - How cloud services are protected
□ Backup Systems - How data is preserved
□ Monitoring Capabilities - How threats are detected
□ Recovery Systems - How services are restored

Technical View:
□ Multi-factor Authentication (MFA) Implementation
□ Encryption (Data at rest/in transit)
□ Firewall/IDS/IPS Configuratio
□ EDR/XDR Deployment
□ Cloud Security Architecture
□ Security Information and Event Management (SIEM)
□ Vulnerability Management System
□ Patch Management Process

Example from Chapter 1:
□ API Security Controls
□ Transaction Monitoring
□ Authentication Protocols
□ Real-time Alert Systems

2. Administrative Controls

Business View:
□ Security Policies & Procedures
□ Employee Training Programs

□ Incident Response Plans
□ Change Management Process
□ Business Continuity Plans
□ Risk Management Program
□ Security Awareness Training
□ Documentation Standards

Technical View:
□ Access Control Policies
□ Configuration Managemen
□ Security Baseline Standards
□ Incident Response Procedures
□ Disaster Recovery Plans
□ Technical Training Program
□ Change Control Process
□ Security Testing Procedures

Example from Chapter 3:
□ Phishing Awareness Training
□ Data Handling Procedures
□ Access Review Process
□ Incident Escalation Protocols

3. Physical Controls

Business View:
□ Facility Access Controls
□ Data Center Security
□ Equipment Protection
□ Environmental Controls
□ Physical Media Handling
□ Visitor Management
□ Asset Management
□ Secure Disposal Process

Technical View:
□ Access Card Systems
□ Video Surveillance
□ Environmental Monitoring
□ Fire Suppression Systems
□ Power Management
□ Hardware Inventory
□ Media Destruction
□ Physical Security Logs

Example from Chapter 2:
□ Manufacturing Floor Access
□ Equipment Security
□ Production Environment Controls
□ Physical Asset Protection

4. Third-Party Controls

Business View:
□ Vendor Risk Assessment
□ Contract Requirements
□ Access Management
□ Performance Monitoring
□ Compliance Verificatio
□ Service Level Agreements
□ Incident Response Requirements
□ Regular Reviews

Technical View:
□ Third-party Access Controls
□ Security Requirements
□ Integration Security
□ Monitoring Capabilities

□ Incident Response Integration
□ Data Protection Standards
□ Change Management Process
□ Security Testing Requirements

Example from Chapter 2:
□ Vendor Update Verificatio
□ Supply Chain Security
□ Partner Integration Controls
□ Third-party Monitoring

5. Compliance Controls

Business View:
□ Regulatory Requirements
□ Industry Standards
□ Audit Preparations
□ Documentation Management
□ Reporting Requirements
□ Privacy Compliance
□ Security Certification
□ Compliance Monitoring

Technical View:
□ Technical Compliance Controls
□ Audit Logging
□ Evidence Collection
□ Control Testing
□ Compliance Reporting
□ Security Assessments
□ Gap Analysis
□ Remediation Tracking

Example from Chapter 3:
□ HIPAA Requirements
□ Patient Data Protection
□ Compliance Documentation
□ Audit Trail Maintenance

Implementation Guidelines:

For Business Leaders:
□ Review all control categories
□ Prioritize based on risk
□ Allocate resources
□ Monitor implementation
□ Verify effectiveness
□ Update as needed

For Technical Teams:
□ Assess current controls
□ Identify gaps
□ Implement solutions
□ Test effectiveness
□ Document results
□ Maintain controls
Review Schedule:
□ Monthly Technical Review
□ Quarterly Business Review
□ Annual Comprehensive Assessment
□ Post-Incident Review
□ Change-triggered Review

Success Metrics:
□ Control Implementation Rate
□ Control Effectiveness

□ Incident Prevention
□ Response Efficienc
□ Compliance Status
□ Resource Utilization

3) BUDGET TEMPLATES

Executive Overview:
Strategic security investment requires careful financi l planning across multiple categories. These templates provide a framework for both business leaders and technical teams to plan and track security investments.

1. Capital Expenditures (CAPEX)

Annual Security Infrastructure Budget Template:

Hardware/Infrastructure:
(Key: Item | Estimated Cost | Business Impact | Risk Mitigation Value)

Security Appliances | $________ | □High □Med □Low | □High □Med □Low
Network Equipment | $________ | □High □Med □Low | □High □Med □Low
Endpoint Devices | $________ | □High □Med □Low | □High □Med □Low
Physical Security Systems| $________ | □High □Med □Low | □High □Med □Low
Total Hardware | $________ | □High □Med □Low | □High □Med □Low

Security Software/Platforms:
(Key: Item | Estimated Cost | Business Impact | Risk Mitigation Value)

SIEM Platform | $________ | □High □Med □Low | □High □Med □Low
EDR/XDR Solutions | $________ | □High □Med □Low | □High □Med □Low
Access Control Systems | $________ | □High □Med □Low | □High □Med □Low
Security Tools | $________ | □High □Med □Low | □High □Med □Low
Total Software | $________ | □High □Med □Low | □High □Med □Low

2. Operational Costs (OPEX)

Monthly Operating Expenses Template:

Licensing & Subscriptions:
(Key: Item | Monthly Cost | Annual Cost | Priority Level)

Security Software | $________ | $________ | □High □Med □Low
Cloud Services | $________ | $________ | □High □Med □Low
Monitoring Tools | $________ | $________ | □High □Med □Low
Support Services | $________ | $________ | □High □Med □Low
Total Licensing | $________ | $________ | □High □Med □Low

Maintenance & Support:
(Key: Item | Monthly Cost | Annual Cost | Priority Level)

Regular Maintenance | $________ | $________ | □High □Med □Low
Emergency Support | $________ | $________ | □High □Med □Low
Updates & Patches | $________ | $________ | □High □Med □Low
Help Desk Services | $________ | $________ | □High □Med □Low
Total Maintenance | $________ | $________ | □High □Med □Low

3. Personnel Expenses

Annual Staff Budget Template:

Internal Team:
(Key: Position | Salary Range | Benefits (30%) | Total Cost)

Security Manager | $________ | $________ | $________
Security Engineers | $________ | $________ | $________
Analysts | $________ | $________ | $________
Support Staff | $________ | $________ | $________
Total Internal | $________ | $________ | $________

Professional Services:
(Key: Service | Monthly Rate | Annual Cost | Priority Level)

Security Consultants	$________	$________	□High □Med □Low
Incident Response	$________	$________	□High □Med □Low
Training Services	$________	$________	□High □Med □Low
Audit Support	$________	$________	□High □Med □Low
Total Professional	$________	$________	□High □Med □Low

4. Vendor/Partner Costs

Annual Partner Budget Template:

Managed Services:
(Key: Service | Monthly Cost | Annual Cost | Critical Service)

SOC Services	$________	$________	□Yes □No
Threat Intelligence	$________	$________	□Yes □No
Vulnerability Management	$________	$________	□Yes □No
Cloud Security	$________	$________	□Yes □No
Total Managed Services	$________	$________	□Yes □No

Assessment Services:
(Key: Service | Frequency | Annual Cost | Compliance Required)

Security Assessments	________	$________	□Yes □No
Penetration Testing	________	$________	□Yes □No
Compliance Audits	________	$________	□Yes □No
Risk Assessments	________	$________	□Yes □No
Total Assessments	________	$________	□Yes □No

5. Contingency Funds

Annual Emergency Fund Template:

Incident Response:
(Key: Category | Reserved Amount | Used YTD | Remaining)

Emergency Response | $________ | $________ | $________
Crisis Management | $________ | $________ | $________
Recovery Operations | $________ | $________ | $________
Business Continuity | $________ | $________ | $________
Total Emergency Funds | $________ | $________ | $________

Unplanned Requirements:
(Key: Category | Reserved Amount | Used YTD | Remaining)

Security Incidents | $________ | $________ | $________
Regulatory Changes | $________ | $________ | $________
Emergency Projects | $________ | $________ | $________
Urgent Upgrades | $________ | $________ | $________
Total Unplanned | $________ | $________ | $________

Real-World Examples:

1. Financial Services (Chapter 1):
API Security Investment Example:
Capital Investment | $2.5M | High Impact | High Mitigation
Monthly Monitoring | $75K | High Priority| Critical Service
Incident Response Team | $1.2M/year| High Priority| Yes Required
ROI: Prevented $2.3M potential loss

2. Manufacturing (Chapter 2):
Supply Chain Security Example:
Capital Investment | $1.8M | High Impact | High Mitigation
Vendor Monitoring | $45K/month| High Priority| Critical Service
Security Integration | $850K/year| High Priority| Yes Required
ROI: Protected $15M production line

3. Healthcare (Chapter 3):
Patient Data Security Example:
Capital Investment | $3.2M | High Impact | High Mitigation
Compliance Monitoring | $95K/month| High Priority| Critical Service
Staff Training | $450K/year| High Priority| Yes Required
ROI: Protected 5,000+ patient records

Budget Planning Guidelines:

For Business Leaders:
□ Align with risk assessment
□ Consider compliance requirements
□ Balance security vs. operations
□ Plan for growth
□ Include contingencies

For Technical Teams:
□ Identify technical requirements
□ Research solution costs
□ Consider integration needs
□ Plan maintenance costs
□ Include training needs

Review Schedule:
□ Monthly Expense Review
□ Quarterly Budget Analysis
□ Annual Budget Planning

□ Post-Incident Review
□ Technology Refresh Planning

Success Metrics:
□ Budget Utilization
□ Security Improvement
□ Incident Prevention
□ Cost Efficiency
□ Risk Reduction

4) IMPLEMENTATION TIMELINE

Executive Overview: Successful security implementations require careful timeline planning and milestone tracking. This section provides structured templates for planning, tracking, and managing security implementation projects across different time horizons.

1. Project Phases Template

Planning Phase (0-30 Days): (Key: Task | Duration | Dependencies | Owner | Status)

Risk Assessment | 1-2 weeks | None | Risk Team | □Not Started □In Progress □Complete **Security Design** | 2-3 weeks | Risk Ass. | Arch Team | □Not Started □In Progress □Complete **Resource Planning** | 1-2 weeks | Sec Design| Project Team | □Not Started □In Progress □Complete **Vendor Selection** | 2-3 weeks | Sec Design| Procurement | □Not Started □In Progress □Complete **Budget Approval** | 1 week | All Above | Executive | □Not Started □In Progress □Complete

Implementation Phase (31-90 Days): (Key: Task | Duration | Dependencies | Owner | Status)

Infrastructure Setup | 3-4 weeks | Budget | Tech Team | □Not Started □In Progress □Complete Security Controls | 4-6 weeks | Infra | Sec

Team | □Not Started □In Progress □Complete Integration | 2-3 weeks | Controls | Tech Team | □Not Started □In Progress □Complete Initial Testing | 2 weeks | Integrate | QA Team | □Not Started □In Progress □Complete Staff Training | Ongoing | Controls | Training | □Not Started □In Progress □Complete

Testing Phase (91-120 Days): (Key: Task | Duration | Dependencies | Owner | Status)

Security Testing | 2-3 weeks | Controls | Sec Team | □Not Started □In Progress □Complete User Acceptance | 2 weeks | Training | Business | □Not Started □In Progress □Complete Performance Testing | 1-2 weeks | Security | Tech Team | □Not Started □In Progress □Complete Compliance Review | 1 week | All Tests | Compliance | □Not Started □In Progress □Complete Final Adjustments | 1 week | Review | Project Team | □Not Started □In Progress □Complete

Review Phase (121-180 Days): (Key: Task | Duration | Dependencies | Owner | Status)

Performance Monitor | Ongoing | Launch | Tech Team | □Not Started □In Progress □Complete Security Assessment | 1-2 weeks | 30 Days | Sec Team | □Not Started □In Progress □Complete User Feedback | Ongoing | Launch | Business | □Not Started □In Progress □Complete Optimization | 2-3 weeks | Assessment| Project Team | □Not Started □In Progress □Complete Documentation | 1-2 weeks | All Above | Admin Team | □Not Started □In Progress □Complete

2. Key Milestones Template

Business Milestones: (Key: Milestone | Target Date | Status | Dependencies | Owner)

Project Kickoff | _________ | □Not Started □Complete | None | Project Lead Budget Approval | _________ | □Not Started □Complete |

Risk Analysis | Executive User Training | _________ | □Not Started □Complete | System Ready | Training Team Business Validation | _________ | □Not Started □Complete | Training Done | Business Lead Final Sign-off | _________ | □Not Started □Complete | All Complete | Executive

Technical Milestones: (Key: Milestone | Target Date | Status | Dependencies | Owner)

Design Approval | _________ | □Not Started □Complete | Requirements | Architect Infrastructure Ready| _________ | □Not Started □Complete | Design | Tech Lead Controls Implemented| _________ | □Not Started □Complete | Infrastructure| Security Lead Testing Complete | _________ | □Not Started □Complete | Implementation| QA Lead Security Verified| _________ | □Not Started □Complete | Testing | Security Lead

3. Resource Allocation Timeline

Technical Resources: (Key: Resource | Start Date | End Date | Allocation % | Priority)

Security Team | _________ | _________ | _____% | □High □Med □Low Network Team | _________ | _________ | _____% | □High □Med □Low System Engineers | _________ | _________ | _____% | □High □Med □Low QA Team | _________ | _________ | _____% | □High □Med □Low Support Team | _________ | _________ | _____% | □High □Med □Low

Business Resources: (Key: Resource | Start Date | End Date | Allocation % | Priority)

Project Management | _________ | _________ | _____% | □High □Med □Low Business Analysts | _________ | _________ | _____% | □High □Med □Low Training Team | _________ | _________ | _____% | □High □Med □Low User Groups | _________ | _________ | _____% | □High

□Med □Low Documentation | _________ | _________ | _____% | □High □Med □Low

4. Dependencies Tracking

Technical Dependencies: (Key: Task | Prerequisite | Impact | Risk Level | Status)

Security Controls | Infrastructure | High | □High □Med □Low | □Not Started □Complete Integration | Controls | High | □High □Med □Low | □Not Started □Complete Testing | Integration | Medium | □High □Med □Low | □Not Started □Complete Deployment | Testing | High | □High □Med □Low | □Not Started □Complete Monitoring | Deployment | Medium | □High □Med □Low | □Not Started □Complete

Business Dependencies: (Key: Task | Prerequisite | Impact | Risk Level | Status)

Training | System Ready | High | □High □Med □Low | □Not Started □Complete User Testing | Training | Medium | □High □Med □Low | □Not Started □Complete Business Process | Integration | High | □High □Med □Low | □Not Started □Complete Documentation | Process Change | Medium | □High □Med □Low | □Not Started □Complete Sign-off | All Complete | High | □High □Med □Low | □Not Started □Complete

Real-World Examples:

1. API Security Implementation (Chapter 1): Planning: 3 weeks - Risk assessment completed in week 1 - Design approved in week 2 - Vendor selected in week 3 Implementation: 6 weeks - Infrastructure setup in weeks 1-2 - Security controls in weeks 3-4 - Testing in weeks 5-6 Result: Prevented $2.3M potential loss

2. Supply Chain Security (Chapter 2): Planning: 4 weeks - Vendor assessment in weeks 1-2 - Integration design in weeks 3-4 Implementation: 8

weeks - System updates in weeks 1-3 - Security controls in weeks 4-6 - Testing in weeks 7-8 Result: Protected production line integrity

3. Healthcare Data Protection (Chapter 3): Planning: 3 weeks - Compliance review in week 1 - System design in week 2 - Resource allocation in week 3 Implementation: 6 weeks - Security controls in weeks 1-2 - Integration in weeks 3-4 - Testing in weeks 5-6 Result: Protected 5,000+ patient records

Implementation Guidelines:

For Business Leaders: □ Review timeline feasibility □ Approve resource allocation □ Monitor key milestones □ Address escalations □ Validate business impact

For Technical Teams: □ Detail technical dependencies □ Plan resource requirements □ Track implementation progress □ Document technical decisions □ Validate security controls

Success Metrics:

Timeline Metrics: □ Milestone completion rate □ Resource utilization □ Dependencies cleared □ Risk mitigation effectiveness □ Business impact achieved

5) RESOURCE PLANNING TOOLS

Executive Overview:

Effective security implementation requires precise resource planning and allocation. These tools help business leaders and technical teams identify, allocate, and track resources needed for successful security programs.

1. Staffing Requirements Matri

Security Team Roles:
(Key: Role | Required Skills | FTE Count | Internal/External | Priority)

CISO/Security Director | Leadership, Strategy | ____ | Int Ext | High Med Low
Security Engineers | Technical, Systems | ____ | Int Ext | High Med Low
Security Analysts | Monitoring, Response | ____ | Int Ext | High Med Low
Risk Analysts | Assessment, Planning | ____ | Int Ext | High Med Low
Compliance Specialists | Regulatory, Audit | ____ | Int Ext | High Med Low

Technical Support Roles:
(Key: Role | Required Skills | FTE Count | Internal/External | Priority)

Network Engineers | Infrastructure, Config | ____ | Int Ext | High Med Low
System Administrators | Systems, Platforms | ____ | Int Ext | High Med Low
Application Developers| Development, Security | ____ | Int Ext | High Med Low
QA Engineers | Testing, Validation | ____ | Int Ext | High Med Low
Support Staff | User Support, Training | ____ | Int Ext | High Med Low

2. Technology Resource Allocation

Infrastructure Resources:
(Key: Resource | Capacity | Utilization | Availability | Cost)

Servers/Systems | ________ | _____% | _____hrs/day | $_______
Network Equipment | ________ | _____% | _____hrs/day | $_______
Security Appliances | ________ | _____% | _____hrs/day | $_______
Storage Systems | ________ | _____% | _____hrs/day | $_______
Backup Infrastructure| ________ | _____% | _____hrs/day | $_______

Software Resources:
(Key: Resource | Licenses | Usage | Availability | Cost)

Security Platforms | ________ | _____% | _____hrs/day | $_______
Monitoring Tools | ________ | _____% | _____hrs/day | $_______
Analysis Software | ________ | _____% | _____hrs/day | $_______
Management Systems | ________ | _____% | _____hrs/day | $_______
Support Applications | ________ | _____% | _____hrs/day | $_______

3. Training & Development Plan

Security Training:
(Key: Training Type | Target Group | Duration | Cost | Priority)

Security Awareness | All Staff | ___hrs | $_____ | High Med Low
Technical Security | IT Team | ___hrs | $_____ | High Med Low
Incident Response | Security Team| ___hrs | $_____ | High Med Low
Compliance Training | Key Staff | ___hrs | $_____ | High Med Low
Tool-specific | Users | ___hrs | $_____ | High Med Low

Certification Plan
(Key: Certification | Target Role | Timeline | Cost | Priority)

Security Cert. | Security Team| ___mos | $_____ | High Med Low
Technical Cert. | IT Team | ___mos | $_____ | High Med Low
Compliance Cert. | Compliance | ___mos | $_____ | High Med Low
Industry Cert. | Management | ___mos | $_____ | High Med Low
Vendor Cert. | Support Team | ___mos | $_____ | High Med Low

4. Vendor/Partner Resource Plan

Managed Services:
(Key: Service | Resource Type | Availability | SLA | Cost)

Security Monitoring | 24/7 Team | ___hrs | ___% | $_____/month
Incident Response | On-call Team | ___hrs | ___% | $_____/month
Threat Intelligence | Analysis Team| ___hrs | ___% | $_____/month
Technical Support | Help Desk | ___hrs | ___% | $_____/month
Compliance Support | Specialists | ___hrs | ___% | $_____/month

Professional Services:
(Key: Service | Resource Type | Duration | Deliverables | Cost)

Security Assessment | Consultants | ___wks | ________ | $_____
Implementation | Engineers | ___wks | ________ | $_____
Training Delivery | Trainers | ___wks | ________ | $_____
Audit Support | Auditors | ___wks | ________ | $_____
Project Management | PM Team | ___wks | ________ | $_____

5. Project Resource Tracking

Technical Resources:
(Key: Resource | Assignment | Utilization | Performance | Status)

Security Team | _________ | _____% | High Med Low | Active Complete
Network Team | _________ | _____% | High Med Low | Active Complete
System Team | _________ | _____% | High Med Low | Active Complete
Development Team | _________ | _____% | High Med Low | Active Complete
Support Team | _________ | _____% | High Med Low | Active Complete

Business Resources:
(Key: Resource | Assignment | Utilization | Performance | Status)

Project Management | _________ | _____% | High Med Low | Active Complete
Business Analysis | _________ | _____% | High Med Low | Active Complete
Training Team | _________ | _____% | High Med Low | Active Complete
Documentation Team | _________ | _____% | High Med Low | Active Complete
Quality Assurance | _________ | _____% | High Med Low | Active Complete

Real-World Examples:

1. Financial Services (Chapter 1):
Security Team Structure:
- 1 CISO
- 3 Security Engineers
- 2 Security Analysts
- 1 Risk Analyst
- 1 Compliance Specialist
Technology Resources:
- API Security Platform
- Real-time Monitoring Tools
- Threat Intelligence Platform
Training Requirements:
- API Security Training
- Threat Detection Training
- Compliance Training

2. Manufacturing (Chapter 2):
Security Team Structure:
- 1 Security Director
- 2 OT Security Engineers
- 2 Security Analysts
- 1 Supply Chain Specialist

Technology Resources:
- OT Security Platform
- Supply Chain Monitoring
- Vendor Management System

Training Requirements:
- OT Security Training
- Supply Chain Security
- Vendor Management

3. Healthcare (Chapter 3):

Security Team Structure:
- 1 CISO
- 2 Security Engineers
- 3 Security Analysts
- 2 Compliance Specialists

Technology Resources:
- PHI Protection Systems
- Access Control Platform
- Compliance Monitoring

Training Requirements:
- HIPAA Compliance
- Privacy Protection
- Security Awareness

Implementation Guidelines:

For Business Leaders:

Review resource requirements

Approve staffing plan

Allocate budget

Monitor utilization

Assess effectiveness

For Technical Teams:
Detail technical needs
Plan capacity requirements
Track resource usage
Measure performance
Optimize allocation

Success Metrics:

Resource Metrics:
Utilization rates
Performance levels
Cost efficienc
Project completion
Quality measures

Review Schedule:
Weekly resource tracking
Monthly performance review
Quarterly capacity planning
Annual resource planning
Project-based reviews

APPENDIX A

SECURITY IMPLEMENTATION GUIDE 2. Implementation Steps

6) PRE-IMPLEMENTATION CHECKLIST

Executive Overview: Before beginning any security implementation, organizations must verify readiness across multiple dimensions. This checklist ensures all prerequisites are met and risks are addressed before project initiation.

1. Project Readiness Assessment

Business Requirements: (Key: Requirement | Status | Verified By | Date)

□ Business Case Approved | □Complete □Pending | _________ | _________ □ Budget Allocated | □Complete □Pending | _________ | _________ □ Executive Sponsorship | □Complete □Pending | _________ | _________ □ Success Criteria Defined | □Complete □Pending | _________ | _________ □ ROI Metrics Established | □Complete □Pending | _________ | _________

Technical Requirements: (Key: Requirement | Status | Verified By | Date)

□ Architecture Review | □Complete □Pending | _________ | _________
□ System Requirements | □Complete □Pending | _________ | _________
□ Integration Points | □Complete □Pending | _________ | _________
□ Technical Dependencies | □Complete □Pending | _________ | _________ □ Security Standards | □Complete □Pending | _________ | _________

2. Resource Verificatio

Internal Resources: (Key: Resource | Availability | Capacity | Status)

□ Project Team | _____% | _____hrs | □Ready □Not Ready □ Technical Staff | _____% | _____hrs | □Ready □Not Ready □ Security Team | _____% | _____hrs | □Ready □Not Ready □ Business Users | _____% | _____hrs | □Ready □Not Ready □ Support Staff | _____% | _____hrs | □Ready □Not Ready

External Resources: (Key: Resource | Availability | Contract Status | Start Date)

□ Vendors | _____% | □Signed □Pending | _________ □ Consultants | _____% | □Signed □Pending | _________ □ Security Partners | _____% | □Signed □Pending | _________ □ Auditors | _____% | □Signed □Pending | _________ □ Training Resources | _____% | □Signed □Pending | _________

3. Risk Evaluation

Business Risks: (Key: Risk | Impact | Mitigation | Status)

□ Operational Impact | □High □Med □Low | ____________ | □Addressed □Pending □ Resource Constraints | □High □Med □Low | ____________

| □Addressed □Pending □ Budget Overrun | □High □Med □Low | ____________ | □Addressed □Pending □ Timeline Delays | □High □Med □Low | ____________ | □Addressed □Pending □ Change Resistance | □High □Med □Low | ____________ | □Addressed □Pending

Technical Risks: (Key: Risk | Impact | Mitigation | Status)

□ Integration Issues | □High □Med □Low | ____________ | □Addressed □Pending □ Performance Impact | □High □Med □Low | ____________ | □Addressed □Pending □ Security Gaps | □High □Med □Low | ____________ | □Addressed □Pending □ System Compatibility | □High □Med □Low | ____________ | □Addressed □Pending □ Data Migration | □High □Med □Low | ____________ | □Addressed □Pending

4. Stakeholder Alignment

Key Stakeholders: (Key: Role | Engagement Status | Sign-off Required | Status)

□ Executive Sponsor | □Engaged □Pending | □Yes □No | □Approved □Pending □ Business Owner | □Engaged □Pending | □Yes □No | □Approved □Pending □ Technical Lead | □Engaged □Pending | □Yes □No | □Approved □Pending □ Security Lead | □Engaged □Pending | □Yes □No | □Approved □Pending □ Compliance Officer | □Engaged □Pending | □Yes □No | □Approved □Pending

Communication Status: (Key: Stakeholder Group | Informed | Feedback | Status)

□ Executive Team | □Yes □No | □Received □Pending | □Complete □Pending □ Technical Teams | □Yes □No | □Received □Pending | □Complete □Pending □ End Users | □Yes □No | □Received □Pending | □Complete □Pending □ Support Teams | □Yes □No | □Received □Pending | □Complete □Pending □ External Partners | □Yes □No | □Received □Pending | □Complete □Pending

5. Technical Prerequisites

Infrastructure: (Key: Component | Readiness | Testing | Status)

□ Network Infrastructure | □Ready □Not Ready | □Tested □Pending | □Complete □Pending □ Security Systems | □Ready □Not Ready | □Tested □Pending | □Complete □Pending □ Storage Systems | □Ready □Not Ready | □Tested □Pending | □Complete □Pending □ Backup Systems | □Ready □Not Ready | □Tested □Pending | □Complete □Pending □ Monitoring Tools | □Ready □Not Ready | □Tested □Pending | □Complete □Pending

Integration Points: (Key: Integration | Documentation | Testing | Status)

□ API Connections | □Complete □Pending | □Tested □Pending | □Ready □Not Ready □ Data Flows | □Complete □Pending | □Tested □Pending | □Ready □Not Ready □ Authentication | □Complete □Pending | □Tested □Pending | □Ready □Not Ready □ Security Controls | □Complete □Pending | □Tested □Pending | □Ready □Not Ready □ Monitoring Systems | □Complete □Pending | □Tested □Pending | □Ready □Not Ready

Real-World Examples:

1. Financial Services (Chapter 1): Pre-Implementation Verification: □ API Security Architecture Review □ Transaction Monitoring Readiness □ Integration Testing Complete □ Compliance Requirements Met Result: Successful API security implementation

2. Manufacturing (Chapter 2): Pre-Implementation Verification: □ Supply Chain System Review □ Vendor Integration Testing □ Production Impact Assessment □ Safety Controls Verified Result: Secure supply chain implementation

3. Healthcare (Chapter 3): Pre-Implementation Verification: □ HIPAA Compliance Review □ Patient Data Protection Controls □ Clinical System Integration □ Privacy Impact Assessment Result: Compliant security implementation

Implementation Guidelines:

For Business Leaders: □ Review business readiness □ Verify resource availability □ Confirm budget allocation □ Ensure stakeholder alignment □ Validate success criteria

For Technical Teams: □ Verify technical prerequisites □ Test integration points □ Validate security controls □ Document configurations □ Prepare support procedures

Success Metrics:

Readiness Indicators: □ All prerequisites met □ Resources confirmed □ Risks addressed □ Stakeholders aligned □ Technical environment ready

7) STAKEHOLDER COMMUNICATION PLANS

Executive Overview: Effective security implementation requires clear, consistent communication across all stakeholder groups. These templates and protocols ensure appropriate information sharing and engagement throughout the implementation process.

1. Stakeholder Matrix

Executive Leadership: (Key: Role | Communication Type | Frequency | Format | Priority)

CEO/Board | Status Updates | Monthly | Meeting Report | High Med Low CFO/Finance | Budget/ROI | Monthly | Meeting Report | High Med Low CTO/Technology | Technical Review | Bi-weekly |

Meeting Report | High Med Low CISO/Security | Security Review | Weekly | Meeting Report | High Med Low COO/Operations | Impact Review | Monthly | Meeting Report | High Med Low

Technical Teams: (Key: Team | Communication Type | Frequency | Format | Priority)

Security Team | Implementation | Daily | Meeting Update | High Med Low IT Infrastructure | Integration | Weekly | Meeting Update | High Med Low Development | Requirements | Weekly | Meeting Update | High Med Low QA/Testing | Progress | Weekly | Meeting Update | High Med Low Support Team | Training/Updates | Bi-weekly | Meeting Update | High Med Low

2. Communication Templates

Executive Updates: (Key: Component | Content | Frequency | Distribution)

Project Status: Overall Progress | ___% Complete | Key Milestones Met/Missed Budget Status | $____ vs Plan | Variance Analysis Risk Updates | High/Med/Low | Mitigation Status Resource Status | Allocated/Need | Gap Analysis Timeline Updates | On/Off Track | Adjustment Needs

Technical Updates: Implementation Progress | Technical Milestones | Issues/Resolutions Security Status | Control Implementation| Risk Assessment Integration Status | System Connections | Performance Metrics Testing Results | Pass/Fail Rates | Required Actions Resource Utilization | Team Performance | Additional Needs

3. Notification Protocol

Critical Updates: (Key: Event | Notification Time | Method | Recipients)

Security Incidents | Within 1 hour | Email Call Text | Exec Tech Bus Major Issues | Within 2 hours | Email Call Text | Exec Tech Bus Implementation Delays| Within 4 hours | Email Call Text | Exec Tech Bus Resource Issues | Within 8 hours | Email Call Text | Exec Tech Bus Budget Concerns | Within 24 hours| Email Call Text | Exec Tech Bus

Regular Updates: (Key: Update Type | Frequency | Method | Recipients)

Status Reports | Weekly | Email Meeting | All Select Progress Reviews | Bi-weekly | Email Meeting | All Select Technical Briefings | Weekly | Email Meeting | All Select Budget Reviews | Monthly | Email Meeting | All Select Risk Assessments | Bi-weekly | Email Meeting | All Select

4. Feedback Mechanisms

Stakeholder Feedback: (Key: Type | Method | Frequency | Action Required)

Executive Feedback: Project Direction | Survey Meeting | Monthly | Yes No Resource Allocation | Survey Meeting | Quarterly | Yes No Risk Tolerance | Survey Meeting | Monthly | Yes No Budget Adjustments | Survey Meeting | Monthly | Yes No Timeline Changes | Survey Meeting | As Needed | Yes No

Technical Feedback: Implementation Issues| Survey Meeting | Weekly | Yes No Resource Needs | Survey Meeting | Weekly | Yes No Technical Challenges | Survey Meeting | Daily | Yes No Integration Problems | Survey Meeting | Daily | Yes No Support Requirements | Survey Meeting | Weekly | Yes No

5. Progress Reporting

Executive Dashboard: (Key: Metric | Status | Trend | Action Required)

Project Health: Overall Status | Green Yellow Red | ↑→↓ | Yes No Budget Status | Green Yellow Red | ↑→↓ | Yes No Resource Status | Green Yellow Red | ↑→↓ | Yes No Risk Status | Green Yellow Red | ↑→↓ | Yes No Timeline Status | Green Yellow Red | ↑→↓ | Yes No

Technical Dashboard: Implementation | Green Yellow Red | ↑→↓ | Yes No Integration Status | Green Yellow Red | ↑→↓ | Yes No Security Status | Green Yellow Red | ↑→↓ | Yes No Testing Status | Green Yellow Red | ↑→↓ | Yes No Support Status | Green Yellow Red | ↑→↓ | Yes No

Real-World Examples:

1. Financial Services (Chapter 1): Communication Strategy: Daily technical updates on API security Weekly executive briefings on implementation Real-time incident notifications Monthly compliance updates Result: Clear stakeholder alignment

2. Manufacturing (Chapter 2): Communication Strategy: Supply chain status updates Production impact notification Vendor integration updates Safety compliance reporting Result: Effective cross-team coordination

3. Healthcare (Chapter 3): Communication Strategy: Patient data protection updates Compliance status reporting Clinical system notifications Staff training communications Result: HIPAA-compliant implementation

Implementation Guidelines:

For Business Leaders: Review communication plans Confirm stakeholder lists Validate reporting requirements Ensure feedback mechanisms Monitor effectiveness

For Technical Teams: Establish update protocols Document technical communications Track issue resolution Maintain audit trail Monitor feedback

Success Metrics:

Communication Effectiveness: Stakeholder engagement Feedback implementation Issue resolution time Information accuracy Response rates

TESTING PROTOCOLS

Executive Overview: Comprehensive testing ensures security implementations meet both business requirements and technical specific - tions. These protocols provide structured approaches for validating security controls, functionality, and compliance requirements.

1. Test Plan Templates

Security Testing Plan: (Key: Test Type | Scope | Duration | Resources Required | Status)

Penetration Testing | ____________ | ___days | ____________ | □Not Started □In Progress □Complete Vulnerability Scans | ____________ | ___days | ____________ | □Not Started □In Progress □Complete Access Control Tests | ____________ | ___days | ____________ | □Not Started □In Progress □Complete Integration Testing | ____________ | ___days | ____________ | □Not Started □In Progress □Complete Performance Testing | ____________ | ___days | ____________ | □Not Started □In

Progress □Complete

Compliance Testing Plan: (Key: Requirement | Test Cases | Validation Method | Sign-off Required | Status)

Regulatory Controls | ___cases | ____________ | □Yes □No | □Not Started □Complete Privacy Requirements | ___cases | ____________ | □Yes □No | □Not Started □Complete Industry Standards | ___cases | ____________ | □Yes □No | □Not Started □Complete Internal Policies | ___cases | ____________ | □Yes □No | □Not Started □Complete Audit Requirements | ___cases | ____________ | □Yes □No | □Not Started □Complete

2. Testing Scenarios

Security Control Testing: (Key: Scenario | Expected Result | Actual Result | Pass/Fail)

Authentication: □ Valid Credentials | Access Granted | __________ | □Pass □Fail □ Invalid Credentials | Access Denied | __________ | □Pass □Fail □ MFA Challenge | Prompt Shown | __________ | □Pass □Fail □ Session Timeout | User Logged Out| __________ | □Pass □Fail □ Password Reset | Process Works | __________ | □Pass □Fail

Access Control: □ Role-based Access | Proper Rights | __________ | □Pass □Fail □ Data Restrictions | Access Limited | __________ | □Pass □Fail □ System Controls | Rules Enforced | __________ | □Pass □Fail □ Admin Functions | Admin Only | __________ | □Pass □Fail □ User Permissions | Correct Level | __________ | □Pass □Fail

3. Acceptance Criteria

Business Acceptance: (Key: Criterion | Measurement | Target | Actual | Status)

User Experience: □ System Response | Seconds | < 2 sec | ___sec | □Pass □Fail □ Process Flow | Steps | < 5 steps| ___steps| □Pass □Fail □ Error Handling | Clear Msgs | 100% | ___% | □Pass □Fail □ Feature Complete | Functions | 100% | ___% | □Pass □Fail □ User Satisfaction | Survey | > 90% | ___% | □Pass □Fail

Technical Acceptance: (Key: Criterion | Measurement | Target | Actual | Status)

System Performance: □ Security Controls | Coverage | 100% | ___% | □Pass □Fail □ Integration Tests | Success | 100% | ___% | □Pass □Fail □ Error Rates | Frequency | < 0.1% | ___% | □Pass □Fail □ System Load | Response | < 1 sec | ___sec | □Pass □Fail □ Data Accuracy | Validation | 100% | ___% | □Pass □Fail

4. Documentation Requirements

Test Documentation: (Key: Document | Required Elements | Review Level | Status)

Test Plans: □ Test Objectives | Goals/Scope | □High □Med □Low | □Complete □Pending □ Test Cases | Detailed Steps | □High □Med □Low | □Complete □Pending □ Test Data | Sample Sets | □High □Med □Low | □Complete □Pending □ Expected Results | Success Criteria| □High □Med □Low | □Complete □Pending □ Test Schedule | Timeline | □High □Med □Low | □Complete □Pending

Test Results: □ Test Execution | Results Log | □High □Med □Low | □Complete □Pending □ Issues Found | Detail Report | □High □Med □Low | □Complete □Pending □ Resolutions | Fix Details | □High □Med

□Low | □Complete □Pending □ Retest Results | Verification | □High □Med □Low | □Complete □Pending □ Final Status | Summary Report | □High □Med □Low | □Complete □Pending

5. Sign-off Procedures

Business Sign-off: (Key: Approver | Criteria | Verification | Status

□ Business Owner | Requirements Met | __________ | □Approved □Pending □ Process Owner | Workflow Valid | __________ | □Approved □Pending □ Compliance | Standards Met | __________ | □Approved □Pending □ Risk Management | Risks Addressed | __________ | □Approved □Pending □ Executive Sponsor | Goals Achieved | __________ | □Approved □Pending

Technical Sign-off: (Key: Approver | Criteria | Verification | Status

□ Security Team | Controls Valid | __________ | □Approved □Pending □ IT Infrastructure | Integration OK | __________ | □Approved □Pending □ Development | Code Review OK | __________ | □Approved □Pending □ QA Team | Testing Complete | __________ | □Approved □Pending □ Operations | Support Ready | __________ | □Approved □Pending

Real-World Examples:

1. Financial Services (Chapter 1): Testing Focus: □ API Security Testing □ Transaction Validation □ Performance Testing □ Compliance Verification Result: Secure API Implementation

2. Manufacturing (Chapter 2): Testing Focus: □ Supply Chain Security □ Integration Testing □ Safety Validation □ Vendor Verification Result: Secure Manufacturing Process

3. Healthcare (Chapter 3): Testing Focus: □ PHI Protection □ Access Controls □ HIPAA Compliance □ Clinical Integration Result: Compliant

Healthcare System

Implementation Guidelines:

For Business Leaders: □ Review test objectives □ Validate business requirements □ Monitor test progress □ Review test results □ Approve final sign-o f

For Technical Teams: □ Execute test plans □ Document results □ Address issues □ Validate fixes □ Prepare documentatio

Success Metrics:

Testing Effectiveness: □ Test coverage □ Issue detection □ Resolution rate □ Performance metrics □ User acceptance

8) VALIDATION PROCEDURES

Executive Overview: Validation ensures security implementations meet all requirements and function as intended. These procedures provide structured approaches to verify technical functionality, business requirements, and compliance standards.

1. Validation Requirements

Business Requirements: (Key: Requirement | Success Criteria | Validation Method | Status)

Operational Impact: □ Business Processes | No Disruption | Process Review | □Pass □Fail □Pending □ User Workflows | Maintained/Better | User Testing | □Pass □Fail □Pending □ System Performance | Meet/ Exceed SLA | Metrics Review | □Pass □Fail □Pending □ Resource Usage | Within Budget | Cost Analysis | □Pass □Fail □Pending □ Business Continuity | Maintained | DR Testing | □Pass □Fail □Pending

Technical Requirements: (Key: Requirement | Success Criteria | Validation Method | Status)

Security Controls: □ Access Controls | 100% Effective | Security Test | □Pass □Fail □Pending □ Data Protection | Full Coverage | Data Review | □Pass □Fail □Pending □ System Integration | All Connected | System Test | □Pass □Fail □Pending □ Performance Metrics | Meet Targets | Load Testing | □Pass □Fail □Pending □ Monitoring Systems | Full Coverage | System Check | □Pass □Fail □Pending

2. Success Criteria

Business Success Metrics: (Key: Metric | Target | Actual | Validation Method | Status)

Operational Metrics: □ System Uptime | >99.9% | ____% | Monitoring | □Pass □Fail □ Response Time | <2 sec | ____s | Performance Test | □Pass □Fail □ User Satisfaction | >90% | ____% | User Survey | □Pass □Fail □ Process Efficiency | >95% | ____% | Process Analysis | □Pass □Fail □ Cost Effectiveness | On Budget | $____ | Cost Review | □Pass □Fail

Security Metrics: □ Control Coverage | 100% | ____% | Security Scan | □Pass □Fail □ Incident Response | <15 min | ____m | Response Test | □Pass □Fail □ Policy Compliance | 100% | ____% | Audit Review | □Pass □Fail □ Risk Reduction | >90% | ____% | Risk Assessment | □Pass □Fail □ Security Score | >95% | ____% | Security Rating | □Pass □Fail

3. Performance Metrics

System Performance: (Key: Metric | Baseline | Target | Actual | Status)

Response Times: □ User Actions | ___sec | <2 sec | ___sec | □Pass □Fail □ System Processing | ___sec | <3 sec | ___sec | □Pass □Fail □ Data Retrieval | ___sec | <1 sec | ___sec | □Pass □Fail □ Report Generation |

___sec | <5 sec | ___sec | □Pass □Fail □ Security Checks | ___sec | <0.5 sec | ___sec | □Pass □Fail

Resource Utilization: □ CPU Usage | ____% | <70% | ____% | □Pass □Fail □ Memory Usage | ____% | <80% | ____% | □Pass □Fail □ Storage Usage | ____% | <75% | ____% | □Pass □Fail □ Network Bandwidth | ____% | <60% | ____% | □Pass □Fail □ Database Load | ____% | <65% | ____% | □Pass □Fail

4. Compliance Verificatio

Regulatory Compliance: (Key: Requirement | Validation Method | Evidence | Status)

Industry Standards: □ Data Protection | Audit Review | ________ | □Compliant □Non-Compliant □ Access Controls | Control Test | ________ | □Compliant □Non-Compliant □ Incident Response | Process Review | ________ | □Compliant □Non-Compliant □ Documentation | Doc Review | ________ | □Compliant □Non-Compliant □ Risk Management | Risk Assessment | ________ | □Compliant □Non-Compliant

Internal Policies: □ Security Policies | Policy Review | ________ | □Compliant □Non-Compliant □ User Access | Access Review | ________ | □Compliant □Non-Compliant □ Data Handling | Process Audit | ________ | □Compliant □Non-Compliant □ Change Management | Change Review | ________ | □Compliant □Non-Compliant □ Incident Handling | Process Test | ________ | □Compliant □Non-Compliant

5. Documentation Standards

Required Documentation: (Key: Document | Content Requirements | Review Level | Status)

Technical Documentation: □ System Design | Architecture Details | □High □Med □Low | □Complete □Pending □ Configuration | Settings/

Parameters | □High □Med □Low | □Complete □Pending □ Integration Specs | Connection Details | □High □Med □Low | □Complete □Pending □ Security Controls | Control Details | □High □Med □Low | □Complete □Pending □ Test Results | Validation Evidence | □High □Med □Low | □Complete □Pending

Business Documentation: □ User Guides | Process Instructions | □High □Med □Low | □Complete □Pending □ Training Materials | User Training Docs | □High □Med □Low | □Complete □Pending □ Support Procedures | Support Guidelines | □High □Med □Low | □Complete □Pending □ Business Process | Process Changes | □High □Med □Low | □Complete □Pending □ Compliance Docs | Regulatory Evidence | □High □Med □Low | □Complete □Pending

Real-World Examples:

1. Financial Services (Chapter 1): Validation Focus: □ API Security Validation □ Transaction Integrity □ Performance Metrics □ Compliance Evidence Result: Validated API Security

2. Manufacturing (Chapter 2): Validation Focus: □ Supply Chain Validation □ Production Security □ Safety Compliance □ Integration Verification Result: Secure Manufacturin

3. Healthcare (Chapter 3): Validation Focus: □ HIPAA Validation □ Patient Data Security □ Clinical Integration □ Privacy Controls Result: Compliant Healthcare System

Implementation Guidelines:

For Business Leaders: □ Review validation criteria □ Confirm business requirements □ Verify compliance status □ Approve documentation □ Sign off on validation

For Technical Teams: □ Execute validation tests □ Document results □ Verify technical requirements □ Maintain evidence □ Support compliance verificatio

Success Metrics:

Validation Effectiveness: □ Requirements met □ Performance achieved □ Compliance verified □ Documentation complete □ Sign-o f obtained

9) POST-IMPLEMENTATION REVIEW

Executive Overview: Post-implementation review ensures security implementations achieve intended objectives and identifies opportunities for improvement. This structured review process evaluates success, documents lessons learned, and provides recommendations for future implementations.

1. Review Process

Business Review: (Key: Component | Success Criteria | Actual Results | Status)

Project Objectives: □ Business Goals Met | ____________ | ____________ | □Achieved □Partial □Not Met □ Budget Performance | ____________ | ____________ | □Achieved □Partial □Not Met □ Timeline Adherence | ____________ | ____________ | □Achieved □Partial □Not Met □ Resource Utilization | ____________ | ____________ | □Achieved □Partial □Not Met □ User Adoption | ____________ | ____________ | □Achieved □Partial □Not Met

Technical Review: (Key: Component | Expected Results | Actual Results | Status)

Implementation Success: □ Security Controls | ____________ | ____________ | □Achieved □Partial □Not Met □ System Integration | ____________ | ____________ | □Achieved □Partial □Not Met □ Performance Metrics | ____________ | ____________ | □Achieved □Partial □Not Met □ Technical Standards | ____________ | ____________ | □Achieved □Partial □Not Met □ Support Readiness | ____________ | ____________ | □Achieved □Partial □Not Met

2. Performance Assessment

Business Metrics: (Key: Metric | Target | Actual | Variance | Status)

Operational Performance: □ Process Efficiency | ____% | ____% | ____% | □Exceeds □Meets □Below □ User Productivity | ____% | ____% | ____% | □Exceeds □Meets □Below □ Cost Savings | $____ | $____ | $____ | □Exceeds □Meets □Below □ Risk Reduction | ____% | ____% | ____% | □Exceeds □Meets □Below □ Business Impact | ____% | ____% | ____% | □Exceeds □Meets □Below

Technical Metrics: (Key: Metric | Target | Actual | Variance | Status)

System Performance: □ Security Effectiveness| ____% | ____% | ____% | □Exceeds □Meets □Below □ System Response Time | ____s | ____s | ____s | □Exceeds □Meets □Below □ Integration Success | ____% | ____% | ____% | □Exceeds □Meets □Below □ Uptime/Availability | ____% | ____% | ____% | □Exceeds □Meets □Below □ Error/Incident Rate | ____% | ____% | ____% | □Exceeds □Meets □Below

3. Lessons Learned

Success Factors: (Key: Factor | Impact | Documentation | Future Application)

What Worked Well: □ Project Planning | □High □Med □Low | ____________ | ____________ □ Team Collaboration | □High □Med □Low | ____________ | ____________ □ Risk Management | □High □Med □Low | ____________ | ____________ □ Change Management | □High □Med □Low | ____________ | ____________ □ Technical Execution | □High □Med □Low | ____________ | ____________

Areas for Improvement: (Key: Area | Impact | Resolution | Prevention Strategy)

Challenges Faced: □ Resource Constraints | □High □Med □Low | ____________ | ____________ □ Technical Issues | □High □Med □Low | ____________ | ____________ □ Timeline Delays | □High □Med □Low | ____________ | ____________ □ Integration Problems| □High □Med □Low | ____________ | ____________ □ User Adoption | □High □Med □Low | ____________ | ____________

4. Documentation Requirements

Implementation Records: (Key: Document | Content Required | Review Status | Location)

Business Documentation: □ Project Summary | Final Results | □Complete □Pending | ____________ □ Cost Analysis | Budget vs Actual | □Complete □Pending | ____________ □ Process Changes | Updated Workflows | □Complete □Pending | ____________ □ Training Materials | Updated Guides | □Complete □Pending | ____________ □ Support Procedures | Service Guides | □Complete □Pending | ____________

Technical Documentation: □ System Architecture | Final Design | □Complete □Pending | ____________ □ Security Controls | Implementation | □Complete □Pending | ____________ □ Integration Details | Connections | □Complete □Pending | ____________ □ Test Results | Validation Data | □Complete □Pending | ____________ □ Support Procedures | Technical Guides | □Complete □Pending | ____________

5. Future Recommendations

Strategic Improvements: (Key: Recommendation | Priority | Resource Needs | Timeline)

Business Recommendations: □ Process Optimization | □High □Med □Low | ____________ | ____________ □ Resource Planning | □High □Med □Low | ____________ | ____________ □ Risk Management | □High □Med □Low | ____________ | ____________ □ Change Management | □High □Med □Low | ____________ | ____________ □ User Training | □High □Med □Low | ____________ | ____________

Technical Recommendations: □ Security Enhancement | □High □Med □Low | ____________ | ____________ □ Performance Tuning | □High □Med □Low | ____________ | ____________ □ Integration Updates | □High □Med □Low | ____________ | ____________ □ Monitoring Improve | □High □Med □Low | ____________ | ____________ □ Support Optimization | □High □Med □Low | ____________ | ____________

Real-World Examples:

1. Financial Services (Chapter 1): Post-Implementation Results: □ API Security Enhancement □ Transaction Protection □ Performance Improvement □ Compliance Achievement Result: Secure Financial Operations

2. Manufacturing (Chapter 2): Post-Implementation Results: □ Supply Chain Security □ Production Protection □ Vendor Integration □ Safety Compliance Result: Protected Manufacturing Process

3. Healthcare (Chapter 3): Post-Implementation Results: □ Patient Data Security □ HIPAA Compliance □ Clinical Integration □ Privacy Protection Result: Secure Healthcare Environment

Implementation Guidelines:

For Business Leaders: □ Review business impact □ Assess ROI □ Evaluate user feedback □ Consider improvements □ Plan future investments

For Technical Teams: □ Evaluate technical success □ Document configurations □ Identify improvements □ Plan enhancements □ Optimize performance

Success Metrics:

Review Effectiveness: □ Comprehensive assessment □ Clear documentation □ Actionable insights □ Future planning □ Knowledge transfer

APPENDIX B: INCIDENT RESPONSE TEMPLATES 1. Initial Response

1) FIRST 24 HOURS CHECKLIST

Executive Overview: The first 24 hours following a security incident are critical for effective containment and response. This checklist provides structured guidance for both business and technical teams during the initial response phase.

IMMEDIATE RESPONSE (0-1 Hours): (Key: Action | Owner | Status | Time Completed)

Initial Detection & Notification: Incident Detected/Reported | Security Team | Complete Pending | ________ Initial Severity Assessment | Security Lead | Complete Pending | ________ CISO/Security Director Alert | Security Lead | Complete Pending | ________ IR Team Activation | CISO | Complete Pending | ________ DIS Risk Solutions Notified | Security Lead | Complete Pending | ________

HOUR 1-2: (Key: Action | Owner | Status | Time Completed)

Initial Assessment: Incident Classification | IR Team | Complete Pending | ________ System/Data Impact Review | Technical Lead | Complete Pending | ________ Business Impact Assessment | Business Lead | Complete Pending | ________ Initial Containment Actions | Technical Team | Complete Pending | ________ Evidence Preservation Start | Forensics Team | Complete Pending | ________

HOURS 2-4: (Key: Action | Owner | Status | Time Completed)

Response Mobilization: Executive Notification | CISO | Complete Pending | ________ IR Plan Activation | IR Team Lead | Complete Pending | ________ Resource Allocation | Department Heads | Complete Pending | ________ Communication Plan Start | Comms Team | Complete Pending | ________ Legal/Compliance Alert | Legal Team | Complete Pending | ________

HOURS 4-8: (Key: Action | Owner | Status | Time Completed)

Initial Containment: Containment Verification | Technical Team | Complete Pending | ________ System Impact Analysis | IT Team | Complete Pending | ________ Data Impact Assessment | Security Team | Complete Pending | ________ Business Continuity Check | Business Lead | Complete Pending | ________ Initial Findings Report | IR Team Lead | Complete Pending | ________

HOURS 8-12: (Key: Action | Owner | Status | Time Completed)

Response Coordination: Stakeholder Updates | Comms Team | Complete Pending | ________ Technical Response Plan | Technical Lead | Complete Pending | ________ Resource Assessment | Department Heads | Complete Pending | ________ Evidence Collection | Forensics Team | Complete Pending | ________ Insurance Coordination | Risk Management | Complete Pending | ________

HOURS 12-16: (Key: Action | Owner | Status | Time Completed)

Impact Management: Business Impact Update | Business Lead | Complete Pending | ________ Customer Impact Review | Customer Service | Complete Pending | ________ Regulatory Assessment | Compliance Team | Complete Pending | ________ Partner/Vendor Notice | Vendor Management | Complete Pending | ________ Media Response Plan | PR Team | Complete Pending | ________

HOURS 16-20: (Key: Action | Owner | Status | Time Completed)

Response Progress: Technical Status Update | Technical Lead | Complete Pending | ________ Containment Verification | Security Team | Complete Pending | ________ Recovery Planning Start | IR Team | Complete Pending | ________ Resource Adjustment | Department Heads | Complete Pending | ________ Documentation Review | IR Team Lead | Complete Pending | ________

HOURS 20-24: (Key: Action | Owner | Status | Time Completed)

Day One Wrap-up: 24-Hour Status Report | IR Team Lead | Complete Pending | ________ Response Assessment | CISO | Complete Pending | ________ Next Steps Planning | IR Team | Complete Pending | ________ Resource Planning | Department Heads | Complete Pending | ________ Stakeholder Briefing | Comms Team | Complete Pending | ________

Real-World Examples:

1. Financial Services (Chapter 1): First 24 Hours Response: API Vulnerability Detection Transaction Monitoring Alert Client Account Protection System Containment Result: $2.3M Loss Prevention

2. Manufacturing (Chapter 2): First 24 Hours Response: Supply Chain Breach Alert Production Line Protection Vendor System Isolation Quality Control Check Result: Production Line Security

3. Healthcare (Chapter 3): First 24 Hours Response: Patient Data Breach Detection PHI Access Containment HIPAA Breach Assessment Clinical System Protection Result: Patient Data Security

Implementation Guidelines:

For Business Leaders: Review incident severity Authorize resources Approve communications Monitor business impact Guide strategic decisions

For Technical Teams: Execute containment Collect evidence Implement controls Monitor systems Document actions

Success Metrics:

Response Effectiveness: Detection time Response time Containment success Communication effectiveness Documentation completeness

2) TEAM ACTIVATION PROTOCOLS

Executive Overview: Effective incident response requires rapid team mobilization and clear role definition. These protocols ensure proper team activation, coordination, and execution during security incidents.

1. Team Roles & Responsibilities

Executive Team: (Key: Role | Primary Responsibilities | Activation Trigger | Response Time)

CISO/Security Director - Strategic Direction | Incident Command | Severity 1-2 | Within 30 min - Resource Authorization | Team Activation | Severity 1-2 | Within 30 min - Executive Updates | Status Reports | All Levels | Within 1 hour - Critical Decisions | Response Strategy | All Levels | As Needed - Stakeholder Liaison | Communications | All Levels | As Required.

Incident Response Lead - Team Coordination | Response Command | All Levels | Within 15 min - Status Reporting | Team Updates | All Levels | Every 2 hours - Resource Management | Team Support | All Levels | As Needed - Technical Direction | Response Strategy | All Levels | Continuous - Documentation Review | Quality Control | All Levels | Daily

Technical Teams: (Key: Team | Primary Role | Activation Criteria | Response Time)

Security Team - Incident Analysis | Investigation | All Levels | Within 15 min - Threat Assessment | Risk Evaluation | All Levels | Within 30 min - Control Implementation | Containment | All Levels | Within 1 hour - System Monitoring | Detection | All Levels | Continuous - Technical Response | Remediation | All Levels | As Required

IT Infrastructure Team - System Support | Infrastructure | As Needed | Within 30 min - Network Management | Connectivity | As Needed | Within 30 min - Access Control | Security | As Needed | Within 1 hour - System Recovery | Restoration | As Needed | As Required - Technical Support | Maintenance | As Needed | Continuous

2. Activation Procedures

Severity Level 1 (Critical): (Key: Action | Owner | Notification Method | Timeline)

Initial Alert - Incident Detection | Security Team | Alert System | Immediate - CISO Notification | Security Lead | Call/Text | Within 5 min - Team Activation | CISO/IR Lead | Call/Text | Within 15 min - Executive Alert | CISO | Call | Within 30 min - DIS Notification | Security Lead | Call | Within 1 hour

Severity Level 2 (High): Response Activation - Incident Assessment | Security Team | Alert System | Within 15 min - Team Notification | IR Lead | Call/Text | Within 30 min - Resource Alert | Department Heads | Email/Call | Within 1 hour - Status Update | IR Lead | Email | Within 2 hours - Partner Alert | Business Lead | Email/Call | As Required

3. Escalation Protocols

Business Escalation: (Key: Trigger | Escalation Path | Timeline | Authorization)

Impact Thresholds - Financial Impact | >$100K | CFO Alert | Within 1 hour - Customer Impact | >100 Users | COO Alert | Within 2 hours - Regulatory Impact | Any Breach | Legal Alert | Within 1 hour - Media Risk | Public Exposure | PR Alert | Within 2 hours - Partner Impact | Service Affect | CEO Alert | Within 4 hours

Technical Escalation: Technical Triggers - System Breach | Security Team | CISO Alert | Immediate - Data Exposure | Security Team | IR Lead Alert | Within 15 min - Service Outage | IT Team | CTO Alert | Within 30 min - Control Failure | Security Team | CISO Alert | Within 1 hour - Recovery Issues | IT Team | CTO Alert | Within 2 hours

4. Contact Information Templates

Primary Contacts: (Key: Role | Name | Primary Contact | Backup Contact | Activation Method)

Leadership Team - CISO | ____________ | __________ | __________ | Call Text Email - IR Lead | ____________ | __________ | __________ | Call Text Email - Security Lead | ____________ | __________ | __________ | Call Text Email - Technical Lead | ____________ | __________ | __________ | Call Text Email - Business Lead | ____________ | __________ | __________ | Call Text Email

Support Teams - Security Team | ____________ | __________ | __________ | Call Text Email - IT Support | ____________ | __________ | __________ | Call Text Email - Legal Team | ____________ | __________ | __________ | Call Text Email - PR Team | ____________ | __________ | __________ | Call Text Email - HR Team | ____________ | __________ | __________ | Call Text Email

5. Response Team Checklists

Team Assembly: (Key: Action | Responsibility | Timeline | Status)

Initial Response Team - Command Center Setup | IR Lead | 30 min | Complete Pending - Team Notification | Security Lead | 15 min | Complete Pending - Resource Assignment | IR Lead | 1 hour | Complete Pending - Tools/Access Setup | IT Team | 1 hour | Complete Pending - Communications Test | All Teams | 30 min | Complete Pending

Extended Response Team - Specialist Activation | IR Lead | 2 hours | Complete Pending - Partner Engagement | Business Lead | 4 hours | Complete Pending - Support Team Alert | Department Heads | 2 hours | Complete Pending - Vendor Notification | Procurement | 4 hours | Complete Pending - External Resources | CISO | As Needed | Complete Pending

Real-World Examples:

1. Financial Services (Chapter 1): Team Activation: API Security Team Transaction Monitoring Client Services Compliance Team Result: Coordinated Response

2. Manufacturing (Chapter 2): Team Activation: Supply Chain Security Production Control Quality Assurance Vendor Management Result: Integrated Response

3. Healthcare (Chapter 3): Team Activation: Privacy Team Clinical Systems Compliance/Legal Patient Services Result: HIPAA-Compliant Response

Implementation Guidelines:

For Business Leaders: Review activation criteria Authorize resources Monitor response Guide communications Assess business impact

For Technical Teams: Monitor alerts Initiate response Deploy resources Track progress Document actions

Success Metrics:

Activation Effectiveness: Response time Team assembly Resource deployment Communication flow Coordination e fectiveness

3) COMMUNICATION TEMPLATES

Executive Overview: Clear, timely communication is critical during security incidents. These templates ensure consistent, appropriate messaging across all stakeholder groups while maintaining necessary confidentiality and compliance requirements.

1. Initial Notification Templates

Executive Notification: (Key: Component | Content | Timing | Distribution Method)

URGENT: Security Incident Notification Time of Detection: [TIME] Initial Classification: [SEVERIT 1-5]

Summary: • Incident Type: [SPECIFY] • Systems Affected: [LIST] • Business Impact: [DESCRIBE] • Current Status: [UPDATE]

Initial Actions Taken: • [ACTION 1] • [ACTION 2] • [ACTION 3]

Required Decisions: □ Resource Authorization □ Business Continuity Actions □ External Communications □ Regulatory Notification

Next Update Expected: [TIME]

Technical Team Notification: SECURITY INCIDENT - IMMEDIATE RESPONSE REQUIRED Incident ID: [NUMBER] Classification: [TYPE]

Technical Details: • Affected Systems: [LIST] • Attack Vector: [SPECIFY] • Current Status: [UPDATE] • Containment Status: [STATUS]

Required Actions: □ System Analysis □ Containment Measures □ Evidence Preservation □ Impact Assessment

Report to: [LOCATION] Tools Required: [LIST] Access Details: [SPECIFY]

2. Status Update Templates

Executive Update: INCIDENT STATUS UPDATE #[NUMBER] Time: [TIME] Overall Status: □Contained □Active □Resolving

Current Situation: • Impact Assessment: [UPDATE] • Business Operations: [STATUS] • Customer Impact: [DETAILS] • Resource Status: [UPDATE]

Key Metrics: • Systems Affected: [NUMBER] • Users Impacted: [NUMBER] • Recovery Timeline: [ESTIMATE] • Resource Utilization: [PERCENTAGE]

Next Steps: 1. [ACTION] 2. [ACTION] 3. [ACTION]

Technical Update: TECHNICAL STATUS REPORT #[NUMBER] Time: [TIME]

System Status: • Affected Systems: [LIST] • Containment Status: [UPDATE] • Recovery Progress: [PERCENTAGE] • Security Posture: [STATUS]

Technical Metrics: • Attack Vectors: [LIST] • Compromise Indicators: [DETAILS] • System Performance: [METRICS] • Security Controls: [STATUS]

3. Stakeholder Communications

Customer Notification: IMPORTANT SECURITY UPDATE Priority: [LEVEL]

Dear [CUSTOMER],

We are writing to inform you of a security incident affecting [SPECIFY].

Impact to Your Services: • [DETAIL] • [DETAIL] • [DETAIL]

Actions We're Taking: • [ACTION] • [ACTION] • [ACTION]

What You Should Do: 1. [STEP] 2. [STEP] 3. [STEP]

Contact Information: Support: [NUMBER] Email: [ADDRESS] Updates: [WEBSITE]

Internal Staff Update: SECURITY INCIDENT UPDATE Classification: [INTERNAL USE ONLY]

Current Situation: • [UPDATE] • [UPDATE] • [UPDATE]

Impact on Operations: • [DETAIL] • [DETAIL] • [DETAIL]

Your Actions Required: □ [ACTION] □ [ACTION] □ [ACTION]

4. Regulatory Notification

Initial Regulatory Notice: SECURITY INCIDENT NOTIFICATION Reference: [NUMBER] Classification: [TYPE

Incident Details: • Date/Time of Discovery: [DATETIME] • Nature of Incident: [DESCRIPTION] • Systems/Data Affected: [DETAILS] • Current Status: [UPDATE]

Response Actions: • [ACTION] • [ACTION] • [ACTION]

Compliance Impact: • Regulations Affected: [LIST] • Data Breach Status: [ASSESSMENT] • Notification Requirements: [DE AILS]

Follow-up Timeline: • Next Update: [DATE] • Investigation Completion: [ESTIMATE] • Final Report: [DATE]

5. Media Response Templates

Press Statement: FOR IMMEDIATE RELEASE Contact: [NAME] Phone: [NUMBER] Email: [ADDRESS]

[COMPANY] Addresses Security Incident

[LOCATION] - [DATE] - [COMPANY] is actively responding to a security incident affecting [SYSTEMS/SERVICES].

Current Status: • [UPDATE] • [UPDATE] • [UPDATE]

Customer Impact: • [DETAIL] • [DETAIL] • [DETAIL]

Our Response: • [ACTION] • [ACTION] • [ACTION]

Social Media Updates: Tweet 1: [COMPANY] is investigating a security incident affecting [SERVICES]. Customer security is our priority. Updates: [LINK]

Tweet 2: Update on [INCIDENT]: [STATUS]. More information: [LINK] Customer support: [CONTACT]

LinkedIn Post: [COMPANY] Security Update We are actively responding to a security incident affecting [SERVICES]. Our teams are working to [ACTION]. Customer support available at [CONTACT]. Regular updates will be posted at [LINK].

Real-World Examples:

1. Financial Services (Chapter 1): API Security Incident: • Initial Alert: "Critical API security incident detected" • Status Update: "API vulnerability contained, transactions secure" • Customer Notice: "Enhanced security measures implemented" Result: Clear stakeholder communication

2. Manufacturing (Chapter 2): Supply Chain Breach: • Vendor Alert: "Critical supply chain security incident" • Production Update: "Manufacturing systems secured" • Quality Notice: "Product integrity maintained" Result: Coordinated response messaging

3. Healthcare (Chapter 3): Patient Data Incident: • HIPAA Notice: "Potential PHI exposure detected" • Clinical Update: "Patient care systems secured" • Patient Notice: "Data security measures enhanced" Result: Compliant breach notificatio

Implementation Guidelines:

For Business Leaders: □ Review communication strategy □ Approve external messages □ Monitor stakeholder response □ Guide message timing □ Ensure compliance

For Technical Teams: □ Provide technical details □ Verify accuracy □ Update status regularly □ Document communications □ Track notification

Success Metrics:

Communication Effectiveness: □ Message timing □ Stakeholder reach □ Response accuracy □ Compliance adherence □ Documentation completeness

4) DOCUMENTATION FORMS

Executive Overview: Proper documentation is essential for incident tracking, evidence preservation, and compliance requirements. These standardized forms ensure consistent, complete documentation throughout the incident response process.

Business Context:

SEVERITY DEFINITIONS:

Business View: - Critical: Severe business disruption, immediate action required - High: Significant impact, prompt response needed - Medium: Limited impact, scheduled response appropriate - Low: Minimal impact, routine handling acceptable

Technical View: - Critical: System compromise, data breach, service failure - High: Multiple system impact, significant exposure - Medium: Single system impact, limited exposure - Low: Minor system issue, no data exposure

IMPACT DEFINITIONS:

Business View: - Critical: Major financial loss, severe reputational damage - High: Substantial financial impact, significant disruption - Medium: Moderate financial impact, limited disruption - Low: Minor financial impact, minimal disruptio

Technical View: - Critical: Multiple systems compromised, widespread impact - High: Single critical system compromised, significant scope - Medium: Limited system impact, contained scope - Low: Isolated technical issue, minimal scope

1. Incident Tracking Form

INCIDENT DETAILS: (Key: Field | Content | Updated By | Time Stamp)

Incident ID: IR-[YEAR]-[NUMBER] Date Reported: __________ Time Reported: __________ Reported By: ____________ Department: _____________

Initial Assessment: Severity Level: Critical High Medium Low Category: Security Privacy Compliance Operational Systems Affected: ________________________ Business Impact: ________________________

Initial Response: First Responder: ____________ Response Time: ____________ Initial Actions: ____________ Escalation Required: Yes No Escalated To: ____________

2. Evidence Collection Form

EVIDENCE DETAILS: (Key: Item | Description | Location | Collector | Time)

Evidence ID: EV-[INCIDENT ID]-[NUMBER] Collection Date: __________ Collection Time: __________ Collected By: ____________ Location: _______________

Evidence Type: System Logs Network Traffic Email/Communications System Images Physical Evidence

Collection Method: Tool Used: ______________ Process: _______________ Hash Value: ____________ Storage Location: _______ Access Controls: ________

3. Chain of Custody Form

CUSTODY TRACKING: (Key: Evidence ID | Handler | Action | DateTime)

Evidence Details: Evidence ID: __________ Description: __________ Initial Handler: _______ Collection Location: ___

Custody Changes: From: __________ To: __________ Date/Time: __________________ Purpose: ____________________ Condition: __________________ Storage Location: ____________

Verification: Received By: ________________ Signature: __________________ Date/Time: _________________ Condition Check: ____________

4. Impact Assessment Form

IMPACT DETAILS: (Key: Category | Scope | Severity | Mitigation)

Business Impact: Financial Impact: $_____________ Operational Impact: ___________ Customer Impact: _____________ Reputational Impact: __________ Recovery Time: ______________

Technical Impact: Systems Affected: ____________ Data Compromised: ___________ Service Disruption: __________ Recovery Resources: _________ Security Posture: ___________

Compliance Impact: Regulations Affected: ________ Reporting Required: Yes No Notification Deadline: _______ Documentation Needed: _______

5. Resolution Documentation Form

RESOLUTION DETAILS: (Key: Action | Owner | Completion | Verification

Incident Resolution: Resolution Date: __________ Resolution Time: __________ Resolved By: ____________ Verification By: ________

Resolution Actions: Technical Fixes: _________ Business Recovery: _______ Control Updates: ________ Process Changes: ________

Post-Incident: Lessons Learned: ________ Process Updates: ________ Training Needs: _________ Control Improvements: ____

Real-World Examples:

1. Financial Services (Chapter 1): Incident: API Security Breach Evidence Collected: - API Access Logs - Transaction Records - System Configurations Resolution: API Security Enhancement

2. Manufacturing (Chapter 2): Incident: Supply Chain Compromise Evidence Collected: - Vendor Access Logs - Production System Data - Component Records Resolution: Supply Chain Security

3. Healthcare (Chapter 3): Incident: Patient Data Exposure Evidence Collected: - Access Logs - PHI Access Records - System Configurations Resolution: Enhanced Data Protection

Implementation Guidelines:

For Business Leaders: Review documentation requirements Ensure completeness Verify business impact Approve resolutions Maintain records

For Technical Teams: Document technical details Preserve evidence Track changes Maintain chain of custody Record technical actions

Success Metrics:

Documentation Quality: Completeness Accuracy Timeliness Compliance Accessibility

APPENDIX B

INCIDENT RESPONSE TEMPLATES 2. Industry-Specific Response Plans

Executive Overview: Different industries face unique security challenges requiring specialized incident response approaches. These plans provide industry-specific guidance while maintaining core incident response principles and compliance requirements.

1. FINANCIAL SERVICES IR PLAN

Business Context:

Response Priorities: Business View: - Critical: Financial transaction disruption, client asset exposure - High: Trading system impact, client data exposure - Medium: Non-critical service disruption, limited exposure - Low: Internal system impact, no client exposure

Technical View: - Critical: Payment/trading system breach, API compromise - High: Multiple system breach, significant data exposure - Medium: Single system impact, contained exposure - Low: Minor system issue, no data exposure

Response Requirements:

Immediate Actions (0-1 Hour): (Action | Owner | Priority | Compliance Requirement)

Transaction Systems: Payment System Check | Security Team | Critical | SEC/FINRA Trading System Review | Trading Tech | Critical | SEC/FINRA Client Account Audit | Account Team | Critical | SEC/FINRA API Security Check | Security Team | Critical | SEC/FINRA Fraud Detection Review | Risk Team | Critical | SEC/FINRA

Client Protection: Account Freeze Protocol | Operations | Critical | SEC/FINRA Client Data Review | Security Team | High | GLBA Transaction Monitoring | Risk Team | High | SEC/FINRA Client Communication | Client Services | High | SEC/FINRA Regulatory Reporting | Compliance | High | SEC/FINRA

Containment Actions (1-4 Hours): System Isolation | IT Team | Critical | SEC/FINRA Access Control Review | Security Team | High | GLBA Data Flow Analysis | Security Team | High | GLBA Partner System Check | Vendor Team | High | SEC/FINRA Backup Verification | IT Team | High | SEC/FINRA

2. HEALTHCARE IR PLAN

Business Context:

Response Priorities: Business View: - Critical: Patient care impact, PHI exposure - High: Clinical system disruption, limited PHI exposure - Medium: Non-clinical system impact, no PHI exposure - Low: Administrative system impact, no patient impact

Technical View: - Critical: Clinical system breach, PHI breach - High: Multiple system breach, potential PHI exposure - Medium: Single system impact, no PHI exposure - Low: Minor system issue, no data exposure

Response Requirements:

Immediate Actions (0-1 Hour): (Action | Owner | Priority | Compliance Requirement)

Patient Care Systems: Clinical System Check | Clinical Tech | Critical | HIPAA PHI Access Review | Privacy Team | Critical | HIPAA Patient Care Impact | Medical Staff | Critical | HIPAA EMR System Audit | Security Team | Critical | HIPAA Treatment Continuity | Clinical Ops | Critical | HIPAA

Data Protection: PHI Exposure Check | Privacy Team | Critical | HIPAA Access Log Review | Security Team | High | HIPAA System Isolation | IT Team | High | HIPAA Backup Verification | IT Team | High | HIPAA Partner System Check | Vendor Team | High | HIPAA

Containment Actions (1-4 Hours): System Quarantine | IT Team | Critical | HIPAA Access Control Review | Security Team | High | HIPAA Data Flow Analysis | Security Team | High | HIPAA Breach Assessment | Privacy Team | High | HIPAA Patient Notification | Legal Team | High | HIPAA

3. MANUFACTURING IR PLAN

Business Context:

Response Priorities: Business View: - Critical: Production line impact, safety risk - High: Quality control impact, supply chain disruption - Medium: Non-production system impact - Low: Administrative system impact

Technical View: - Critical: OT system breach, safety system compromise - High: Multiple system breach, production impact - Medium: Single system impact, limited scope - Low: Minor system issue, no production impact

Response Requirements:

Immediate Actions (0-1 Hour): (Action | Owner | Priority | Compliance Requirement)

Production Systems: Safety System Check | Safety Team | Critical | OSHA Production Line Audit | Operations | Critical | ISO Quality Control Check | Quality Team | Critical | ISO OT System Review | Security Team | Critical | NIST Supply Chain Check | Supply Chain | Critical | ISO

Safety Protocols: Safety System Verify | Safety Team | Critical | OSHA Equipment Check | Maintenance | High | OSHA Process Control Audit | Operations | High | ISO Worker Safety Check | Safety Team | High | OSHA Environmental Check | EHS Team | High | EPA

Containment Actions (1-4 Hours): System Isolation | IT/OT Team | Critical | NIST Process Quarantine | Operations | High | ISO Quality Hold | Quality Team | High | ISO Vendor System Check | Supply Chain | High | ISO Partner Notification | Vendor Team | High | ISO

4. TECHNOLOGY IR PLAN

Business Context:

Response Priorities: Business View: - Critical: Service outage, client system impact - High: Service degradation, multiple client impact - Medium: Limited service impact, single client - Low: Internal system impact, no client exposure

Technical View: - Critical: Core service breach, infrastructure compromise - High: Multiple service breach, significant exposure - Medium: Single service impact, limited exposure - Low: Minor system issue, no service impact

Response Requirements:

Immediate Actions (0-1 Hour): (Action | Owner | Priority | Compliance Requirement)

Service Systems: Core Service Check | Operations | Critical | SLA Infrastructure Audit | IT Team | Critical | SLA Client System Review | Support Team | Critical | SLA Integration Check | Security Team | Critical | SLA Backup Service Check | IT Team | Critical | SLA

Client Protection: Client Impact Review | Client Services | Critical | SLA Service Monitoring | Operations | High | SLA Data Protection Check | Security Team | High | GDPR Client Communication | Support Team | High | SLA Partner Notification | Vendor Team | High | SLA

Containment Actions (1-4 Hours): Service Isolation | IT Team | Critical | SLA Access Control Review | Security Team | High | GDPR Data Flow Analysis | Security Team | High | GDPR Client System Check | Support Team | High | SLA Recovery Planning | Operations | High | SLA

Real-World Examples:

1. Financial Services (Chapter 1): Incident Response: API Security Breach Transaction System Impact Client Data Protection Regulatory Reporting Result: $2.3M Loss Prevention

2. Healthcare (Chapter 3): Incident Response: Patient Data Breach Clinical System Protection HIPAA Compliance Patient Care Continuity Result: Protected 5,000+ Records

3. Manufacturing (Chapter 2): Incident Response: Supply Chain Breach Production System Security Quality Control Protection Safety System Verification Result: Protected Production Lin

Implementation Guidelines:

For Business Leaders: Review industry requirements Ensure compliance Authorize resources Monitor business impact Guide communications

For Technical Teams: Follow industry protocols Implement controls Document actions Maintain compliance Track progress

Success Metrics:

Response Effectiveness: Industry compliance Response time Impact mitigation Client protection Documentation completeness

APPENDIX C

RISK ASSESSMENT TOOLS 1. Assessment Frameworks

1) THREAT MODELING TEMPLATES

Executive Overview: Effective threat modeling identifies, analyzes, and prioritizes potential security threats to systems and data. These templates provide structured approaches for both business and technical teams to model threats across different scenarios.

Business Context:

THREAT LEVELS:

Business View: - Critical: Direct threat to business operations/assets - High: Significant threat to key business functions - Medium: Moderate threat to business processes - Low: Minor threat to non-critical operations

Technical View: - Critical: Active exploitation, known threat actors - High: Known vulnerabilities, potential exploitation - Medium: Theoretical vulnerabilities, limited exposure - Low: Minimal technical exposure, unlikely exploit

1. Asset Identification Template

Critical Business Assets: (Key: Asset | Value | Impact | Protection Level)

Data Assets: Customer Data | $_______ | High Med Low | Critical Standard Financial Records | $_______ | High Med Low | Critical Standard Intellectual Property | $_______ | High Med Low | Critical Standard Business Plans | $_______ | High Med Low | Critical Standard Employee Information | $_______ | High Med Low | Critical Standard

System Assets: Core Applications | $_______ | High Med Low | Critical Standard Network Infrastructure | $_______ | High Med Low | Critical Standard Security Systems | $_______ | High Med Low | Critical Standard Backup Systems | $_______ | High Med Low | Critical Standard Communication Systems | $_______ | High Med Low | Critical Standard

2. Threat Identification Matri

External Threats: (Key: Threat | Likelihood | Impact | Risk Level)

Cyber Attacks: Ransomware | High Med Low | High Med Low | Critical High Med Low Data Breach | High Med Low | High Med Low | Critical High Med Low API Attacks | High Med Low | High Med Low | Critical High Med Low DDoS Attacks | High Med Low | High Med Low | Critical High Med Low Social Engineering | High Med Low | High Med Low | Critical High Med Low

Internal Threats: Insider Actions | High Med Low | High Med Low | Critical High Med Low System Failures | High Med Low | High Med Low | Critical High Med Low Process Errors | High Med Low | High Med Low | Critical High Med Low Configuration Issues | High Med Low | High Med Low | Critical High Med Low Access Control Gaps | High Med Low | High Med Low | Critical High Med Low

3. Attack Vector Analysis

Entry Points: (Key: Vector | Exposure | Controls | Risk Level)

Network Vectors: Internet Connection | High Med Low | ____________ | Critical High Med Low Remote Access | High Med Low | ____________ | Critical High Med Low Wireless Networks | High Med Low | ____________ | Critical High Med Low Partner Connections | High Med Low | ____________ | Critical High Med Low Cloud Services | High Med Low | ____________ | Critical High Med Low

Application Vectors: Web Applications | High Med Low | ____________ | Critical High Med Low Email Systems | High Med Low | ____________ | Critical High Med Low Mobile Apps | High Med Low | ____________ | Critical High Med Low APIs | High Med Low | ____________ | Critical High Med Low Third-party Systems | High Med Low | ____________ | Critical High Med Low

4. Impact Analysis Template

Business Impact: (Key: Impact Area | Severity | Duration | Cost)

Operational Impact: Service Disruption | High Med Low | _____ hrs | $_______ Data Loss | High Med Low | _____ hrs | $_______ Customer Impact | High Med Low | _____ hrs | $_______ Reputation Damage | High Med Low | _____ hrs | $_______ Regulatory Issues | High Med Low | _____ hrs | $_______

Technical Impact: System Downtime | High Med Low | _____ hrs | $_______ Data Corruption | High Med Low | _____ hrs | $_______ Security Breach | High Med Low | _____ hrs | $_______ Recovery Time | High Med Low | _____ hrs | $_______ Resource Drain | High Med Low | _____ hrs | $_______

5. Mitigation Planning

Control Measures: (Key: Control | Priority | Cost | Implementation Time)

Technical Controls: Access Controls | High Med Low | $_______ | _____ days Encryption | High Med Low | $_______ | _____ days Monitoring Systems | High Med Low | $_______ | _____ days Backup Solutions | High Med Low | $_______ | _____ days Security Tools | High Med Low | $_______ | _____ days

Process Controls: Security Policies | High Med Low | $_______ | _____ days User Training | High Med Low | $_______ | _____ days Incident Response | High Med Low | $_______ | _____ days Change Management | High Med Low | $_______ | _____ days Audit Procedures | High Med Low | $_______ | _____ days

Real-World Examples:

1. Financial Services (Chapter 1): Threat Model: API Security Threats Transaction Systems Client Data Protection Regulatory Compliance Result: Protected $2.3M in Assets

2. Manufacturing (Chapter 2): Threat Model: Supply Chain Threats Production Systems Quality Control Safety Systems Result: Protected Production Line

3. Healthcare (Chapter 3): Threat Model: Patient Data Threats Clinical Systems HIPAA Requirements Treatment Systems Result: Protected 5,000+ Records

Implementation Guidelines:

For Business Leaders: Review threat models Assess business impact Allocate resources Approve controls Monitor effectiveness

For Technical Teams: Identify threats Analyze vectors Design controls Implement protection Test effectiveness

Success Metrics:

Modeling Effectiveness: Threat identification Risk assessment Control effectiveness Implementation success Cost efficienc

2) VULNERABILITY ASSESSMENT CHECKLISTS

Executive Overview:

Regular vulnerability assessments are critical for identifying and addressing security weaknesses. These checklists provide structured approaches for evaluating vulnerabilities across different system components and security domains.

Business Context:

VULNERABILITY SEVERITY:

Business View:
- Critical: Immediate exploitation risk, direct business impact
- High: Near-term risk, significant business impac
- Medium: Potential risk, moderate business impact
- Low: Limited risk, minimal business impact

Technical View:
- Critical: Easily exploitable, system compromise likely
- High: Exploitable with moderate effort, significant exposur
- Medium: Limited exploitation potential, contained impact
- Low: Theoretical vulnerability, minimal exposure

1. System Security Checklist

Operating Systems:
(Key: Component | Status | Vulnerability Level | Last Check)
Core Systems:

□ Patch Status | □Current □Outdated | □Critical □High □Med □Low | ________
□ Security Updates | □Current □Outdated | □Critical □High □Med □Low | ________
□ Configuration | □Secure □At Risk | □Critical □High □Med □Low | ________
□ Access Controls | □Secure □At Risk | □Critical □High □Med □Low | ________
□ System Hardening | □Complete □Pending | □Critical □High □Med □Low | ________

Security Tools:
□ Antivirus | □Active □Inactive | □Critical □High □Med □Low | ________
□ Endpoint Protection | □Active □Inactive | □Critical □High □Med □Low | ________
□ Monitoring Tools | □Active □Inactive | □Critical □High □Med □Low | ________
□ Backup Systems | □Active □Inactive | □Critical □High □Med □Low | ________
□ Security Logging | □Active □Inactive | □Critical □High □Med □Low | ________

2. Network Security Checklist

Infrastructure:
(Key: Component | Configuration | Vulnerability Level | Last Audit)

Perimeter Security:
□ Firewalls | □Secure □At Risk | □Critical □High □Med □Low | ________
□ IDS/IPS Systems | □Active □Inactive | □Critical □High □Med □Low | ________
□ VPN Access | □Secure □At Risk | □Critical □High □Med □Low | ________
□ Network Segregation | □Complete □Partial | □Critical □High □Med □Low | ________
□ Remote Access | □Secure □At Risk | □Critical □High □Med □Low | ________

Network Monitoring:
□ Traffic Analysis | □Active □Inactive | □Critical □High □Med □Low | ________
□ Threat Detection | □Active □Inactive | □Critical □High □Med □Low | ________
□ Log Management | □Active □Inactive | □Critical □High □Med □Low | ________
□ Alert Systems | □Active □Inactive | □Critical □High □Med □Low | ________
□ Performance Monitor| □Active □Inactive | □Critical □High □Med □Low | ________

3. Application Security Checklist

Application Components:
(Key: Element | Security Status | Vulnerability Level | Last Test)

Web Applications:
□ Authentication | □Secure □At Risk | □Critical □High □Med □Low | ________
□ Authorization | □Secure □At Risk | □Critical □High □Med □Low | ________
□ Input Validation | □Secure □At Risk | □Critical □High □Med □Low | ________
□ Session Management | □Secure □At Risk | □Critical □High □Med □Low | ________
□ Error Handling | □Secure □At Risk | □Critical □High □Med □Low | ________

API Security:
□ Authentication | □Secure □At Risk | □Critical □High □Med □Low | ________
□ Rate Limiting | □Active □Inactive | □Critical □High □Med □Low | ________
□ Input Validation | □Secure □At Risk | □Critical □High □Med □Low | ________
□ Output Encoding | □Secure □At Risk | □Critical □High □Med □Low | ________
□ Error Handling | □Secure □At Risk | □Critical □High □Med □Low | ________

4. Data Security Checklist

Data Protection:
(Key: Data Type | Protection Status | Vulnerability Level | Last Review)

Sensitive Data:
□ Customer Data | □Secure □At Risk | □Critical □High □Med □Low | ________
□ Financial Data | □Secure □At Risk | □Critical □High □Med □Low | ________
□ Employee Data | □Secure □At Risk | □Critical □High □Med □Low | ________
□ Business Data | □Secure □At Risk | □Critical □High □Med □Low | ________
□ Intellectual Property| □Secure □At Risk | □Critical □High □Med □Low | ________

Data Controls:
□ Encryption | □Active □Inactive | □Critical □High □Med □Low | ________
□ Access Controls | □Secure □At Risk | □Critical □High □Med □Low | ________
□ Data Classification| □Complete □Partial | □Critical □High □Med □Low | ________
□ Data Backup | □Active □Inactive | □Critical □High □Med □Low | ________
□ Data Recovery | □Tested □Untested | □Critical □High □Med □Low | ________

5. Physical Security Checklist

Facility Security:
(Key: Control | Status | Vulnerability Level | Last Inspection)

Access Controls:
□ Entry Points | □Secure □At Risk | □Critical □High □Med □Low | ________
□ Security Systems | □Active □Inactive | □Critical □High □Med □Low | ________
□ Surveillance | □Active □Inactive | □Critical □High □Med □Low | ________
□ Access Logs | □Active □Inactive | □Critical □High □Med □Low | ________
□ Visitor Management | □Active □Inactive | □Critical □High □Med □Low | ________

Environmental Controls:
□ Power Systems | □Secure □At Risk | □Critical □High □Med □Low | ________
□ Climate Control | □Active □Inactive | □Critical □High □Med □Low | ________
□ Fire Protection | □Active □Inactive | □Critical □High □Med □Low | ________
□ Water Detection | □Active □Inactive | □Critical □High □Med □Low | ________
□ Emergency Systems | □Active □Inactive | □Critical □High □Med □Low | ________

Real-World Examples:

1. Financial Services (Chapter 1):
Vulnerability Assessment:
□ API Security Review
□ Transaction Systems Check
□ Data Protection Audit
□ Compliance Verificatio
Result: API Security Enhancement

2. Manufacturing (Chapter 2):
Vulnerability Assessment:
□ OT Systems Review
□ Supply Chain Security
□ Production Systems Check
□ Safety Systems Audit
Result: Enhanced Production Security

3. Healthcare (Chapter 3):
Vulnerability Assessment:
□ PHI Protection Review
□ Clinical Systems Check
□ HIPAA Compliance Audit
□ Patient Data Security
Result: Strengthened Data Protection

Implementation Guidelines:

For Business Leaders:
□ Review assessment scope
□ Authorize resources
□ Prioritize remediation

□ Monitor progress
□ Validate results

For Technical Teams:
□ Conduct assessments
□ Document finding
□ Implement fixe
□ Verify remediation
□ Update documentation

Success Metrics:

Assessment Effectiveness:
□ Coverage completeness
□ Finding accuracy
□ Remediation rate
□ Control effectiveness
□ Documentation quality

3) IMPACT ANALYSIS TOOLS

Executive Overview: Impact analysis provides structured evaluation of security incidents across multiple business dimensions. These tools enable organizations to quantify and assess potential impacts, supporting informed decision-making and resource allocation.

Business Context:

IMPACT SEVERITY:

Business View: - Critical: Severe business disruption, major fina - cial loss - High: Significant disruption, substantial financial impact - Medium: Limited disruption, moderate financial impact - Low: Minimal disruption, negligible financial impac

Technical View: - Critical: Multiple systems compromised, widespread impact - High: Critical system compromised, significant scope - Medium: Limited system impact, contained scope - Low: Isolated technical issue, minimal scope

1. Business Impact Analysis Template

Critical Business Functions: (Key: Function | Criticality | Maximum Downtime | Recovery Priority)

Core Operations: Primary Services | Critical High Med Low | ___ hours | 1 2 3 4 Support Services | Critical High Med Low | ___ hours | 1 2 3 4 Customer Service | Critical High Med Low | ___ hours | 1 2 3 4 Partner Services | Critical High Med Low | ___ hours | 1 2 3 4 Internal Operations | Critical High Med Low | ___ hours | 1 2 3 4

Dependencies: IT Systems | Critical High Med Low | ___ hours | 1 2 3 4 Data Access | Critical High Med Low | ___ hours | 1 2 3 4 Third-party Services| Critical High Med Low | ___ hours | 1 2 3 4 Staff Access | Critical High Med Low | ___ hours | 1 2 3 4 Physical Facilities | Critical High Med Low | ___ hours | 1 2 3 4

2. Financial Impact Assessment

Direct Costs: (Key: Category | Estimated Cost | Timeframe | Impact Level)

Immediate Costs: Response Costs | $_________ | ___days | Critical High Med Low System Recovery | $_________ | ___days | Critical High Med Low Data Recovery | $_________ | ___days | Critical High Med Low Business Continuity | $_________ | ___days | Critical High Med Low Emergency Measures | $_________ | ___days | Critical High Med Low

Long-term Costs: Security Upgrades | $________ | ___months | Critical High Med Low Process Changes | $________ | ___months | Critical High Med Low Training/Awareness | $________ | ___months | Critical High Med Low Monitoring Tools | $________ | ___months | Critical High Med Low Compliance Measures | $________ | ___months | Critical High Med Low

3. Operational Impact Evaluation

Service Disruption: (Key: Service | Duration | Users Affected | Business Impact)

Critical Services: Core Systems | ___hours | ___users | Critical High Med Low Customer Access | ___hours | ___users | Critical High Med Low Data Access | ___hours | ___users | Critical High Med Low Communication | ___hours | ___users | Critical High Med Low Partner Services | ___hours | ___users | Critical High Med Low

Resource Impact: Staff Productivity | ___hours | ___staff | Critical High Med Low System Performance | ___hours | ___systems| Critical High Med Low Process Efficiency | ___hours | ___processes| Critical High Med Low Partner Operations | ___hours | ___partners| Critical High Med Low Customer Service | ___hours | ___customers| Critical High Med Low

4. Reputational Impact Analysis

Stakeholder Impact: (Key: Group | Impact Level | Duration | Recovery Time)

External Stakeholders: Customers | Critical High Med Low | ___months | ___months Partners | Critical High Med Low | ___months | ___months Investors | Critical High Med Low | ___months | ___months Regulators | Critical High Med Low | ___months | ___months Public | Critical High Med Low | ___months | ___months

Media Impact: Traditional Media | Critical High Med Low | ___months | ___months Social Media | Critical High Med Low | ___months | ___ months Industry Press | Critical High Med Low | ___months | ___months Customer Forums | Critical High Med Low | ___months | ___months Employee Channels | Critical High Med Low | ___months | ___months

5. Compliance Impact Assessment

Regulatory Requirements: (Key: Requirement | Violation Level | Penalty Risk | Response Time)

Compliance Areas: Data Protection | Critical High Med Low | $_______ | ___days Industry Standards | Critical High Med Low | $_______ | ___days Security Rules | Critical High Med Low | $_______ | ___days Privacy Laws | Critical High Med Low | $_______ | ___days Reporting Rules | Critical High Med Low | $_______ | ___days

Documentation Requirements: Incident Reports | Required Optional | ___days | Complete Pending Customer Notices | Required Optional | ___days | Complete Pending Regulatory Filings | Required Optional | ___days | Complete Pending Audit Trail | Required Optional | ___days | Complete Pending Response Records | Required Optional | ___days | Complete Pending

Real-World Examples:

1. Financial Services (Chapter 1): Impact Analysis: $2.3M Financial Exposure 1,547 Client Accounts Trading System Impact Regulatory Reporting Result: Comprehensive Impact Assessment

2. Manufacturing (Chapter 2): Impact Analysis: Production Line Impact Supply Chain Disruption Quality Control Issues Safety Implications Result: Multi-dimensional Impact Evaluation

3. Healthcare (Chapter 3): Impact Analysis: Patient Data Exposure Clinical Operations HIPAA Compliance Treatment Impact Result: Healthcare-specific Impact Assessment

Implementation Guidelines:

For Business Leaders: Review impact scope Assess business risk Authorize resources Monitor recovery Validate results

For Technical Teams: Measure technical impact Document findings Implement solutions Track recovery Update procedures

Success Metrics:

Analysis Effectiveness: Impact accuracy Response time Recovery success Cost accuracy Documentation quality

4) RISK SCORING MODELS

Executive Overview:

Risk scoring provides a standardized approach to evaluating and prioritizing security risks. These models enable consistent risk assessment and informed decision-making across different business contexts and technical scenarios.

Business Context:

RISK LEVELS:

Business View:
- Critical: Immediate business threat, severe impact likely
- High: Significant business risk, substantial impact possibl
- Medium: Moderate business concern, manageable impact
- Low: Minor business risk, limited impact expected

Technical View:
- Critical: Exploitable vulnerability, immediate threat
- High: Known vulnerability, active threat potential
- Medium: Potential vulnerability, limited threat activity
- Low: Theoretical vulnerability, minimal threat evidence

1. Quantitative Scoring Framework

Risk Score Calculation:
(Key: Factor | Weight | Rating | Score)

Primary Factors:
Impact Rating:
Financial Loss | Weight: 30% | Rating 1-5: ___ | Score: ___
Operational Impact | Weight: 25% | Rating 1-5: ___ | Score: ___
Data Exposure | Weight: 25% | Rating 1-5: ___ | Score: ___
Reputation Impact | Weight: 20% | Rating 1-5: ___ | Score: ___

Likelihood Factors:
Threat Level | Weight: 30% | Rating 1-5: ___ | Score: ___
Vulnerability | Weight: 25% | Rating 1-5: ___ | Score: ___
Control Strength | Weight: 25% | Rating 1-5: ___ | Score: ___
Detection Ability | Weight: 20% | Rating 1-5: ___ | Score: ___

2. Qualitative Assessment Matrix

Risk Assessment Grid:
(Key: Impact | Likelihood | Risk Level | Required Action)

Critical Impact:
Almost Certain | Score: 25 | Critical | Immediate Action
Likely | Score: 20 | Critical | <24 Hour Response
Possible | Score: 15 | High | <72 Hour Response
Unlikely | Score: 10 | High | Weekly Review
Rare | Score: 5 | Medium | Monthly Review

High Impact:
Almost Certain | Score: 20 | Critical | <24 Hour Response
Likely | Score: 16 | High | <72 Hour Response
Possible | Score: 12 | High | Weekly Review
Unlikely | Score: 8 | Medium | Monthly Review
Rare | Score: 4 | Low | Quarterly Review

3. Risk Prioritization Model

Priority Assignment:
(Key: Risk Score | Priority Level | Response Time | Resource Level)

Critical Risks (Score 20-25):
System Breach | Priority 1 | <4 Hours | High Med Low
Data Exposure | Priority 1 | <4 Hours | High Med Low
Service Outage | Priority 1 | <4 Hours | High Med Low
Compliance Breach | Priority 1 | <4 Hours | High Med Low
Safety Risk | Priority 1 | <4 Hours | High Med Low

High Risks (Score 15-19):
Security Gaps | Priority 2 | <24 Hours | High Med Low
Control Failures | Priority 2 | <24 Hours | High Med Low
System Issues | Priority 2 | <24 Hours | High Med Low
Process Failures | Priority 2 | <24 Hours | High Med Low
Access Problems | Priority 2 | <24 Hours | High Med Low

4. Treatment Selection Guide

Risk Treatment Options:
(Key: Risk Level | Treatment | Cost | Implementation Time)
Critical Risk Treatments:
Risk Mitigation | Required | $______ | ___ days
Risk Transfer | Optional | $______ | ___ days

Risk Acceptance | Restricted | \$______ | ___ days
Risk Avoidance | Required | \$______ | ___ days
Risk Sharing | Optional | \$______ | ___ days

Control Selection:
Technical Controls | Required | \$______ | ___ days
Process Controls | Required | \$______ | ___ days
Physical Controls | Required | \$______ | ___ days
Admin Controls | Required | \$______ | ___ days
Compensating | Optional | \$______ | ___ days

5. Monitoring & Reporting Templates

Risk Monitoring:
(Key: Risk | Metrics | Frequency | Threshold)

Key Risk Indicators:
Security Events | Count/Time | Daily | >10/day
System Uptime | Percentage | Hourly | <99.9%
Control Failures | Count/Week | Weekly | >5/week
Incident Response | Time/Event | Per Event | >1 hour
Compliance Status | Violations | Monthly | Any

Reporting Requirements:
Executive Report | Monthly | Format: Dashboard | Owner: CISO
Technical Report | Weekly | Format: Detailed | Owner: Security
Audit Report | Quarterly | Format: Compliance| Owner: Audit
Trend Analysis | Monthly | Format: Analytics | Owner: Risk
Status Updates | Weekly | Format: Summary | Owner: Security

Real-World Examples:

1. Financial Services (Chapter 1):
Risk Score:
API Vulnerability: 23 (Critical)
Impact: Financial Loss
Likelihood: Almost Certain
Result: Immediate Action Required

2. Manufacturing (Chapter 2):
Risk Score:
Supply Chain: 18 (High)
Impact: Production Loss
Likelihood: Likely
Result: 24-Hour Response Required

3. Healthcare (Chapter 3):
Risk Score:
Data Breach: 21 (Critical)
Impact: Patient Privacy
Likelihood: Almost Certain
Result: Immediate Action Required

Implementation Guidelines:

For Business Leaders:
Review risk scores
Approve treatments
Allocate resources
Monitor progress
Validate results
For Technical Teams:
Calculate risk scores

Implement controls
Monitor effectiveness
Track metrics
Update assessments

Success Metrics:

Scoring Effectiveness:
Score accuracy
Response time
Control effectiveness
Risk reduction
Documentation quality

APPENDIX C

RISK ASSESSMENT TOOLS 2. Industry-Specific Risk Matrices

Executive Overview:
Different industries face unique security challenges and regulatory requirements. These matrices provide sector-specific guidance for threat assessment, compliance management, and risk tolerance determination.

Business Context:

INDUSTRY RISK LEVELS:

Business View:
- Critical: Industry-wide impact, regulatory intervention likely
- High: Sector-specific impact, regulatory reporting require
- Medium: Limited industry impact, standard compliance needs
- Low: Minimal sector impact, routine compliance requirements

Technical View:
- Critical: Industry-targeted attack, active exploitation
- High: Sector-specific vulnerabilit , known threats
- Medium: Common vulnerability, standard threats
- Low: General technical risk, basic security needs

1. Financial Services Matrix

Sector-Specific Threats:
(Key: Threat | Likelihood | Impact | Required Controls)

Critical Systems:
Payment Systems | High Med Low | Critical High Med | SEC/FINRA
Trading Platforms | High Med Low | Critical High Med | SEC/FINRA
Client Accounts | High Med Low | Critical High Med | SEC/FINRA
Transaction APIs | High Med Low | Critical High Med | SEC/FINRA
Settlement Systems | High Med Low | Critical High Med | SEC/FINRA

Compliance Requirements:
SEC Requirements | Reporting Time: 24hrs | Audit Frequency: Quarterly
FINRA Compliance | Reporting Time: 24hrs | Audit Frequency: Quarterly
BSA/AML Rules | Reporting Time: 72hrs | Audit Frequency: Monthly
PCI DSS Standards | Reporting Time: 24hrs | Audit Frequency: Annual
State Regulations | Reporting Time: Varies| Audit Frequency: Annual

Risk Tolerance Guidelines:
Financial Impact:
Critical: >$1M | Response Time: 1hr | Escalation: Immediate
High: $100K-$1M | Response Time: 4hrs | Escalation: Same Day
Medium: $10K-$100K| Response Time: 24hrs| Escalation: Next Day
Low: <$10K | Response Time: 72hrs| Escalation: Weekly

2. Healthcare Matrix

Sector-Specific Threats:
(Key: Threat | Likelihood | Impact | Required Controls)

Critical Systems:
Patient Records | High Med Low | Critical High Med | HIPAA

Clinical Systems | High Med Low | Critical High Med | HIPAA
Treatment Delivery | High Med Low | Critical High Med | HIPAA
Pharmacy Systems | High Med Low | Critical High Med | HIPAA
Lab Systems | High Med Low | Critical High Med | HIPAA

Compliance Requirements:
HIPAA Privacy | Reporting Time: 60days| Audit Frequency: Annual
HIPAA Security | Reporting Time: 60days| Audit Frequency: Annual
State Health Laws | Reporting Time: Varies| Audit Frequency: Annual
FDA Regulations | Reporting Time: 15days| Audit Frequency: Annual
Joint Commission | Reporting Time: 72hrs | Audit Frequency: Annual

Risk Tolerance Guidelines:
Patient Impact:
Critical: >1000 | Response Time: 1hr | Escalation: Immediate
High: 100-1000 | Response Time: 4hrs | Escalation: Same Day
Medium: 10-100 | Response Time: 24hrs| Escalation: Next Day
Low: <10 | Response Time: 72hrs| Escalation: Weekly

3. Manufacturing Matrix

Sector-Specific Threats:
(Key: Threat | Likelihood | Impact | Required Controls)

Critical Systems:
Production Lines | High Med Low | Critical High Med | ISO
Quality Control | High Med Low | Critical High Med | ISO
Supply Chain | High Med Low | Critical High Med | ISO
Safety Systems | High Med Low | Critical High Med | OSHA
OT Systems | High Med Low | Critical High Med | NIST

Compliance Requirements:
ISO Standards | Reporting Time: 24hrs | Audit Frequency: Annual
OSHA Requirements | Reporting Time: 8hrs | Audit Frequency: Annual

EPA Regulations | Reporting Time: 24hrs | Audit Frequency: Annual
Quality Standards | Reporting Time: 24hrs | Audit Frequency: Quarterly
Safety Regulations| Reporting Time: 4hrs | Audit Frequency: Monthly

Risk Tolerance Guidelines:
Production Impact:
Critical: >24hrs | Response Time: 1hr | Escalation: Immediate
High: 12-24hrs | Response Time: 4hrs | Escalation: Same Day
Medium: 4-12hrs | Response Time: 12hrs| Escalation: Next Day
Low: <4hrs | Response Time: 24hrs| Escalation: Weekly

4. Technology Services Matrix

Sector-Specific Threats:
(Key: Threat | Likelihood | Impact | Required Controls)

Critical Systems:
Cloud Services | High Med Low | Critical High Med | SOC2
Data Centers | High Med Low | Critical High Med | ISO
Network Services | High Med Low | Critical High Med | NIST
Client Systems | High Med Low | Critical High Med | SLA
Security Services | High Med Low | Critical High Med | SOC2

Compliance Requirements:
SOC2 Standards | Reporting Time: 24hrs | Audit Frequency: Annual
ISO 27001 | Reporting Time: 24hrs | Audit Frequency: Annual
NIST Framework | Reporting Time: 24hrs | Audit Frequency: Annual
Client SLAs | Reporting Time: Varies| Audit Frequency: Quarterly
Data Protection | Reporting Time: 72hrs | Audit Frequency: Annual

Risk Tolerance Guidelines:
Service Impact:
Critical: >99.99% | Response Time: 15min | Escalation: Immediate
High: >99.9% | Response Time: 1hr | Escalation: Same Day

Medium: >99% | Response Time: 4hrs | Escalation: Next Day
Low: >95% | Response Time: 24hrs | Escalation: Weekly

Real-World Examples:

1. Financial Services (Chapter 1):
Risk Matrix Application:
API Security Breach
SEC/FINRA Compliance
Client Data Protection
Result: Rapid Response Protocol

2. Healthcare (Chapter 3):
Risk Matrix Application:
Patient Data Exposure
HIPAA Compliance
Clinical System Protection
Result: Compliant Response Process

3. Manufacturing (Chapter 2):
Risk Matrix Application:
Supply Chain Breach
Production Impact
Safety Compliance
Result: Integrated Response Plan

Implementation Guidelines:

For Business Leaders:
Review industry requirements
Assess compliance needs
Set risk tolerances
Allocate resources
Monitor effectiveness

For Technical Teams:
Implement controls
Monitor compliance
Track metrics
Document responses
Maintain standards

Success Metrics:

Matrix Effectiveness:
Industry alignment
Compliance status
Response efficienc
Risk reduction
Control effectiveness

APPENDIX D

REGULATORY COMPLIANCE CHECKLIST 1.

Industry Regulations

Executive Overview: Regulatory compliance requires systematic adherence to multiple frameworks and standards. These checklists provide structured guidance for maintaining compliance across different regulatory requirements and industry standards.

Business Context:

COMPLIANCE LEVELS:

Business View: - Critical: Mandatory requirements, severe penalties for non-compliance - High: Required controls, significant penalties for non-compliance - Medium: Expected controls, moderate penalties for non-compliance - Low: Recommended controls, minimal compliance impact

Technical View: - Critical: Required technical controls, immediate implementation - High: Necessary security measures, prioritized implementation - Medium: Standard security controls, scheduled implementation - Low: Basic security measures, routine implementation

1. HIPAA Requirements

Privacy Rule Requirements: (Key: Requirement | Implementation Status | Verification Method | Review Frequency

Patient Rights: Notice of Privacy Practices | Complete Partial None | Audit Review | Quarterly Access to Records | Complete Partial None | Process Check| Monthly Amendment Rights | Complete Partial None | Audit Review | Quarterly Disclosure Accounting | Complete Partial None | Log Review | Monthly Restriction Requests | Complete Partial None | Process Check| Monthly

Security Rule Requirements: Administrative Safeguards: Security Management | Complete Partial None | Audit Review | Monthly Workforce Security | Complete Partial None | Staff Review | Quarterly Information Access | Complete Partial None | Access Audit | Monthly Security Awareness | Complete Partial None | Training Log | Quarterly Security Incidents | Complete Partial None | Event Log | Monthly

2. SEC Guidelines

Cybersecurity Requirements: (Key: Requirement | Implementation Status | Documentation | Review Frequency)

Risk Assessment: Threat Analysis | Complete Partial None | Risk Report | Quarterly Vulnerability Assessment | Complete Partial None | Scan Results | Monthly Impact Analysis | Complete Partial None | Risk Matrix | Quarterly Control Evaluation | Complete Partial None | Audit Report | Quarterly Risk Monitoring | Complete Partial None | Status Report| Monthly

Reporting Requirements: Incident Disclosure | Complete Partial None | Form 8-K | As Required Material Changes | Complete Partial None | SEC Filings | As Required Annual Assessment | Complete Partial None | Form 10-K | Annual Quarterly Updates | Complete Partial None | Form 10-Q | Quarterly Risk Disclosures | Complete Partial None | Risk Reports | Quarterly

3. PCI DSS Standards

Security Requirements: (Key: **Control** | Implementation Status | Validation Method | Review Frequency)

Network Security: **Firewall Configuration** | Complete Partial None | Config Review| Monthly **Password Management** | Complete Partial None | Access Audit | Monthly **Data Protection** | Complete Partial None | Data Scan | Weekly **Encryption** | Complete Partial None | Tech Review | Monthly **Anti-Virus** | Complete Partial None | System Check | Weekly

Access Controls: Access Restriction | Complete Partial None | Access Review| Monthly ID Management | Complete Partial None | User Audit | Monthly Physical Security | Complete Partial None | Site Review | Quarterly Activity Monitoring | Complete Partial None | Log Review | Weekly Security Testing | Complete Partial None | Test Results | Quarterly

4. GDPR Compliance

Data Protection Requirements: (Key: Requirement | Implementation Status | Evidence Required | Review Frequency)

Data Subject Rights: Access Rights | Complete Partial None | Process Doc | Monthly Rectification Rights | Complete Partial None | Process Doc | Monthly Erasure Rights | Complete Partial None | Process Doc | Monthly Portability Rights | Complete Partial None | Process Doc

| Monthly Objection Rights | Complete Partial None | Process Doc | Monthly

Security Measures: Data Protection | Complete Partial None | Controls Doc | Monthly Breach Notification | Complete Partial None | Process Doc | Monthly Impact Assessment | Complete Partial None | DPIA Reports | Quarterly Records Management | Complete Partial None | Records Log | Monthly Third Party Controls | Complete Partial None | Contracts | Quarterly

5. NIST Frameworks

Core Functions: (Key: Function | Implementation Status | Evidence Required | Review Frequency)

Framework Components: Identify | Complete Partial None | Asset Inventory| Quarterly Protect | Complete Partial None | Control Doc | Monthly Detect | Complete Partial None | Monitor Logs | Weekly Respond | Complete Partial None | IR Plans | Quarterly Recover | Complete Partial None | DR Plans | Quarterly

Control Categories: Access Control | Complete Partial None | Access Review | Monthly Awareness Training | Complete Partial None | Training Logs | Quarterly Data Security | Complete Partial None | Security Audit| Monthly Info Protection | Complete Partial None | Control Review| Monthly Response Planning | Complete Partial None | Plan Review | Quarterly

Real-World Examples:

1. Financial Services (Chapter 1): Compliance Application: SEC Guidelines Implementation PCI DSS Compliance NIST Framework Alignment Result: Comprehensive Compliance

2. Healthcare (Chapter 3): Compliance Application: HIPAA Requirements Data Protection Controls Privacy Rule Implementation Result: Healthcare Compliance

3. Manufacturing (Chapter 2): Compliance Application: NIST Framework Security Controls Industry Standards Result: Manufacturing Compliance

Implementation Guidelines:

For Business Leaders: Review requirements Allocate resources Monitor compliance Address gaps Maintain documentation

For Technical Teams: Implement controls Configure systems Monitor compliance Document evidence Maintain security

Success Metrics:

Compliance Effectiveness: Requirement coverage Control effectiveness Documentation completeness Audit readiness Response capability

APPENDIX D

REGULATORY COMPLIANCE CHECKLIST 2. Compliance Documentation

Executive Overview: Proper documentation is essential for demonstrating regulatory compliance and maintaining audit readiness. These templates and guidelines ensure consistent, complete documentation across all compliance requirements.

Business Context:

DOCUMENTATION LEVELS:

Business View: - Critical: Required regulatory evidence, mandatory documentation - High: Important compliance records, significant audit evidence - Medium: Supporting documentation, routine compliance records - Low: Supplementary records, general business documentation

Technical View: - Critical: Technical compliance evidence, required system records - High: Security control documentation, configuration records - Medium: Standard technical records, system documentation - Low: Basic technical logs, routine system records

1. Audit Templates

Internal Audit Checklist: (Key: Component | Status | Evidence Required | Review Frequency)

Policy Review: Security Policies | Complete Pending | Policy Documents | Quarterly Privacy Policies | Complete Pending | Policy Documents | Quarterly Compliance Policies | Complete Pending | Policy Documents | Quarterly Operational Policies | Complete Pending | Policy Documents | Quarterly HR Policies | Complete Pending | Policy Documents | Quarterly

Control Testing: Access Controls | Complete Pending | Test Results | Monthly Security Controls | Complete Pending | Test Results | Monthly Data Controls | Complete Pending | Test Results | Monthly Network Controls | Complete Pending | Test Results | Monthly Physical Controls | Complete Pending | Test Results | Monthly

2. Documentation Requirements

Policy Documentation: (Key: Document | Required Elements | Approval Level | Review Cycle)

Security Policies: Information Security | Complete Pending | Executive | Annual Access Control | Complete Pending | Security | Annual Data Protection | Complete Pending | Privacy | Annual Incident Response | Complete Pending | Security | Annual Business Continuity | Complete Pending | Executive | Annual

Procedure Documentation: Security Procedures | Complete Pending | Security | Semi-Annual Access Procedures | Complete Pending | Security | Semi-Annual Incident Procedures | Complete Pending | Security | Semi-Annual Backup Procedures | Complete Pending | IT | Semi-Annual Recovery Procedures | Complete Pending | IT | Semi-Annual

3. Control Documentation

Technical Controls: (Key: Control | Implementation Evidence | Testing Frequency | Review Level)

System Controls: Access Management | Configuration Docs | Monthly | High Med Low System Security | Security Settings | Monthly | High Med Low Network Security | Network Config | Monthly | High Med Low Data Protection | Protection Methods | Monthly | High Med Low Monitoring Systems | Monitor Config | Monthly | High Med Lo

Administrative Controls: Policies | Policy Documents | Quarterly | High Med Low Procedures | Process Documents | Quarterly | High Med Low Training | Training Records | Quarterly | High Med Low Risk Management | Risk Documents | Quarterly | High Med Low Compliance | Compliance Records | Quarterly | High Med Low

4. Incident Documentation

Incident Records: (Key: Record Type | Required Content | Retention Period | Access Level)

Security Incidents: Initial Report | Incident Details | 3 Years | High Med Low Investigation | Analysis Results | 3 Years | High Med Low Response Actions | Action Records | 3 Years | High Med Low Resolution | Resolution Details| 3 Years | High Med Low Post-Incident | Review Results | 3 Years | High Med Low

Compliance Incidents: Violation Report | Violation Details | 5 Years | High Med Low Impact Assessment | Impact Analysis | 5 Years | High Med Low Corrective Actions | Action Plans | 5 Years | High Med Low Regulatory Reports | Report Documents | 5 Years | High Med Low Follow-up Actions | Action Records | 5 Years | High Med Low

5. Reporting Guidelines

Compliance Reports: (Key: Report Type | Content Requirements | Frequency | Distribution)

Regular Reports: Status Reports | Compliance Status | Monthly | Management Metrics Reports | Key Metrics | Monthly | Management Audit Reports | Audit Results | Quarterly | Executive Risk Reports | Risk Status | Quarterly | Executive Board Reports | Board Summary | Quarterly | Board

Incident Reports: Initial Reports | Incident Details | As Needed | Management Progress Reports | Status Updates | As Needed | Management Final Reports | Resolution Details| As Needed | Executive Regulatory Reports | Required Details | As Required| Regulators Summary Reports | Executive Summary | As Needed | Board

Real-World Examples:

1. Financial Services (Chapter 1): Documentation Example: API Security Controls Transaction Monitoring SEC Compliance Records Result: Complete Audit Trail

2. Healthcare (Chapter 3): Documentation Example: HIPAA Compliance Patient Data Protection Privacy Controls Result: Regulatory Compliance

3. Manufacturing (Chapter 2): Documentation Example: Supply Chain Security Quality Control Records Safety Documentation Result: Industry Compliance

Implementation Guidelines:

For Business Leaders: Review requirements Approve resources Monitor compliance Review reports Validate documentation

For Technical Teams: Maintain records Document controls Track changes Update documentation Support audits

Success Metrics:

Documentation Effectiveness: Completeness Accuracy Timeliness Accessibility Audit readiness

APPENDIX E

INSURANCE CONSIDERATIONS 1. Coverage Analysis

Executive Overview: Effective cyber insurance requires understanding policy components, coverage structures, and claims processes. This analysis provides guidance for evaluating and implementing comprehensive cyber insurance coverage.

Business Context:

COVERAGE LEVELS:

Business View: - Critical: Essential coverage, core business protection - High: Important coverage, significant risk transfer - Medium: Standard coverage, general risk protection - Low: Basic coverage, minimal risk transfer

Technical View: - Critical: Primary security incidents, major breaches - High: Significant technical failures, system compromises - Medium: Standard technical issues, limited incidents - Low: Basic technical problems, minor incidents

1. Policy Types

Primary Coverage Components: (Key: Coverage Type | Required Limits | Retention | Priority)

First-Party Coverage: **Breach Response** | $_______ | $_______ | Critical High Med Low **Business Interruption** | $_______ | $_______ | Critical High Med Low **Data Recovery** | $_______ | $_______ | Critical High Med Low **Cyber Extortion** | $_______ | $_______ | Critical High Med Low **System Failure** | $_______ | $_______ | Critical High Med Low

Third-Party Coverage: **Privacy Liability** | $_______ | $_______ | Critical High Med Low **Network Security** | $_______ | $_______ | Critical High Med Low **Regulatory Defense** | $_______ | $_______ | Critical High Med Low **Media Liability** | $_______ | $_______ | Critical High Med Low **Technology E&O** | $_______ | $_______ | Critical High Med Low

2. Coverage Limits

Tower Structure: (Key: Layer | Limit | Carriers | Premium)

Primary Layer: First $25M | Carrier A | __% Share | $_______ Premium Claims Made Basis | Yes No | Retro Date: _______ Defense Costs | Inside Outside Limits Consent Provisions | Required Not Required Choice of Counsel | Panel Non-Panel

Excess Layers: $25M xs $25M | Multiple Carriers | __% Share | $_______ Premium $50M xs $50M | Multiple Carriers | __% Share | $_______ Premium $50M xs $100M | Multiple Carriers | __% Share | $_______ Premium $50M xs $150M | Multiple Carriers | __% Share | $_______ Premium

3. Retention Structures

Self-Insured Retention: (Key: Coverage | Retention Amount | Aggregate | Time Element)

Primary Retentions: Privacy Breach | $_______ | $_______ Aggregate | __ Hours System Failure | $_______ | $_______ Aggregate | __ Hours Cyber Extortion | $_______ | $_______ Aggregate | __ Hours Business Income | $_______ | $_______ Aggregate | __ Hours Data Recovery | $_______ | $_______ Aggregate | __ Hours

Maintenance Deductibles: Third Party Claims | $_______ | Per Claim Regulatory Actions | $_______ | Per Action Media Claims | $_______ | Per Claim Tech E&O Claims | $_______ | Per Claim System Damage | $_______ | Per Occurrence

4. Claims Processes

Initial Response: (Key: Action | Timeline | Documentation | Responsibility)

Immediate Steps: **Incident Detection** | Within __ Hours | IR Documentation | Security Team **Carrier Notice** | Within __ Hours | Written Notice | Risk Management **Broker Notice** | Within __ Hours | Written Notice | Risk Management **Legal Notice** | Within __ Hours | Written Notice | Legal Team **Response Team** | Within __ Hours | Team Activation | IR Team

Documentation Requirements: **Incident Details** | Complete Pending | Required Format **Loss Estimates** | Complete Pending | Required Format **Response Actions** | Complete Pending | Required Format **Recovery Costs** | Complete Pending | Required Format **Business Impact** | Complete Pending | Required Format

5. Coverage Verificatio

Pre-Incident Review: (Key: Element | Status | Last Review | Next Review)

Policy Review: Coverage Terms | Complete Pending | _______ | _______ Exclusions | Complete Pending | _______ | _______ Conditions | Complete Pending | _______ | _______ Endorsements | Complete Pending | _______ | _______ Definitions | Complete Pending | _______ | _______

Claims Readiness: Response Plans | Complete Pending | _______ | _______ Contact Lists | Complete Pending | _______ | _______ Documentation Forms | Complete Pending | _______ | _______ Vendor Agreements | Complete Pending | _______ | _______ Legal Resources | Complete Pending | _______ | _______

Real-World Examples:

1. Financial Services (Chapter 1): Coverage Application: API Security Incident $2.3M Exposure Transaction Systems Result: Full Coverage Response

2. Manufacturing (Chapter 2): Coverage Application: Supply Chain Breach Production Impact Business Interruption Result: Comprehensive Coverage

3. Healthcare (Chapter 3): Coverage Application: Patient Data Breach HIPAA Violation Privacy Liability Result: Regulatory Coverage

Implementation Guidelines:

For Business Leaders: Review coverage needs | Assess limits adequacy | Verify retentions | Understand process | Maintain readiness

For Technical Teams: Document systems | Track security controls | Maintain evidence | Support claims | Update documentation

Success Metrics:

Coverage Effectiveness: Coverage adequacy | Claims efficiency | Response time | Documentation quality | Recovery success

APPENDIX E

INSURANCE CONSIDERATIONS 2. Industry-Specific Insurance

Executive Overview: Different industries face unique cyber risks requiring specialized insurance coverage. These guidelines provide industry-specific coverage considerations and claims examples for each sector's unique exposures.

Business Context: Each industry sector has specific operational risks, technical exposures, and business considerations that should inform cyber insurance coverage decisions. Coverage should align with the organization's risk profile and business objectives

1. Healthcare Cyber Coverage

Primary Coverage: PHI Breach Response Regulatory Defense Patient Notification Clinical Systems Business Interruptio

Specialized Coverage: Medical Device Coverage Bodily Injury Extension Clinical Trial Protection Healthcare Professional Services Medical Billing Coverage

Claims Examples: Patient Data Breach | Ransomware Attack | System Outage/Failure | Clinical System Failure | Patient Notificatio

2. Financial Services Protection

Primary Coverage: Financial Fraud Coverage Transaction Systems Protection Client Data Protection Regulatory Defense Business Interruption

Specialized Coverage: Trading Platform Protection Payment System Coverage Investment Loss Protection Social Engineering Fraud Cryptocurrency Coverage

Claims Examples: API Security Breach | Client Data Exposure | Trading System Outage | Payment System Breach | Financial Fraud

3. Manufacturing Coverage

Primary Coverage: Supply Chain Disruption Production Systems OT Security Quality Control Systems Business Interruption

Specialized Coverage: Product Liability Extension Supply Chain Security Industrial Control Systems Product Recall Coverage Vendor System Protection

Claims Examples: Supply Chain Breach | Production Line Halt | Quality Control Failure | Safety System Compromise | Vendor System Breach

4. Technology E&O/Cyber Blend

Primary Coverage: Professional Services Technology Products System Security Client Data Protection Service Interruption

Specialized Coverage: Software Performance Integration Failure Cloud Service Interruption Intellectual Property Project Failure

Claims Examples: Service Delivery Failure | Data Breach | System Integration Error | Client System Damage | Project Delay

Implementation Guidelines:

For Business Leaders: Review business operations and risks Assess coverage needs Evaluate coverage options Consider business impact Plan incident response

For Technical Teams: Document critical systems Implement security controls Maintain incident records Support claims process Track security incidents

Real-World Examples:

1. Healthcare (Chapter 3): Coverage Application: Patient Data Breach Response Clinical Systems Protection Business Continuity Result: Protected 5,000+ Patient Records

2. Financial Services (Chapter 1): Coverage Application: API Security Incident Transaction Systems Client Protection Result: Protected $2.3M in Transactions

3. Manufacturing (Chapter 2): Coverage Application: Supply Chain Security Production Systems Quality Control Result: Protected Production Operations

Success Metrics:

Coverage Effectiveness: Business protection | Claims handling | Response time | Recovery success | Operational resilience

GLOSSARY

A

API (Application Programming Interface)
A set of protocols and tools for building software applications that specify how software components should interact.

Authentication
The process of verifying the identity of a user, system, or entity attempting to access a resource.

Access Control
The selective restriction of access to resources, including systems, data, and physical locations.

B

Business Continuity
The capability of an organization to continue delivery of products or services at acceptable predefined levels following a disruptive incident.

Business Interruption
The disruption of normal business operations due to a cyber incident or other disaster.

Breach Notification
The legal requirement to inform affected parties and relevant authorities about a data breach or security incident.

C

Cyber Insurance
Insurance coverage specifically designed to protect businesses from internet-based risks and technology-related risks.

Cloud Security
The protection of data, applications, and infrastructure associated with cloud computing environments.

Compliance
Adherence to laws, regulations, standards, and internal policies governing data protection and security.

D

Data Breach
An incident where confidential or sensitive information is accessed, stolen, or exposed without authorization.

Data Protection
Safeguarding important information from corruption, compromise, or loss through various security measures.

DDoS (Distributed Denial of Service)
An attack that attempts to make a network resource unavailable by overwhelming it with traffic from multiple sources

Deperimeterization (commonly known as "Zero Trust")
A security approach that eliminates the traditional network perimeter, requiring strict identity verification and access controls for every user and device, regardless of location or network position.

E

Endpoint Security
The practice of securing network endpoints like laptops, desktops, and mobile devices from cyber threats.

Encryption
The process of converting information into code to prevent unauthorized access.

Evidence Preservation
The process of maintaining the integrity of data and systems for investigation or compliance purposes.

F

Firewall
A network security system that monitors and controls incoming and outgoing network traffic

First Party Coverage
Insurance coverage for direct losses suffered by the policyholder in a cyber incident.

Forensics
The application of scientific methods to collect, preserve, and analyze digital evidence.

H

HIPAA
Health Insurance Portability and Accountability Act; U.S. legislation that provides data privacy and security provisions for safeguarding medical information.

I

Incident Response
The organized approach to addressing and managing the aftermath of a security breach or cyberattack.

Integration Security
The protection of data and systems during the connection and communication between different technology components.

J

JSON (JavaScript Object Notation)

A lightweight data-interchange format easy for humans to read and write and easy for machines to parse and generate.

K

Kill Chain

A model for describing the stages of a cyberattack, from reconnaissance to data exfiltration

L

Layer 7

The application layer in the OSI model, where common internet user protocols operate.

M

Malware

Malicious software designed to disrupt, damage, or gain unauthorized access to computer systems.

Multi-Factor Authentication (MFA)

A security system that requires multiple forms of verification to grant access to a resource.

N

Network Segmentation

The practice of dividing a computer network into segments to improve security and performance.

O

OAuth

An open standard for access delegation, commonly used for secure authorization.

OT Security
The protection of operational technology systems used in industrial and manufacturing environments.

P

Penetration Testing
An authorized simulated cyberattack on a computer system to evaluate system security.

PHI (Protected Health Information)
Individual health information that is protected under HIPAA privacy rules.

Q

Quantum Computing
Computing using quantum-mechanical phenomena to perform operations on data.

R

Ransomware
Malware that encrypts files and demands payment for the decryption key.

Risk Assessment
The process of identifying, analyzing, and evaluating potential security risks to an organization.

S

Social Engineering
The psychological manipulation of people into performing actions or divulging confidential information

Supply Chain Security
The protection of the supply chain from theft, damage, or compromise of products, services, or information.

T

Third Party Coverage

Insurance coverage for losses suffered by others for which the policy-holder is legally liable.

Two-Factor Authentication

A security process requiring two distinct forms of identification to access resources.

U

URL Filtering

The practice of blocking access to specific websites or web content

V

Vulnerability

A weakness in a system that could be exploited to compromise security.

VPN (Virtual Private Network)

Encrypted connection over the Internet from a device to a network.

W

Web Application Security

The protection of websites, web applications, and web services from security threats.

Z

Zero Day

A previously unknown security vulnerability being exploited before developers have an opportunity to create a patch.

INDEX

RESOURCES

The following resources provided valuable insights for the development of The Zero Day Files and offer readers additional information for implementing security and risk management strategies.

Industry Organizations & Reports

Cybersecurity Resources: • SANS Institute (www.sans.org) - Security awareness training - Technical research - Implementation guides

• MITRE ATT&CK Framework (attack.mitre.org) - Threat modeling - Attack techniques - Defense strategies

• OWASP Foundation (owasp.org) - Application security - Web security testing - Security tools

Insurance Industry Resources: • Cyber Risk Insurance Forum (cyrisk.org) - Market trends - Coverage analysis - Claims data

• NetDiligence Cyber Claims Study - Claims analysis - Cost metrics - Industry trends

Risk Management Resources: • RIMS (rims.org) - Risk management strategies - Industry benchmarks - Professional development

Government & Regulatory Resources

Security Frameworks: • NIST Cybersecurity Framework (nist.gov/cyberframework) - Security guidelines - Implementation guidance - Assessment tools

• FedRAMP (fedramp.gov) - Cloud security standards - Assessment guides - Implementation resources

Healthcare: • HHS Security Risk Assessment Tool (healthit.gov) - HIPAA compliance - Risk assessment - Security planning

Financial Services: • SEC Cybersecurity Guidance (sec.gov) - Regulatory requirements - Disclosure obligations - Risk management

Manufacturing: • NIST Manufacturing Extension Partnership (nist.gov/mep) - Security guidelines - Implementation resources - Best practices

Technical Resources

Security Standards: • ISO/IEC 27001 (iso.org) - Information security management - Risk assessment - Control implementation

• CIS Controls (cisecurity.org) - Security benchmarks - Implementation guides - Assessment tools

Cloud Security: • Cloud Security Alliance (cloudsecurityalliance.org) - Security guidance - Best practices - Implementation tools

Implementation Guides: • NIST Special Publications (csrc.nist.gov) - Security guidelines - Technical implementations - Assessment methods

Industry-Specific Resource

Healthcare Security: • H-ISAC (h-isac.org) - Threat intelligence - Best practices - Industry alerts

Financial Services: • FS-ISAC (fsisac.com) - Threat intelligence - Industry guidance - Best practices

Manufacturing: • MFG-ISAC (mfgisac.org) - Security guidance - Industry alerts - Best practices

Technology Services: • CompTIA (comptia.org) - Security standards - Implementation guides - Best practices

Professional Organizations

Security Associations: • (ISC)² (isc2.org) - Professional standards - Security practices - Implementation guidance

• ISACA (isaca.org) - Security governance - Risk management - Control frameworks

Insurance Organizations: • PLUS (plusweb.org) - Professional liability - Cyber insurance - Risk management

Risk Management: • IRM (theirm.org) - Risk frameworks - Implementation guides - Best practices

Additional Reading

Security Publications: • Dark Reading (darkreading.com) • SecurityWeek (securityweek.com) • The Hacker News (thehackernews.com)

Insurance Publications: • Business Insurance (businessinsurance.com) • Insurance Journal (insurancejournal.com) • Risk & Insurance (riskandinsurance.com)

Research Organizations: • Ponemon Institute (ponemon.org) • Forrester Research (forrester.com) • Gartner (gartner.com)

Note: These resources are current as of publication. Readers are encouraged to verify current web addresses and availability of resources. While these sources informed the development of this book, inclusion does not constitute endorsement of any specific organization or product.

www.ingramcontent.com/pod-product-compliance
Lightning Source LLC
LaVergne TN
LVHW052215200926
848481LV00001B/111